The Amazing Story of
The Fantasticks

The Amazing Story of

The Fantasticks

America's Longest-Running Play

Donald C. Farber
and
Robert Viagas

Limelight Editions

Published in 2005 by
    Limelight Editions
    512 Newark Pompton Turnpike
    Pompton Plains, New Jersey 07444, USA

Originally published in 1991

For sales, please contact
    Limelight Editions
    c/o Hal Leonard Corp.
    7777 West Bluemound Road
    Milwaukee, Wisconsin 53213, USA
    Tel. 800-637-2852
    Fax 414-774-3259

Website: www.limelighteditions.com

Printed in Canada

Vocal selections and other music from *The Fantasticks* available through Hal Leonard Publishing Corporation

Library of Congress Cataloging-in-Publication Data

Farber, Donald C.
  The amazing story of The fantasticks : America's longest running play / Donald C. Farber and Robert Viagis [sic].-- 1st pbk. ed.
      p. cm.
  Updated with a new chapter about the play's closing in 2003.
  Includes index.
  ISBN 0-87910-313-2
  1. Schmidt, Harvey. Fantasticks. I. Viagas, Robert. II. Title.
ML410.S26143F4 2004
782.1'4--dc22
                          2005007713

To Ann Farber and Catherine Ryan
"You are love."

Contents

Acknowledgments

Like *The Fantasticks*, this book was assembled almost despite itself, and thanks mainly to happy coincidences at every turn.

Special acknowledgment must be made to publisher Mel Zerman and writer Andrea Kott, whose chance conversation over dinner in spring of 1989 tapped the first in a long line of dominoes.

The authors were aided and encouraged by their wives, Ann Farber and Catherine Ryan, both of whom reviewed each chapter and suggested substantial improvements.

But the breadth and depth of the story is owed to the creators and members of the original cast who opened their diaries, letters, financial records, filing cabinets, and hearts to the authors.

Interviews with Harvey Schmidt were conducted at the Sullivan Street Playhouse and at his 74th Street apartment in Manhattan; interviews with Rita Gardner, at Cafe Borgia and on the sidewalks of Greenwich Village; the interview with George Curley, at J.R.'s restaurant in New York's theater district. Most of the other people were interviewed at their homes or offices.

Without the cooperation of the following additional people, this book would have been impossible: Dianne Averill, Word Baker, S. Miles Baron, Rubin Blum, Jillana Devine, Mildred Dunnock, Jules and Mickie Field, John and Elizabeth Fuller, Fred Golden, Ronny Graham, Sam Houston, Tom Jones, Ira Kapp, Carol Kopp, Janice Mars, Robert Miller, Julius Monk, Kenneth Nelson, Dorothy Olim, Jerry Orbach, David Powers,

Charles Nelson Reilly, Robert Ryan, Harvey Sabinson, John Schak, Beverly Mann Statter, Blair Stauffer, Julian Stein, Tommy Tune, Keith Urmy, Anthony and Lillian Viagas, Allan J. Wilson, Joseph Wishy, Ed Wittstein and all the others who tried to remember.

Special thanks, also, to the Billy Rose Theatre Collection of the New York Public Library, and to the Southern Methodist University Oral History Program.

The Fantasticks
(*Original Production*)

Presented by Lore Noto
Book and lyrics by Tom Jones
Music by Harvey Schmidt
Suggested by a play by Edmund Rostand
Directed by Word Baker
Musical direction and arrangements by Julian Stein
Sets, costumes and lighting by Ed Wittstein
Choreography by Lathan Sanford
Associate Producers: Sheldon Baron, Dorothy Olim, Robert Alan Gold

Original Cast

Narrator (El Gallo)—Jerry Orbach
The Girl (Luisa)—Rita Gardner
The Boy (Matt)—Kenneth Nelson
The Boy's Father (Hucklebee)—William Larsen
The Girl's Father (Bellomy)—Hugh Thomas
An Actor (Henry Albertson/Lodevigo)—"Thomas Bruce" (Tom Jones)
The Man Who Dies (Mortimer/Socrates)—George Curley
The Mute—Richard (Blair) Stauffer
Handyman—Jay Hampton

Other Credits

Beverly Mann at the Harp
Production State Manager: Geoffry Brown
Assistant to Mr. Noto: Noel Weiss
Press Agents: Harvey Sabinson, David Powers
Attorney: Donald C. Farber
Advertising Representative: Fred Golden, Ingram Ash
Sets Constructed by Richard Thayer
Costumes Executed by Susan Sweetzer and Anthea Giannakouros
Musical Transcription by Ben Pickering
General Understudy: Jay Hampton
Standby for Miss Gardner: Sybil Lamb

Preface

When we wrote the first edition of *The Amazing Story of The Fantasticks* in 1991, the little musical on Sullivan Street was still running—as we assumed (or wished) it would keep doing forever. And it did run for another ten years, making the final total forty-one years, eight months and ten days.

But even the longest-running musical in history had a final performance—the 17,162nd, as it turned out. It came on January 13, 2003, and both of us were in attendance at the Sullivan Street Playhouse, among the small but devoted group that needed to bear witness, and the original production—and, as it turned out, the Playhouse itself—slipped into history.

The first eighteen chapters comprise this book's original text. For this second edition, at publisher John Cerullo's request, we've left them as they were written, speaking of the show in the present tense, as if it were still running. Because, in a real sense, it is. The show continues to get dozens of productions around the world each year.

The final chapter, "The Closing Night of *The Fantasticks*," was written in 2002 and 2004 and draws on a paper that co-author Robert Viagas submitted at a symposium at Hofstra University in 2003. The final chapter brings the story of the show and its creators up-to-date—another part of the cycle of life that is central to the show.

Many of the things we describe herein exist now only in the memories of those who loved the show. And in these pages. *The Fantasticks* was a show that celebrated the power of the passionate imagination. Let our book whet your imagination, so you can envision the show as it was—"Not with your eyes, for they are wise." But see it and hear it with your mind's eye and your mind's ear.

We'll help you try to remember. And follow . . .

—Donald C. Farber and Robert Viagas
December 2004

The Amazing Story of
The Fantasticks

HENRY: Perhaps you recall my Hamlet?

EL GALLO: Of course.

HENRY: (Stunned) You remember? Would you like to see the clippings?

EL GALLO: Perhaps later.

HENRY: As you wish. I preserve them. Who knows— I may write a book someday.

1

August 1959

"Remember me—in light!"

A N odd figure paced the lob-
by of the Minor Latham Theatre, glowing with the August 1959
heat in a pure white linen suit, fanning himself with a Panama
straw hat. The apparition was prim, theatrically cordial and
very determined. He had come to see a new play in this
fantastic getup—and he had brought his lawyer.

With darting eyes and a habit of talking out of the side of his
mouth, the Mysterious Man in White sought to acquire two
seats for that day's dress rehearsal.

The new play's creators, Tom Jones, Harvey Schmidt and
Word Baker, couldn't believe it. Just when they needed it most,
the gods of comedy and tragedy had sent them an eccentric
millionaire.

Or so they thought.

In fact, the gods had sent them a small clutch of producers
who were curious about their show, a one-act musical that
they'd been writing, on and off, for nearly a decade, but which
they had finished in a pell-mell theatrical tumble in just the
previous three weeks.

Director Word Baker was the happy-go-lucky one; easy-
going, social, a natural leader. Composer Harvey Schmidt was
the quiet, soulful one; a shy Southern gentleman. Librettist

Tom Jones was the intense one; motivated and driven, a periodic geyser of poetry.

Since their days together as students at the University of Texas at Austin, the three had been toying with the idea of fashioning a musical out of Edmond Rostand's 1890 play *Les Romanesques*. Neatly turning *Romeo and Juliet* on its head, the play tells the story of two duplicitous dads who concoct a feud in order to fool their romance-obsessed children into falling in love.

The show remained a dream for the trio throughout the Korean War, as they returned to jobs in the South, and as they followed the Yellow Brick Road to Manhattan and succeeded in commercial art (Schmidt), teaching (Jones) and directing Off-Broadway (Baker). As three Texans in the Wonderland of Beat-era 1950s Manhattan, they finally finished it.

But now, with the possibility of their big break standing in the lobby with his lawyer, Jones took a deep breath, walked up to the Man in White and said something he never thought he'd say to a prospective producer.

"All things considered, you'd be better off going to a movie."

* * *

The Barnard College campus on Broadway at 119th Street is on Manhattan's upper West Side, formerly a middle class residential neighborhood then in the process of being settled by Latin American immigrants in the latest chapter of the New York melting pot. Their clashes with earlier settlers inspired the 1957 musical *West Side Story*. Barnard's campus, like that of adjacent Columbia University, is positioned on the IRT subway line that runs north to the Bronx and south to Greenwich Village.

Barnard was considered to be distant enough from the city's traditional theater centers that it might as well have been in another city. It was far enough that it could support a stock playhouse—normally a staple of the boondocks—with only a little irony. Actress Mildred Dunnock, producer of a summer-long weekly series of new plays and revivals, didn't hesitate to advertise it as "a summer theater on Broadway."

It seemed a blue-moon notion that any commercial producer—let alone three—could be induced to trek to the remote reaches of Morningside Heights and see a new play. That such a producer might consider moving the show to a commercial run Off-Broadway constituted a Mickey-and-Judy-league miracle.

One of the most obscure offerings of the summer was a triple-bill of one-act plays, including William Inge's *The Mall* and Jack Dunphy's *The Gay Apprentice*. The Jones-Schmidt-Baker musical was listed last on the poster and ads, but eventually served as the curtain-raiser.

The triple-bill was scheduled to run August 4 to 8, preceded by a few days of rehearsal.

But the day before the first dress rehearsal, disaster had struck. Susan Watson, the play's ingenue, was suffering from strained vocal cords and could barely manage a hoarse whisper. On top of that, she had fallen from the ladder that served as the tiny musical's only scenery and had bruised her ribs, making dancing impossible.

That's why, when the Mysterious Man in White showed up and politely insisted on seeing the musical, Jones became, in his word, "furious."

"Who is this man? How did he get here?" Jones recalls thinking. "I tried to explain that this was our first run-through and that our leading lady was ill and the show was not going to be seen in its final form, and we were not ready for the pressure of an audience."

The Man in White smiled at him tolerantly. "Go on," he said, "It's all right." He would make allowances. He knew all about rehearsals.

* * *

Beyond Manhattan, America was still riding on the rush of its postwar wealth and power. Everything was big: sideburns, car fins, birth rates, suburbs, Ike's interest in golf, America's ego, Reds-under-the-beds paranoia, defense budgets. All the things that would come back as kitsch in the late 1980s were simply a way of life.

But the weather was changing. Holden Caulfield's notion of the phoniness of life kept nagging at the conscience. That year's Edsels weren't selling. Too gross.

Even in theater, Rodgers and Hammerstein's latest show,

Flower Drum Song, suffered from bloat, and there was something perfunctory about the way ticket-buyers went for the brand name. There was a desire for something compact, modest, sincere and, if the crowds in the beatnik coffeehouses were any barometer, something poetic.

The booming generation that later would exalt peace, love, youth and poetry was just reaching its adolescence. It was 1959—before "Silent Spring," Vietnam, assassinations and race riots—a perfect time to be alive.

*   *   *

Having hushed Jones's fears and having elbowed his way into the dress rehearsal of the little musical, what did the Mysterious Man in White see?

A boy, a girl, a cardboard moon, a ladder—little more. On a bare wooden stage, eight actors cast a parable "about the funny pain of growing up," as it was described.

Recited completely in verse, the wry love story was fresh, modest and unpretentious. The orchestra consisted of the composer sitting at a piano on the right side of the stage with his back to the audience. Sets and costumes seemed to materialize out of the pretty score, woven seemingly from tiny but correct sparkles and flourishes. If the play needed a wall, a few words and the audience's mind's eye supplied it. Shears and a watering can implied two flourishing backyard plots. A dissonant chord on the piano blew in all of winter.

With images of vegetation and gardening springing through every crack, there was a wholesome organic feeling to it. It had a sweetness that rarely cloyed and an integrity that never became self-righteous. It claimed to be nothing but a pleasant illusion gathered around a few grains of truth.

The proceedings were so informal that, to compensate for its limping leading lady, the choreographer stepped in to do her dances, and the composer sang her songs.

"So there's Susan Watson mouthing all these things and this disembodied voice with a Texas accent coming from over on one side," Schmidt said. "Lore just flipped over the show. He thought all this was part of the play, that it was some really avant-garde thing, much more than it ended up being."

Lore Noto, as the Man in White introduced himself afterward, was in love with the show and wanted to produce it Off-Broadway as soon as possible.

Like all producers, he had some suggestions—but just a few. Foremost among them was that the show be expanded from one act to two in order to make a full evening. That was a tough call, because one of the other would-be presenters, a TV producer named Joseph Wishy, liked the one-act just as it was and offered to mount it on a double-bill with some of Jones and Schmidt's earlier songs and sketches. The three authors figured, why tinker with success?

But what ultimately sold the trio on the still-somewhat-mysterious white-suited apparent-millionaire Lore Noto was his most mysterious action of all.

Librettist Tom Jones remembers Noto saying " 'I will only do it if you three make all the artistic decisions.' That's unheard of in this business! 'I'll step in if you have a disagreement, but I want you to have creative control.' That's what made us go with him."

There would be plenty of obstacles on the road to getting their little musical one hundred twenty-odd blocks south to Off-Broadway, but the first task was telling the other would-be impresarios that Noto would produce the show.

"Tom and I invited Joe Wishy up to my apartment to break the news to him," Schmidt recalls. "He was full of ideas. We were having this huge rain storm, and just as we were about to tell him that we had decided to go with Lore, suddenly the lights went out. I still remember him sitting framed by this big window facing out on the street. When we told him, he burst into tears.

"I'll never forget that image: lightning flashing behind him in the dark, and him sitting there weeping because he wouldn't be doing *The Fantasticks*."

2

1951 and Before

"Please, God, please—Don't let me be normal."

ALL roads in *The Fantasticks* lead to Tom Jones. Which you might not guess from examining the circumstances of his childhood. There was no confetti, no whirling girlies, no tipsy gypsies in Coleman, Texas, during the 1930s. There was just dry grit hanging in the air, sticking to windshields and gumming up the eyes.

There also was the smell of the turkey hatchery Jones's father ran in the town, some one hundred fifty miles northwest of the state capital at Austin. Jones's mother, a housewife, worked hard to cover the windows, wash faces and keep the food clean when the Dust Bowl storms got particularly bad.

It was best to be indoors on those days. To pass the time, Jones indulged two of his favorite pastimes. One was reading, the other was listening to comedies and dramas on the radio.

He was used to being a shut-in. When he was two years old in 1930, Jones came down with a severe attack of pneumonia that nearly killed him. Penicillin wouldn't become widely available until after World War II, so Jones was hospitalized for weeks while the infection ran its course. In the process, doctors cut out a rib to drain the pus from his chest.

"It was very traumatic," Jones recalls. "It left me convinced that I was in some way scarred, mutilated, unacceptable. I'm convinced that at least part of my compulsion to pretend was the necessity to compensate for that feeling."

Jones recalls concocting and leading elaborate games of make-believe for his pals. Usually his flights of fancy involved costumes, masks, swords and feats of bravery. And the aggression wasn't all theatrical.

"It was a pretty tough world," Jones said. "A real hick farm world of pretty rough old boys. I didn't feel that I could compete in some of the rougher activities of life. But I found that I could tell stories, or enact the stories that I heard on the radio. When they gave school plays I could do them. It was my way of fitting in."

Among his more startling roles was the Stage Manager in Thornton Wilder's deceptively simple slice of small-town life, *Our Town.* Scrawny, with an outsized head and big eyes, the brown-haired twelve-year-old Tommy Jones was the only child in a cast full of adults. "It must have been strange," he recalls, "this little, squeaky, voice-changing, wise philosopher."

With its supernaturally wise narrator who could stop and start the action, and with its love story about a boy and a girl who grow up next door to each other, it was a play Jones never would forget.

Jones's main connection with the world beyond Texas, however, was the movies. There were three cinemas in Coleman at that time, including one that opened only on Saturdays to accommodate farmers. Jones recalls being no fan of musicals, though he was drawn to "movies where the heroes were the strongest. Because I felt mutilated and inadequate from my illness, I identified out of necessity with Tarzan, Robin Hood, Zorro, et cetera."

His only exposure to live theater were traveling medicine shows, full of wily fakers trying to gull the rubes, and touring productions of a now-extinct species of American entertainment known as the Toby Show.

"The central character was always named Toby," Jones said. The lineage of that character goes back to Roman times, at least. It was your freckle-faced red-headed country bumpkin who in the end outsmarts the city slickers. He did it in dozens of different plays with dozens of different plots and locales."

Among the Tobys Jones got to see was one of Texas's foremost practitioners, Harley Sadler, near the end of his career. Looking back later, "I realized how brilliant this performer was. He was a great comic actor, at least as great as Bert Lahr. The things they were doing were so dated at that time, but he was great, and a great clown doesn't date."

Aside from Sadler's performance, Jones remembers being captivated by the entire atmosphere of the Toby Shows. Vaudeville actors plyed their trade on improvised stages beneath tents. To the light of lanterns, bands played amid the smell of hay, spread to keep down the dust.

Jones remembers Sadler stepping out of character to conduct a prize drawing. Holders of the right numbered Cracker Jack box could win a kewpie doll, a baseball or a trove of other wonders designed to enchant World War II era children. Then it was back to watching Toby—in the elderly Sadler's case, costumed, wigged and rouged to resemble a young farmhand—outwit another city slicker, usually from the East.

"It was not exactly classic drama," Jones said, "although perhaps more classic than I realized at the time."

Some part of Jones must have realized it. By the time he graduated seventh grade and entered high school, he was certain that he wanted to make his life in the theater.

"It was a great shock to my parents as you could imagine," he said, "because there really was no such thing around. But I never changed that under any circumstance, ever, in my life. It's the only thing that I ever considered being or doing."

When he was old enough, Jones got a job as one of the ushers at Coleman's Howell Theater, which gave him a chance to see films four times a day on weekends. Wednesdays, the Howell hosted an amateur night, for which the adolescent Jones would emcee and do comedy routines.

He also discovered girls. "My memories of girls of that time were adolescent bodies bearing the slight, delicious odor of perspiration mixed with gardenia smells of corsages" he said, "—heady, provocative, mysterious implications. Pale bodies and junior/senior corsages make a potent combination."

Potent or not, the fragrant maidens of Coleman were not enough to hold him there. A shining world beckoned down the road beyond the Howell. One of Jones's older friends had graduated to the University of Texas, which then had its only branch in Austin. When Jones learned that several of his high school contemporaries were matriculating there as well, his college plans were set. The decision was as simple as that.

There were a number of schools teaching drama in Texas in 1946. His life would have been quite different had he gone to any of the others.

Then as now, Texas had a glorious view of itself and of its destiny among American states and the world. If Texas was to have a university town, then it would be the Adelphi and Heidelberg of the South. If it was to train students in theater, it would train them to its own standards—not those of New York or Hollywood. And it would consider those students to be at least the equal of those from any other university. This attitude gave students a self-confidence and assertiveness that would serve them well in the world.

Among Jones's better-known contemporaries at the University of Texas were Fess Parker, later TV's *Davy Crockett*; future gossip columnist Liz Smith; actors Barbara Barrie, Rip Torn and Jayne Mansfield, plus Kathryn Grandstaff, who married Bing Crosby.

These and other people he met there continued to shape his life for the next forty-five years. Three of the nine original *Fantasticks* cast members were alumni. Besides Jones (who played The Actor under the name Thomas Bruce), they were Bill Larsen (Hucklebee) and Jay Hampton (The Handyman), though they did not come to the university until after Jones.

"It was a great, incredible experience to leave Coleman, Texas, where nobody did what I did and everybody thought I was crazy," Jones said, "and to go to a place where there were other people who did what I did—in fact, it was part of the lifestyle."

Jones's first influence was a teacher named Gordon Minter. "He was a wonderful teacher, very schmaltzy," Jones said. "He loved the razzle-dazzle of show biz. He would tell all these great show biz stories, and indeed I did well under him. I liked him very much, and he took me under his wing. If I had gone on like that under his influence I'm sure that I might have become a successful sitcom writer or director in Hollywood.

"But when Mr. Payne came, it opened up a new perception."

The "Mr. Payne" he refers to was B. Iden Payne, whose name can be found alone on the dedication page of the published script of *The Fantasticks*.

Payne arrived at the University of Texas about a year after Jones did, one of the faculty's most eminent acquisitions. A native of Great Britain, Payne had been director of the Abbey Players in Dublin when J. M. Synge's *The Playboy of the Western World* opened there to a riot in 1907. He served as director of the Shakespeare Memorial Theatre, Stratford-on-Avon, from 1935 to 1942, and was named director of New York's Theatre Guild Shakespeare Company in 1944. He had directed Ethel Barrymore, Maude Adams, Otis Skinner and many others at the pinnacle of his profession in New York and London, yet when he died in 1976, *The New York Times* called him "a leading figure in the growth of repertory and little theater in Britain and the United States."

He took credit for giving John Barrymore his first major serious role in Galsworthy's *Justice*, and for casting fourteen-year-old Helen Hayes in her first important part, in *Dear Brutus*.

Years later, when Jones met Hayes, he broke the ice by reminiscing about Payne. "She's older than I," Jones said, "but we have the same perspective: youthful idolators of this god-like man."

A specialist in the works of Shakespeare, Payne staged the Bard's plays in a replica of the Globe theater at the 1932 World's Fair in Chicago. Through his students he left a legacy of Globe-style theaters around the country, including the Old Globe in San Diego. Payne himself was one of the godfathers of the Goodman Theatre in Chicago and helped start one of the first drama departments at an American university, at Carnegie Tech.

Most significantly, as an authority on Elizabethan stage techniques, he was determined to root out the notion that complicated sets and scenery were necessary to theater. For Payne, if the text is rich enough, no further stage dressing is needed but the actors to speak it. He was emphatic about this and pounded it into his students.

"It's all quite standard now" Jones said. "But his idea of doing Shakespeare on essentially a bare stage was a revolutionary idea in this century and especially in this country. That's the way it was done originally, of course, and his whole thing was to return to that and see what's there. But he came along after two hundred and fifty years of *A Midsummer Night's Dream* with castles and painted forests."

By the time Payne accepted the post of drama department chairman at the University of Texas in 1946, he was coming to the evening of his career. But the spirit that had animated his long resume was still blazing. He influenced two generations of theater artists, including one of his most admiring disciples, director/choreographer/dancer Tommy Tune.

Jones said, "Mr. Payne was fond of saying 'The first rule of the theater is . . .'—but it was always a different first rule. The bottom line of anything he taught was his great passion for the theater. And respect for it, which made us all view it in a different way: As a noble profession, potentially. As something valuable to oneself and to *life*. And to all people."

Payne cut an eccentric figure in Austin, always wearing a tie and jacket even in the summer heat. He had poor eyesight and was the subject of some disrespectful merriment among his students because of it. Not helping was his theory that the best therapy for the eyes was staring directly into the noon sun. Though he became virtually blind, he continued to direct well into his eighties.

Under Payne's tutelage, Jones drew on his childhood expertise before an audience and plunged into acting studies. "But I was a terrible actor," Jones later told an audience at the 92nd Street YM-YWHA in New York. "I wasn't a bad showman, necessarily, but I was a really bad actor because I never wanted to look at the other actors. I always wanted to look at the audience. My whole thing was, I wanted to get applause when I went off stage. That was my whole technique. My motto as an actor was, 'The show must *not* go on.' I had to stop it.

"Combined with that was another childish manifestation: When I get nervous, I start belching and I can't stop. There weren't too many parts written for belchers, that I could find."

So Jones refocused his studies with the intention of taking instruction from his adored British mentor in how to become a director. This subtle change in Jones's academic emphasis proved to be another of the crucial forks in the road that led to *The Fantasticks*.

For one thing, Jones almost immediately crossed paths with

another directing student, Charlie Baker. For reasons that, for the moment, will stay in the future, Baker later adopted his mother's maiden name as his first name.

"Word Baker was this skinny, pimply little kid like me—or so he seemed," Jones said. "I was astonished to discover not only that he'd been in the Army during World War II, but he had a wife and two daughters. I was totally inexperienced, so that impressed me enormously. Everything Word did at the university was magic. He was very funny and everything he did worked out well. He did some acting and some directing and designing, too. All of it. He quickly became very impressive to all of us."

Born in Honey Grove, Texas, in 1923, Baker was just five years older than Jones, but he was nearly a generation ahead in terms of life experience. He began directing almost immediately. When he was five, he received a Mother Goose book as a gift and assigned all the neighborhood children to learn the poems and recite them in a backyard theater. He borrowed a kimono so he could do a children's version of *Madame Butterfly*.

He married his high school sweetheart, Joanna Alexander, and the two of them went to North Texas Teachers College under National Youth Administration scholarships. But the lure of the stage was strong. Baker got a part in *College Capers*, an amateur show performed between movies at local cinemas. It cut into his studies so severely that he soon flunked out of college. Baker was drafted in 1943 and sent to California where he was assigned to the 389th Anti-Aircraft Artillery Battalion. Attached to the 13th Air Force, the 389th saw action in the Pacific and participated in the invasion of Morotai.

After the war, Baker got a job as an assistant county auditor in Honey Grove and helped organize the Honey Grove Town Theater. A childhood friend urged him to follow his stage instinct and enroll at the U of Texas. Promising his wife that he'd make straight A's, Baker matriculated in 1948, where he soon met Jones.

Under B. Iden Payne and his colleague, James Moll, Jones and Baker embarked on a diversified course of study that gave them experience not only in directing, but in acting, designing and handling everything from props to lighting.

Among the enticements for enterprising and diverse young drama students like Jones and Baker was the university's Curtain Club. Its purpose was primarily social, but it did offer at least one unusual outlet for the theatrical imagination.

When Jones met Baker in 1947, the Broadway musical *Oklahoma!* was only four years old, and many of the milestone American musical plays like *South Pacific* and *West Side Story* lay in the future. Musicals were still frowned upon as inferior to straight drama and even comedy. As a result, musicals were largely ignored in classrooms at the college level.

But they certainly weren't ignored at the Curtain Club. Each Friday the club would host a talent showcase in the tradition of *Babes in Arms* and the *Our Gang* comedies. The students would perform scenes and songs from the current movies, plays and musicals. Sometimes the skits and songs were original.

It was at one of these Curtain Club revues that Jones succumbed to the peer pressure of his Renaissance-man pal Baker and made his debut as a lyricist. His first song, a *cri de coeur* of youthful angst cowritten with U of Texas student Tom Ribbink, carried the ineffable title "Out of the Night Comes My Lament of Sorrow." Jones observed, "We had a fantastic piece of staging that was very original: We had a girl sing it by a lamppost. We thought that was some kind of revolutionary breakthrough. I worked with several people turning out terrible songs like that."

Between the inspiring classroom work with Payne and the boisterous informality of the Curtain Club, Jones and Baker had some glorious fun and began to come of age.

"I began to realize that there was a kind of theater that I liked, and a kind of theater that I didn't like," Jones said. "The kind of the theater that I liked was exemplified by Shakespeare, but also included Moliére, the Greeks and Thornton Wilder."

B. Iden Payne's lessons had fallen on fertile soil. "I began to realize that there were certain similarities between these things," Jones said. "First of all, they weren't realistic, weren't naturalistic. I realized that something in me responded to that. I didn't believe plays that had realistic scenery. I kept wanting to say 'That's not a real tree I see through the window. That's not a real door; I know what it looks like from the other side.' But if you trimmed away all that and just gave me the characters and the story, I could believe anything. If you didn't *ask* me to believe anything, I could believe everything.

"I also liked the soliloquys and so forth: the presentational theater as opposed to the realistic theater. I liked the potential for linguistic magic—not just people talking the way they really talked, but in a way that was heightened, that could evoke an excitement just because of the language itself, in addition to the emotions of the characters.

"I think I knew instinctively that that went back to the origins of what the theater was. Way back in the beginning when people gathered and a story was told. I liked the fact that you could do anything. Not being literally realistic, you didn't have to waste a lot of time with exposition. You could go to the meat of the matter, and you could go skipping anyplace you wanted to because you were freer.

"Lastly, I liked it because it was schmaltzy, because it was so theatrical. Nobody has ever been more dramatic and more outrageously theatrical than Shakespeare. He did things that you wouldn't dare do in a literally realistic play. He pulls out all the stops and goes all the way.

"Gradually it dawned on me that the one place where these elements were possible and natural in my time was in the musical theater. If people try to use linguistic magic in a regular play, they get nervous. It isn't part of the convention of our time. Ditto soliliquys. But in musicals, that's what you expect. That's the natural stock in trade. Well, I thought, if you have all these things I've been talking about, plus you have music and dancing—and naked girls—my God, what more could you ask out of life?"

* * *

By 1948, Jones's devotion to the Curtain Club's weekly revels was repaid with election to the club presidency. One of the president's duties was to audition aspirants for club membership. Today, Jones says he still cannot remember the single most important audition he conducted: that of an introverted, piano-playing art student named Harvey Schmidt.

Schmidt was born in 1929 in a cottage adjoining the campus of Southern Methodist University where his father, a Methodist minister, was working toward a masters degree. They were descended from German immigrants who had farmed Texas since the nineteenth century.

Schmidt recalls the house fondly, but his family didn't stay there long. As a minister, his father moved the family every two or three years, so Schmidt lived in many parts of Texas, though mostly in little towns around Houston, which he recalls as his "mother navel city" when he was growing up.

Today home to its own opera company, resident theater and a host of other first-class arts organizations, Houston in the 1930s and 1940s already was considered second only to Dallas as a cultural wellspring of Texas.

"People growing up today can't imagine how different the world was before television," Schmidt said. "We had movies, radio and some live performances, and I loved them all because they were all separate. TV smears them all together. It also makes everything real. In those days you didn't know quite what was real and what was fantasy. Movies showed you New York and Hollywood—they showed them in a false way, but they looked better than they ever actually were. I'd see in these old '30s musicals where everybody'd be dancing on black glass floors and that supposedly was New York. I thought, well, that looks swell."

Yet his first movie experience was a traumatic one. While waiting on line to see the 1938 Tommy Kelly *The Adventures of Tom Sawyer*, Schmidt saw a man being removed from the theater while suffering an epileptic fit. The nine-year-old Schmidt was terrified to go in, thinking that there was something in the movie so frightening that it could provoke such a reaction. When the part came where Injun Joe is stalking Tom and Becky through a dark cavern, Schmidt tried to leave, thinking the convulsion-inducing sequence had arrived.

"A few years later, you couldn't get me out of the movies," he said. He found he was no less impressed by their ability to provoke strong responses of other kinds.

A precocious artist, Schmidt's drawing so impressed his first grade teacher that the teacher announced to the class that he could grow up to be a commercial artist in New York. "That sounded good to me," Schmidt said, "so I always claimed I'd do that."

Schmidt's acute visual sense attracted him to movies at first more than theater, and particularly to the color of Vincente Minnelli's MGM musicals. Schmidt recalls Minnelli's 1946 *Ziegfeld Follies* as a special favorite, partly because of the wide open spaces for dancing on Minnelli's sets, and especially for his use of color in striking scenic concepts.

With his mother's encouragement, Schmidt listened each weekend to radio broadcasts of classical music, particularly Toscanini's weekly shows with the NBC Orchestra.

"I'd live for the weekends when I'd get these symphonic broadcasts on the radio," Schmidt said. "I'd just sit there and draw by the hour, happy as could be. We'd hear the Metropolitan Opera on Saturday, too. My mother always made us listen to that every Saturday afternoon. She would tell us how wonderful it was that we were actually able to hear that."

His mother had good reason to train her son's ear. She earned money by giving piano lessons. Unfortunately, Harvey was one of her worst students. Though not clinically dyslexic, Schmidt says he suffers extreme discomfort when faced with having to correlate letters to words, or math symbols with math concepts. The same was true with music and written music.

"She tried to teach me, but there was this dyslexia thing. I wouldn't sit still. I was a very wild child. I was very creative, very interested in things, but I would dance away from the piano and go and do something else."

Which is not to say that he never learned to play. "The minute I'd hear how a song went," he said, "I could play it, just by ear. I had a very good ear."

His imagination ran wild. Walking the deserted country roads, he would invent, compose, orchestrate, choreograph and perform his own movie extravaganzas while singing his creations at the top of his lungs. He recalls being able to "run through wild ideas for mammoth production numbers like those I'd seen in musical films. Only mine were even bigger and grander, because, out of doors, under the sky, I was not restricted by a studio budget!"

But from that day to this, Schmidt never learned to read or write a note. Though he went on to create seven major theater scores, he composed and played them all by ear, making all his changes from memory, and relying on an assistant to transcribe them.

"You can't be taught things anyway, very much," he said. "I used to think you could be, and I kept thinking that when I went to the university I'd be taught how to paint. But nobody ever teaches you. You come to realize that nobody knows anything and you have to do it yourself."

Schmidt's "deep hunger" for the arts drew him to performances of ballet, theater and classical music in Houston. Schmidt figured out a way to slip backstage at the Civic Auditorium and would wander the hallways to get close looks at heroes like Leonard Bernstein and Jeanette MacDonald.

Like New York and Hollywood, World War II was buffed and glamorized by the movies. With no evening TV news, America got its images of war from *Movietone News*, *The March of Time* and from the pages of *Life* magazine—each sometimes weeks after the fact.

"I adored World War II," Schmidt said. "It will always be the most exciting time of my life. I wasn't in it but I loved the movies at that time. The movie theaters were jammed with servicemen, the streets awash with servicemen. There was such an excitement about the whole thing, and it had nothing to do with the horror of people getting killed, somehow."

You could join the Navy at age seventeen, and many of those who didn't join were drafted the following year. As the war dragged on and Schmidt began to approach draft age, his romance with the war began to wane. Still, the excitement of that time etched its music into his mind.

The atom bomb was dropped in August 1945, ending the war. The following spring, Schmidt graduated high school. He worked two years earning college tuition at the Gulf Atlantic Warehouse Company on the Houston ship channel. He began as office boy and worked up to clerk-typist.

In 1948, he finally had the tuition to get into the University of Texas. "It was like going to heaven," Schmidt said, echoing Jones's enthusiasm at finding sympathetic minds.

Though Schmidt was studying commercial art, his love for performance drew him to the Curtain Club, where he had his fateful audition. His acting left a lot to be desired, and overall he wasn't a very appetizing candidate.

He did play the piano, however, and on the strength of that, Schmidt was inducted by acclamation. Though Jones can't recall his first encounter with Schmidt, Schmidt remembers the awesome figure struck by the Curtain Club potentate. Though they have been collaborators now for close to a half-century, Schmidt still speaks and behaves deferentially to his former upperclassman.

Oblivious to the effect he was having, Jones didn't really take notice of Schmidt until he started designing posters for the weekly showcase and for the official drama department productions.

"My first memory and impression of Harvey had to do with Harvey as a designer," Jones said. "He did some posters for the Curtain Club which were sensational. They were so good, we couldn't keep them up. People were taking them and framing them. I was impressed."

Schmidt also designed scenery, but his main task was playing piano. "A lot of it was drama students wanting to be musical comedy stars without the wherewithal to do it," Jones said. "They would get poor Harvey, who was so pliable and docile and eager to please, and rehearse him for hours and hours and hours."

Mightily impressed by Betty Grable movies, their friend Charlie Baker also began doing more work in musicals, and he too turned to the Curtain Club as the only campus outlet. And it was there, in 1948, twelve years before the opening of *The Fantasticks*, that the triumvirate at the center of its creation began working together on a single stage.

And it was in the music rooms of the university's Student Union building that Harvey Schmidt made a momentous discovery.

It all started when Schmidt tried to stretch his limited musical knowledge to fit the demands of the Curtain Club. As 1948 turned into 1949, a new kind of music began to penetrate Texas. The original cast recording of *Oklahoma!*, released as a set of 78s some years earlier, was so successful for Decca Records that it soon became *de rigueur* for the cast of new hit Broadway shows to troop into the recording studio within weeks of their openings.

These records enabled a generation raised on radio to visualize musicals in their own homes, thousands of miles from Broadway. *Finian's Rainbow, Carousel, Brigadoon, Gentlemen Prefer Blondes, South Pacific*—Schmidt vividly remembers the arrival of these records in the university's co-op store.

"The kids in the drama department, they'd come to me and say, 'In next Wednesday's show I want to sing "How Are Things in Glocca Morra?" ' and they'd give me the record and say 'Go learn to play it.' They thought I could play the piano, and I didn't want to let them down. But at that time I could only play songs in the key of C."

His only recourse was to go to the Student Union building where the school maintained listening rooms equipped with both a record player and a piano. Painstakingly, for hours at a time, Schmidt would play the records over and over, imitating the songs by rote, note-by-note, inventing a primitive piano adaptation in his head, then committing the entire score to memory. He did this nearly every week during semesters for two years.

For Schmidt, whose heroes were Bela Bartók and Vincente Minnelli, the cast albums were a double education. Not only did they introduce him to the wonderland of show music in its golden age, they also helped teach him the nuts and bolts of musical technique.

"I didn't understand anything about music; all I knew was that a lot of these things weren't in the key of C. But one day it dawned on me that there were patterns in all this music. Suddenly I saw the whole way the piano could function in different keys. I thought this was my own invention! I had discovered Western Music. It was an incredible musical education, I can tell you, having to do that. I've always said everyone should go to college because you don't know what you're going to learn—but you're going to learn something. Well, I learned that."

Musing on his partner's experience, Tom Jones said, "Would it have been better if he had knocked that off in a week or so in class? We'll never know. Harvey does things at his own pace, in his own unique way."

* * *

One day in summer 1949, Charlie (Word) Baker showed up at the Schmidt parsonage with a car trunk full of sheet music and a wild idea.

One of their professors, James Moll, had been a pianist in speakeasies during the 1930s and had amassed an enormous collection of songs from the first two decades of the century. He'd added to it extensively in the ensuing years, but late in his life he had grown weary of the clutter and was preparing to throw it all away.

Learning of this, Baker convinced the professor to turn over the entire collection to him instead. The notion of all that wonderful music had sparked a plan. For the upcoming fiftieth anniversary of the Curtain Club in 1950, the members would stage a cavalcade of music from the first half of the twentieth century. Baker himself would direct. With the impressive title of "Musical Director," Schmidt would arrange all the fabulous music. Jones would write comedy sketches to tie it all together.

"We knew a lot of the songs ourselves from earlier things that had been done, and a lot of them had been in movies," Schmidt said. "So Tom and Word and I went through it all and structured the whole thing, starting in 1900 and running up through 1950. We had a big Ziegfeld segment, a sleek 1920s Busby Berkeley/Manhattan/Gershwinesque segment and a 1930s Depression Blues segment set in New Orleans."

For the 1910s, they did a silent movie sequence all designed in black and white. For this, Schmidt wrote his own music, incorporating elements of classical music and his beloved Hollywood scores. He also was responsible for arranging all the sheet music for piano and drums—which in many ways was more difficult than learning it from a record. Schmidt called upon his mother and sister Evelyn to play the volumes of music so he could hear how the songs went. Then they would listen to his arrangements and notate them according to his directions.

After the show was assembled, Baker decided something was missing. Despite the superfluity of great American pop music, there was no single song that captured the spirit of the whole show.

"Word wanted to open the show with just a girly chorus line—with something like six girls—singing the most racky-tacky thing you could think of. We didn't really have a song that did that, so I said, well, I'll just write one."

Writing both music and lyrics, Schmidt came back with a 1900s-flavored number titled "Hipsy-Boo" in which the sequined chorus girls wiggled their bottoms and warbled:

> Hello fellas, we're here to greet ya
> With a song and a smile
> Dance all the while
> Hello boys
> We hope that you like
> Our show with girlies and gags
> Music that rags

You'll find that we're pals in the end
And we will always be true-blue
We're the pride of this the-ater
Show your dough and see more later

Hope our kicks do something to you
Because we L (bump) O (bump) V E, love you, boys
And hope you're here to stay
Hope that you won't (bump) stray too far away
'Cause racky-tack ticky-too
We love men with eyes of blue

So glad your wife's at home crocheting
While you're sashaying 'round town
It's a one (bump) two (bump) doin' the Hipsy-Boo
Three, four, honey, you know what it does for you
Goodbye boys, we're glad to have welcomed you
Doin' the old one-two
Givin' a kick for you
Doin' the Hipsy-Boo R-a-a-a-a-g.*

Why "Hipsy-Boo"? Nonce song titles were very popular during the period covered by the revue. Both Jerome Kern and Cole Porter wrote for the *Hitchy-Koo* revue series in the late 1910s and early 1920s. George Gershwin had a hit with "Tee-Oodle-Um-Bum-Bo," Jimmy Durante's "Inka Dinka Doo" was one of his signature numbers, and "Three Little Fishes" was a wartime favorite.

Writing a pastiche of music from this period, it's small wonder Schmidt came up with "Hipsy-Boo." Baker was so enchanted with it, he adopted it as the title of the entire show.

Opening at the four-hundred-seat X-Hall Theater (one of the sequentially lettered prefab buildings left over from World War II) in the spring of 1950, the show was a huge success. "There are professors teaching there today who still talk about it whenever I go back," Schmidt said.

Hipsy-Boo was staged with a circular runway around the orchestra pit to bring the chorus-line cuties closer to the audi-

*From "Hipsy-Boo" © Harvey Schmidt. Reprinted by Permission.

ence. To enhance the burlesque atmosphere, Baker offered free seats to bald men so that the first row of seats would be a solid line of shining pates, a la Minsky's.

"We knew we were a hit because students started shaving their heads to get in, and lining up for hours to be the lucky ones chosen. You usually could get tickets for any student production at the University of Texas. But the tickets to *Hipsy-Boo* were gone in an instant.

"And suddenly, just everywhere we went, we were stars like we've never been since. Quite honestly, we've never had success like that since. Ever."

Said Schmidt, "It really spoiled us and made us very badly want to be in show business."

* * *

But first it was back to classes. Under B. Iden Payne, the students had to be well-grounded not only in the well-known classics, but in all the minor classics whose eddies subtly affected the flow of theater history.

Several of these came up in Payne's course, Period Play Production. Among Payne's many assignments to Jones was to direct a scene from Edmond Rostand's first play, *Les Romanesques*, written in 1890 when he was twenty-two—about Jones's age when he first directed it.

Written partly as a reaction against the ebbing romanticism of the age, *Les Romanesques* is a cheerfully mean-spirited parody of/homage to Shakespeare's *Romeo and Juliet*.

Writing in the book *Edmond Rostand*, Alba dell Fazia Amoia traces the story to the French *Lai de Lastic* (*Lay of the Nightingale*) as well as to the medieval legend of Aucassin and Nicolette and the legend of Pyramus and Thisbe, which was translated from Ovid and updated, also by Shakespeare.

Instead of Shakespeare's warring Montagues and Capulets, Rostand's play has two fathers, Bergamin and Pasquinot, who pretend to feud in order to play on the absurdly romantic rebelliousness of the children, Sylvette and Percinet. They figure that as long as they pretend to keep the young lovers apart in the strictest conditions, the couple inevitably will be attracted to one another. To aid their scheme, the fathers enlist the help of a bandit named Straforel. The play is distinguished chiefly for its flamboyant use of costumed swordsmen and brigands in its comically exaggerated mock abduction scene.

The play was first performed with modest success at the Comédie Française in 1894, and was translated into English by Mary Hendee in 1899 as *The Romancers,* though with little notice.

In 1900, an Englishwoman named Julia Constance Fletcher, writing under the pen name George Fleming, published a new translation "Freely Done into English Verse," which she titled *The Fantasticks,* after the archaic sense of the word meaning "One who is fantastic in conduct or appearance" (Funk and Wagnalls). The word is derived from the Greek, "phantastes," meaning "boaster."

Fleming added the extra "K" on the end in a flight of pure whimsy.

Fleming's *The Fantasticks* was performed at London's Royalty Theatre, May 29, 1900, starring Mrs. Patrick Campbell, a primary interpreter of George Bernard Shaw and one of the foremost actresses of her age. In a gender switch, she played the "Matt" part, Percinet, with Gerald du Maurier as Straforel and George Arliss as Pasquin.

It was tepidly received. Among contemporary reviewers, one wrote ". . . there is a certain prettiness to the main idea and its development, as well as in the acting, that may make *The Fantasticks* acceptable to a lazy audience on a close afternoon in summer."

Nevertheless, it had the poetic richness that B. Iden Payne was looking for. And in 1909, Payne did a production of Fleming's translation in Manchester, repeating it in repertory there for several seasons. When he was teaching directing to Tommy Jones some forty years later, he handed his student some mimeographed pages of this old favorite and told him to stage one of its most remarkable scenes. Summoned by the fathers to carry out a phony abduction, the bandit Straforel proceeds to describe to them the many sorts that are available.

Amoia points out that Straforel is a precursor of Rostand's more famous Cyrano de Bergerac. His abduction speech anticipates Cyrano's funny monologue about the many insults that might be leveled against his outsized nose.

It can be a very funny scene playing on both Straforel's

grandiloquence and the father's chagrin at learning that their carefully-hatched plan actually is quite standard. It also provides an acting and directing challenge since Straforel must conjure extravaganzas of lighting and costume with only the power of his words.

And one more thing. Jones said: "It was the conceit of the woman writing under the name George Fleming to take the word 'rape,' as in *The Rape of the Lock*, and substitute it for the word 'abduction,' as they were called clearly in the French original."

The result goes like this:

Sir! We've the obvious open schoolboy rape
Which only needs black cloaks, no matter what
    their shape;
The rape by cab; — 'tis little in request;—
The rape by day; — the rape by night looks best;—
The pompous rape with coaches of the court,
With powdered lacqueys, wigs of every sort—
(The wigs are extra)—eunuchs, slaves and mutes,
Blacks, bravos, brigands, musketeers — as suits . . .

The comic rape; — the lady must be fond;—
Romantic, in a boat; — requires a pond;—
The rape Venetian; — wants a blue lagoon;
The rape by moonlight, or without a moon—
Moonlight is dear, and always in demand;—
The rape lugubrious, by blue lightning planned . . .

The rape emphatic, and the rape polite;—
The rape with torches, *that's* a charming sight!
The rape in masks — we call that classical;—
The rape gallant, done to sweet music's call;—
The rape in sedan chair, that's new and gay,
That latest thing of all — and *distingué*.

Compare that with part of the slightly Americanized lyric Jones would later write for "It Depends on What You Pay" in his own *The Fantasticks*:

We've the obvious open schoolboy rape,
With little mandolins and perhaps a cape,
The rape by coach; it's little in request.
The rape by day; but the rape by night is best.
Just try to see it.

And you will soon agree, Señors,
Why invite regret,
When you can get the sort of rape
You'll never ever forget!

You can get the rape emphatic.
You can get the rape polite.
You can get the rape with Indians,
A truly charming sight.
You can get the rape on horseback,
They all say it's *distingué.*
So you see the sort of rape
Depends on what you pay.
It depends on what you pay . . .

The comic rape!
Perhaps it's just a trifle too unique (Ha ha)
Romantic rape.
Done while canoeing on a moonlit creek.
The Gothic rape!
I play Valkyrie on a bass bassoon!
The drunken rape!
It's done completely in a cheap saloon.
The rape Venetian — needs a blue lagoon.
The rape with moonlight — or without a moon.
Moonlight is expensive, but it's in demand.
The military rape,
It's done with drummers and a band.
You understand?
It's very grand!
It's done with drums and a great big brass band!*

But that wasn't until many years later. At the time, the scene from Fleming's *The Fantasticks* was one among dozens Jones read, directed, acted or designed under Payne's tutelage. Jones's first version was never seen by an audience. It was done in class, by students, and quickly was followed by a new assignment. He never even saw the complete play, just a one-act version that ended with the happy reunion and the tearing down of the wall—essentially the first act of the musical.

But there was something else that helped stamp it in Jones's memory. Among his many responsibilities to the theater department was running the light board for a high school play competition hosted by the university each year. Owing to the liveliness and brevity of the one-act *Fantasticks*, it was very popular among the teenage thespian societies. Jones got to watch it again and again.

* * *

Having graduated with a BFA in 1949, Jones began his master's program that autumn. As his thesis, he chose to stage an American folk play titled *Roadside*. Its author was Lynn Riggs, a playwright best known for another folk play, *Green Grow the Lilacs*, a cowboy saga that had been adapted by Richard Rodgers and Oscar Hammerstein as *Oklahoma!*

Jones had decided to augment the script with a few songs of his own, so he wrote some lyrics and went hunting for a composer to set them. Jones and Schmidt had worked harmoniously on *Hipsy-Boo*, but their continued collaboration was no *fait accompli*. For one thing, they had never collaborated as songwriters. Jones had done no lyrics for *Hipsy-Boo*, and Schmidt had written the words to his own music.

But while Jones was a star of the theater department, Schmidt was still a commercial art major and therefore technically an outsider. Also, Jones was an upperclassman, and in college, class distinctions, in all senses of the expression, are sharper.

Jones and Schmidt rarely even saw each other. It was only through Charlie Baker, who continued to stage the weekly Curtain Club shows, that the two got together on *Roadside*—or didn't get together, as things turned out.

Shortly after *Hipsy-Boo*, Schmidt entered what he calls his

Salvador Dali period. It was the dawn of the 1950s, and the rebelliousness of the Beat era was still in Schmidt's future. But even then, to express his individuality, he shaved his head bald like the students who had fought to get into *Hipsy-Boo*. Punkers were still able to fluster the middle class with that hairstyle in the 1980s. It's easy to imagine its effect on Austin, Texas, in the Truman era.

Next, Liz Smith, one of Schmidt's idols on the staff of the student magazine, for which he sometimes did artwork, began wearing white overalls. "I liked the way it looked," Schmidt said, "So I took to wearing nothing but white overalls. Mine were smeared with paint because I was always painting. I'd wear the same pair day after day."

This was the vision that confronted Jones when he brought over his lyric and asked Schmidt to set it to music. But he was in for another surprise.

"I was heavily into Harold Arlen at the time," Schmidt said. "I just loved him, and I loved bluesy Gershwinesque chords. I was just discovering how to do them at the piano myself. I was having major breakthroughs at the keyboard."

To Jones's simple country lyric, Schmidt wrote a melody embroidered with sumptuous chords out of Arlen and clangorous dissonances out of Bartók.

When Jones came back to hear their first collaboration, Schmidt said, "I think he was appalled that this person who he barely knew had shaved his head and was wearing white overalls with nothing underneath. Then on top of it, there was that music. He just said, 'I think this is terrible. Not what I had in mind at all.'"

Jones remembers it much the same way, though the years have made him more charitable. "I didn't think very much of what he'd done, but that's because it was more advanced than I was at that point. It was full of more innovation and daring than I perceived. So I got somebody else, someone who did little 'Coming Through the Rye'-type melodies."

During the winter of 1950–51, Jones was invited by the journalism fraternity and sorority to direct their annual satirical musical titled *Time Staggers On*, a play on the title of the newsreel *Time Marches On*.

Jones took the job for a simple reason —it paid. Though it had been born as strictly a political lampoon, *Time Staggers On*, or *TSO* as they all still call it, had evolved into an annual college-themed musical revue.

As director, it was Jones's job to accept submissions of material from anyone in the school. "But," he said, "I really was unhappy with all of the scripts being submitted. It seemed to me that it would be almost impossible not to write something better if one tried to do it oneself. So I began to put together a story and some lyrics."

Jones and Schmidt hadn't seen one another for months after the *Roadside* debacle, but faced with the task of composing a respectable original score for *TSO*, Jones decided to give Schmidt another try.

"By then my hair had grown back," Schmidt said. "I think it helped."

A year had matured them both. "I found that the working relationship was terrific, and the whole thing was very exhilarating," said Jones, who did the staging and choreography, as well as wrote the book and lyrics. In addition to the music and arrangements, Schmidt designed the sets and costumes.

For their first full-scale collaboration, they decided to tell the story of a typical freshman on his first day at the University of Texas. Jones wrote an opening lyric introducing the protagonist, aptly titled "The Freshman Song."

Schmidt said, "He gave me the lyric and I carried it to and from class. I'd work on it as I was walking across the campus, which was huge. When I got through with it after a week or two, I played it for him, and he really liked it a lot. I still think it's one of the nicest songs we ever wrote. Then he started giving me other lyrics, and very quickly we wrote this whole score. It was the first time I'd ever done anything like that."

The script shows strong influence of *On the Town*, the 1944 Leonard Bernstein musical. *TSO* opens with two scrubwomen talking as the dawn comes up on the university, and waiting for the new students to burst on the scene like the sailors in the opening of the Bernstein show.

"When you're that age, you think you can steal from everybody," Schmidt said. "You don't think you're stealing, but you think no one else has noticed these things that you think are so divine. You just use whatever you like, and it never occurs to you that someone else might notice it or figure out you'd lifted it."

The libretto is loaded with college humor—though also with references to the many events shaping the world they were coming into. It also was influenced by the contemporary musicals—especially those choreographed by Agnes De Mille and Jerome Robbins—that integrated dance into the storytelling. "The Registration Ballet" is one of the high points of *TSO*.

Among those satirized were Ronny Dugger, later a well-known Texas publisher, and future New York *Daily News* columnist Liz Smith, who then wrote for the school magazine, the *Ranger*. Smith's character, "Linda Smith," was the fashion editor who played protector for *TSO*'s disoriented protagonist. Jones described "Linda" as "Somewhat older, somewhat cynical, but with heart of gold. In the movies of that time, she would have been the Jean Arthur character, as in *Mr. Smith Goes to Washington*."

As the opening approached, Jones said, "The excitement of musicals began to dawn on me. It wasn't so much the awareness of the potential of the form; I was just exhilarated by that much applause and adoration. That was wonderful. The sense of power that gave! And also, since I didn't really sing very well myself, it was thrill to actually put together a song and have people sing it and have it sound so pretty."

The Jones-Schmidt *Time Staggers On* opened in spring 1951 at the Hogg Auditorium, a space with approximately twelve hundred seats—about the size of a medium-sized Broadway musical theater. If anything, the show was even more popular than *Hipsy-Boo*. All three performances were solidly sold out, with people standing in the back and sitting in the aisles.

The auditorium had windows on either side, and those who couldn't buy tickets crowded around the windows to watch the show from outside. Schmidt remembers a rainstorm blowing in one night, and how the wet faces looked, still pressed against the windows.

3

1951–55

*"I've had an education. / I've been inside a lab: /
Dissected violets. / I know the way things are."*

DESPITE their success at song-
writing, Schmidt said, "We weren't committed as a team or
anything. It was just something we enjoyed doing together."

That, as much as anything, welded Jones to Schmidt to
Baker. The fecundity of the college atmosphere plus the over-
whelming success of their first efforts made them feel safe with
each other. They'd discovered a niche in Austin, an intellectual
and artistic oasis in a redneck land, which nonetheless was
home.

All were content to stay and build lives there. Despite their
desire to trace careers in theater, in early 1951, the three had no
plans to go to New York City. "At the University of Texas,
nobody gave you any illusions about New York or about the
theater," Jones said. "They were scrupulously careful to say,
'You are *not* going to be able to make a living in this field. Get
into something else.' New York held for me nothing but terror
and potential rejection and loss of identity."

As a graduate student, Jones was respected. Not only was he
asked to teach classes to the underclassmen, he was taken
under the wing of other professors, including Lawrence Carra,
later head of the theater department at Carnegie Tech. Carra

was an expert on the Renaissance Italian theater movement called *commedia dell'arte*. He gave Jones books he had written on the subject, illustrated with the colorful costumes of Pantaloon, Harlequin, Columbine and the other stock characters of *commedia*. He explained to Jones how the plots tended to have the same basic situation—a pair of young lovers opposed by grasping fathers but abetted by a wily servant—but that infinite variations could be worked on it.

Texas now boasts several major resident theaters, but in the early 1950s, there was just the annual series—dubbed Theatre '47, Theatre '48, etc.—run by Margo Jones (no relation to Tom) in Dallas, and which also helped spawn Nina Vance's Alley Theatre in Houston. If there had been more, Jones said, he might have gone there to pursue a career.

Schmidt was still at work on his degree, but Jones and Baker graduated in 1951; Baker with a B.A. in fine arts, Jones with a B.F.A. and an M.F.A. in directing. Baker had done his bit in World War II, but Jones, no longer having an education deferral to shield him, was summoned for duty in the armed forces almost immediately.

For Jones, the University of Texas at Austin still represents a kind of Paradise Lost. "I was very happy there," he said. "I might still be there if I hadn't gotten drafted."

Jones graduated just two months after President Harry Truman had relieved General Douglas MacArthur of his command in Korea. MacArthur had been fully prepared to go to war with Communist China over Korea, possibly precipitating World War III—and furthermore had been willing to ignore the directions of the President in order to do so.

That's how desperate the war climate was when Jones was sent to boot camp. With MacArthur out of the way, the war had bogged down into a bloody stalemate, as was later depicted in the book, film and TV show *M*A*S*H*. World War II had been hyped as the war to end all wars. Nevertheless, six years later, American soldiers were dying again. Cease-fire talks opened in July 1951, but the fighting continued for two more years.

Jones was drafted into the infantry and underwent basic training in California. Just as his division was about to be shipped to Korea, Jones found himself tapped for a special assignment.

His writing experience had been noted by his superiors, and he was being transferred to the CIC—Counter Intelligence Corps—at Fort Holabird in Baltimore. But there was no cloak-and-dagger work for Jones. For the Army, a writer with a degree in directing was good for . . . the typing pool, where he stayed for much of his two-year hitch, through 1953.

Jones did get a chance to coach one undercover officer on how to pass himself off as a writer, on an assignment to North Africa. Jones also helped prepare another officer who was going to work on the Voice of America. But aside from cowriting a manual on covert operations and a history of those same operations, Jones's primary contribution to the Korean War effort was typing letters, orders and forms. If little else, it sharpened his typing and organization skills—and kept him gratefully far from the battle lines.

There was one other important thing about Jones's Baltimore posting. It landed him on the East Coast for the first time, a half-day's journey from New York City. On weekends, he would visit University of Texas alumni friends who had gone there to try to break into show business.

New York in the early 1950s was still a Damon Runyon place and still in its classical era as the dominant city of the dominant nation on Earth. The Empire State Building was the tallest building in the world. Irish, Jews and Italians were the most pervasive ethnic groups. In 1951, the New York Yankees won the third of their six consecutive World Series championships.

The theater world Jones encountered was dominated by Arthur Miller and Tennessee Williams. Expanding on the teachings of Russian acting teacher Konstantin Stanislavsky, Lee Strasberg's Actors Studio "Method" served as something like a religion for young actors. Rodgers and Hammerstein set the tone for musicals, though each season still brought new works by Cole Porter, Irving Berlin, Leonard Bernstein, Harold Rome and Frank Loesser.

It also was the high tide of bebop jazz. You could go up to 52nd Street to the original Birdland, the Three Deuces or the Open Door and hear Charlie Parker, Dizzy Gillespie, Charles Mingus, Thelonius Monk and Miles Davis taking apart Western music and putting it back together their own way.

On West 20th Street in April 1951, Jack Kerouac wrote the first draft of *On the Road*. It was only a few months after Allen Ginsberg had met Gregory Corso in a lesbian bar on Third Street. During the time Jones was spending his weekend leaves in New York, starting in late 1951, these and other Beat poets were in the top of their East Coast form. The scene later shifted to San Francisco, but their actions in those few seminal years set the tone for the entire late-'50s Beatnik culture.

These are the names and places that stick in the media memory of the period. The underlying pulse, however, was a supreme cockiness, a firm belief that the world was imperfect, but that it could be put right, and that *these guys knew how.*

The rebellious and self-assured spirit of the time was a magnet for some of the most talented young people in the country, each of whom was convinced that they, too, had all the answers.

This, plus the assumed superiority that comes with being Texan, inspired Jones to stay in touch with his partners in Austin. Their correspondence consisted mainly of excited dialogues about applications of B. Iden Payne's Elizabethan "open stage" concepts. These were relieved by surprisingly little personal chat, though Jones sometimes sent Schmidt a lyric as well. While informal, for a time the letters were the thread that held the trio together. "We never wrote about personal things," Jones said. "We're not close that way. Our private lives were always separate. The things that joined us together were theatrical visions."

* * *

As Jones was getting used to Army life, Baker headed to El Paso for his first teaching job, at the Texas College of Mines and Metallurgy, which was in the process of evolving into Texas Western College. Part of the change of focus included the founding of a drama department. Baker taught acting and directing there, and staged student productions of plays and musicals.

On the receiving end of Jones's letters, Schmidt continued pounding the piano for the Curtain Club while studying drawing and painting. Upon his graduation in June 1952 with a B.F.A. in Art, Schmidt put his training to work, taking a job designing displays at Sakowitz Brothers, a Houston department store. The job came courtesy of an English professor, one of the eponymous Sakowitzes, who wanted Schmidt to make the store look more like their main competitor, Neiman-Marcus.

In the brief months before he, too, was drafted, Schmidt lucked into one of his dream jobs.

"When I was a teenager," he said, "one of things I loved to do when I went to Houston was to buy the Sunday *New York Times*. It was always like a week late because of the way travel was at that time. You'd get these huge fat Sunday *Times*es. And I was astounded by what you could see and do in New York, especially back then. You still had all the big movie theaters, and they had live shows, big bands playing at the Paramount or the Capitol. Well, I would sit and devour these ads."

Featured on his menu were the drawings by Al Hirschfeld that could be found in the Sunday Drama Section (today known as Arts & Leisure). These graceful, swooping caricatures—filled with pointing fingers and the concealed name of Hirschfeld's daughter, Nina—perspicaciously captured the essence of Broadway shows. Hirschfeld's pictures invariably were worth a good deal more than a thousand words, and magically conveyed the spirit of the stage in a career that lasted from the 1920s to the 1990s.

In 1952, Schmidt was invited by the *Houston Post* to perform the same service for the touring versions of Broadway shows that came through that town. He recalls it as a "wonderful job" that had the side benefit of immersing him in the latest of professional theater. He developed a distinctive angular style.

In January of 1953, Schmidt had to relinquish both the cartooning (reluctantly) and the department store (eagerly) to serve his country.

"I kept thinking I wouldn't mind getting drafted because you get to travel, and I'd never been out of Texas," Schmidt said. "I thought, how wonderful! I might go to Europe or at least to New England. But I got drafted and where did they send me? El Paso. I didn't even get out of Texas. But compared to what I'd seen so far, El Paso seemed exotic because it was halfway to Hollywood and right on the border with Mexico."

It was so Spanish, that's why he liked it. And it left Schmidt with a permanent love for Mexican culture and a permanent fascination with the cultural clash between Anglos and Latinos.

It also gave him a chance to visit Charlie Baker at Texas Western. Schmidt made a point of coming over to see his production of *Finian's Rainbow* which they agreed was one of the greatest musicals ever.

A lot of Schmidt's other U of Texas classmates were stationed in El Paso as well, including Schmidt's college roommates, Robert Benton (later Oscar-winning director of *Kramer vs. Kramer* and scriptwriter for *Places in the Heart*) and cartoonist Rowland Wilson.

"College to me was sort of like the way I had imagined New York," Schmidt said. "Nothing in New York has ever been as glamorous as the University of Texas at that time. I mean you had real stars in the drama department there. It was all so cutthroat and serious and high-toned. Even our apartment in Austin was better than any apartment I've ever had in New York.

"On the other hand, the Army was like the way college should have been: nothing but fun. I thought that when you joined the Army, you did nothing but basic training for two years. Well, I learned that that's just a horrible period of six weeks. After that, it was like having a regular job, nine to five. You could go off the post every night of the week and go into town, if you wanted. I loved the Army. I loved all the friends I made there, and they're still all my best friends."

The Army liked Schmidt as well. He quickly learned that "the Army runs on inspections and along with inspections it needs a constant supply of signs to announce things. An artist has a windfall in the Army."

Adapting odd lettering styles he'd picked up from the Neiman-Marcus ads, Schmidt took simple signs that needed to say little more than "Second Battalion" or even "Latrine" with an arrow, and tricked them out into works of art.

"Majors and colonels would squeal with delight," Schmidt said. And they often would pull him out of basic training to make signs for the post.

"I was worried about that because I thought I was going to be shipped to Korea and I wouldn't know how to defend myself; I'd missed bayonet practice, and I wouldn't know how to bayonet someone."

Not to worry. Like Jones's ability to type, Schmidt's ability to paint saved him from the front lines. When Schmidt completed basic training, his superiors created a post especially for him, doing all sorts of artwork from lettering to painting insignia on their helmets when they got promoted. Unlike The Boy's father in *The Fantasticks*, Schmidt didn't learn horticulture in the Navy—but he did spend his Army years painting signs and writing songs.

From 1953 to 1955, the Army gave him a jeep with a driver to pick up his assignments, and a studio in which to execute them. The studio contained a small stage and a piano, and it was there that Schmidt set many of Jones's increasingly urbane lyrics to music. "I would get out on the stage and sing and dance and work on the songs that he would send me," said Schmidt, explaining that the songs were not part of any theater score; just pop tunes or novelty numbers—whatever was on his mind.

When he was done, he'd get several of his Army buddies to help make a recording at a studio in town and then mail it to Jones or Baker. Baker would make his comments and send them along to Jones. In this way, an informal round-robin system was born. It began in fun, but as the men's careers ripened, the round-robin become increasingly purposeful.

* * *

Just as Schmidt was settling into his Beetle Bailey-like Army existence, Jones completed his stint and was released in summer of 1953. He wasn't sure what to do at first, since his two collaborators were stuck in Texas, at least for the time being. So Jones went to work for his father, candling turkey eggs. This task consisted mainly of scraping turkey excrement off them with steel wool and checking their soundness.

By Christmas he had accumulated enough money and resolve to head for New York and, in the Betty Comden and Adoph Green lyrics to that year's Broadway hit, *Wonderful Town*, "to conquer the city . . . to grab up the Pulitzer Prize."

"I decided I would give it six months," Jones said. "And if I wasn't a success in six months, I was going to give up, come back, and—since I had a master's degree—try to get a job teaching at a junior college or something in the speech department or the drama department. Anyway, by this time I had more connections, in a way, with New York than with Texas."

On January 1, 1954, Tom Jones arrived via plane in New York City. His main connection was Gerry Matthews, a Texas actor who had appeared in both *Hipsy-Boo* and *Time Staggers On*. "I couldn't figure out how to get started as an actor or a director or anything, but Gerry and others told me that if I could write something, I might get a chance to direct it."

Jones's first piece was a comedy routine tailored to the talents of Matthews and his friend, actor Tom Poston, later of TV's *Newhart*. Titled "The Movie Matador," Jones's sketch parodied the Actors Studio "Method." It reflected Jones's enthusiasm about his chosen field, and, he said, "It was a sendup of everything theatrical at that time. It was full of topical theatrical references."

In it, Poston, dressed as a matador, sang fragments of satirical lyrics about show business—"Off-Broadway will live again/ At Equity minimem[sic]/ Twenty-five dollars *a week*?"—while Matthews furiously and ineptly strummed a flamenco guitar. "It was more like the Marx Brothers than anything else," Jones said. "It was full of strange, antic, chaotic humor and non sequiturs. Tom would wave his cape and go 'Ah-ha! Oh-oh!' Then stop and say 'It doesn't *feel* right'—making fun of the Method. Then he'd do a chorus from *Oklahoma!*"

Written and directed by Jones, and performed by Poston and Matthews, the routine was accepted for *Talent '54*, the New York stage managers' showcase, once an annual Broadway tradition, held that year in April at the Mark Hellinger Theatre on 51st Street. Others on that year's bill included actors Jerry Stiller and Arte Johnson.

The audience—primarily agents, producers and theatrical reporters—stopped the show for "The Movie Matador."

Reaction was enthusiastic, and Max Gordon, of the legendary Village Vanguard nightclub, asked Jones, Poston and Matthews if they had enough material for an act. Aside from being a major jazz club, the Vanguard hosted poetry readings and small nightclub revues. Among the more famous revuers were lyricists Comden and Green, who wrote for themselves and Judy Holliday at the Vanguard as far back as the early 1940s.

Unfortunately, "The Movie Matador" comprised Jones's entire portfolio. He tried churning out enough new material to satisfy a Village Vanguard Sunday night crowd, but when supper club impresario Julius Monk invited them to appear at his club, the Ruban Bleu, they had no safety net.

" 'Matador' was written for big stages," Jones said. "I didn't know from supper clubs. Or from subtle. And the supper club attitude I didn't know. My stuff was full of wacky things: They'd sing a line, then stop and do a strange comedy bit, then we'd break into a parody of *Oklahoma!* with changed lyrics, and then break into something else—it was like *The Goon Show*, out of which came *Monty Python*. But they didn't know what to make of it in the supper club world, and our option wasn't picked up."

Poston was spotted by a scout from the pre-Johnny Carson *Tonight Show*, then broadcast from New York. Poston went on to become a regular on the show—one of host Steve Allen's informal repertory company of comedians.

But for Jones the ride was over. He tried supporting himself by working at the Lenox Hill Book Shop, a very elegant, very crowded, very small shop in the East Eighties near Madison Avenue. But while the clientele included Moss Hart and other theatrical lights, Jones found the pressure unpleasant. "Working in book shops never turns out to be what you think it's going to be," he said. " 'Oh, have you read the latest . . . ?' It's work."

Jones's home was a single room in the rough, poor West Side Manhattan neighborhood known as Hell's Kitchen. The apartment was near a run-down area of 65th Street later razed to make way for Lincoln Center.

Unable to put up with cramped quarters and the smell of his landlady's cooking, he moved into a Greenwich Village apartment he shared with Poston; then to an apartment in the Jackson Heights section of Queens, sublet from friends who were spending the winter in Europe.

Jones kept his mind active by sending song lyrics to Schmidt. By now, the songs had acquired a reason for being: they were part of an full-fledged nightclub act Jones was assembling for Poston and Matthews. Humiliated by his rejection at the Reuban Bleu, Jones was determined to master the form.

And it was in late summer 1954 that Jones got a fateful telephone call from Louisette Roser, whose apartment Tom Poston had sublet while working on *Talent '54*. She worked at

American National Theatre and Academy (ANTA) and knew of Jones's desire to write for the theater.

Jones recalls, "She said, 'I have just met somebody, a distinguished gentleman, who's looking for somebody to write the lyrics and the book for a musical.' She asked if I would be interested in meeting him, and I said, well, I would, as long as he understands that it's a temporary thing until Harvey comes out of the Army."

The distinguished gentleman was John Donald Robb, an old-money university professor who went by the name J. Donald Robb, in the style of that era's Southern gentlemen. A classmate of Cole Porter's at Yale in the 1920s, Robb had studied music and dabbled in composing while pursuing a law degree. He eventually became a successful corporate lawyer but never lost his interest in music.

After his retirement, he settled in Albuquerque and began teaching at the University of New Mexico. This second career blossomed, and soon he was appointed chairman of the musical department and Dean of the School of Fine Arts.

Perhaps with an eye to his successful fellow Yalie, Porter, who was writing what would turn out to be his last musical, *Silk Stockings*, that year, Robb took a sabbatical with the intention of writing an original musical comedy.

He traveled to New York to hook up with the most promising young lyricist he could find, and soon was shaking hands with Jones at a family home on Shelter Island, an exclusive enclave between the Hamptons and Orient Point on Long Island's east end.

Serious, scholarly and in many ways brilliant, he had the same cultured, academic aura that attracted Jones to B. Iden Payne. The differences in their ages, energy level and temperament were eased by the fact that they slipped into something of a father/son relationship.

They each compiled a list of eight to ten plays they thought might be musicalized successfully. One of the scripts on both their lists was Rostand's *Les Romanesques*, which Jones recalled from his directing classes and from his long hours in the lighting booth of the high school play competition.

Both men having attachements to the Southwest, it occurred to them that the upside-down little Romeo-and-Juliet story might be transposed to Texas or New Mexico, with Anglos and Mexicans substituting for the families of Bergamin and Pasquinot, Rostand's answer to the Montagues and Capulets.

They decided to have fun with their adaptation and placed it in the comically named town of Dead Horse.

They worked on weekends and whenever Jones could find time, but Jones was finding it harder and harder to support himself in Manhattan. Robb and Jones hadn't a glimmer of a producer for their fledgling musical—soon titled *Joy Comes to Dead Horse*—which probably would take months, if not years, to complete. Broadway seemed as far away as it had in Texas. How to pay the rent in the meantime?

* * *

Jones was far from alone in his struggle for acceptance. Uptown, a sunny, slender, boyish actor named Kenneth Nelson was enjoying the afterglow of his first success, playing the juvenile lead in the Broadway musical *Seventeen*. Another actor, a growly character named Lore Noto, was regaling audiences at the Carroll Club on Madison Avenue, and carefully putting aside every spare dollar for an emergency—or an opportunity. An almond-eyed nymph named Rita Schier (later to become Rita Gardner) was singing in TV shows and taking dance lessons.

And on an undistinguished byway off the Village's Bleecker Street, a T-shaped sign hung over a former speakeasy: it read "Jimmy" across the top and "Kelly's" down the shaft, and it advertised a sometimes-nightclub of questionable repute. The nineteenth-century building was a warren of secret passageways and peep-holes. It had spent a half century keeping as low a profile as possible.

Jimmy Kelly's was rooted in Manhattan, but the young actors weren't. For Jones, his six months had stretched into nearly a year. Despite his modest success at the Mark Hellinger, and despite the hazy potential of his *Joy Comes to Dead Horse* project with J. Donald Robb, he simply couldn't support himself on what he made at the bookstore. Just before Christmas 1954, he flew back to Texas and resumed scraping turkey eggs for his father.

So much for an errant son's dream of making a living arranging shadows and scribbling verses. A little bit of the world had happened to him, but his plans weren't completely shelved.

It was his first taste of failure after the intoxicating successes of *Hipsy-Boo* and *Time Staggers On*. Perhaps, for all his expertise, he really needed the humble simplicity of Harvey Schmidt. Knowing that Harvey was coming up for discharge in spring 1955, Jones labored in his father's garden but continued to write comedy material for his brainchild born of the Village Vanguard experience: a genuinely witty and topical nightclub revue.

* * *

Jones was now back in Texas, but he didn't have a chance to see his pal, Charlie Baker. Baker had left his El Paso teaching post and returned to the U of Texas to get his master's degree, but never completed it. He opted instead for what he hoped would be a better teaching job, in Auburn, Alabama, in the Department of Dramatic Arts at Alabama Polytechnic Institute (now Auburn University).

This title was nowhere near as impressive as it sounds. In fact, the Department of Dramatic Arts consisted of precisely two persons, the chairman and one underling. Needless to say, the underling was Baker. The chairman was Telfair B. Peete, an adherent of the old declamatory school of acting. He asked little more of his students than that they memorize their lines and blocking. They got a steady diet of the classics and well-made plays.

"There was a total lack of chemistry, and it was mutual," Baker said of his new boss. "It went from bad to worse from the word go."

It was at Auburn that Baker also crossed paths with Sam Houston—no relation to the Texas hero, but a kid from the hills of northern Alabama. Houston began as an architecture major, then switched to advertising design for two years before settling on English and journalism. He also served as associate editor of *The Plainsman*, the campus newspaper. His descriptions of Baker's aura sound very much like Jones's encomiums for B. Iden Payne. Payne seems to have passed on the secret of weaving fascinated enlightenment.

It began when Houston went to see a production of a student

musical titled *Gold in the Hills*. He was so excited by what he saw that he resolved to audition for the next Dramatic Arts Department play, whatever it was.

When the announcement came that it would be Arthur Miller's *The Crucible*, Houston ran out and bought a copy of the script. After reading it, he decided to try for the role of Rev. Samuel Parris, whose insecurities set the play's murderous machinery in motion.

At the auditions, he had his first encounter with Charlie Baker. "He was a slight fellow, tall, full of life," Houston said. Though only a few years older than most of these students, Baker commanded their respect. "He had characteristics about him that I have never seen in another person," Houston said, "a charisma beyond anything I'd ever heard of. He was incandescent."

Though Baker never talked about Stanislavsky or the Method, Houston said, "When we went through rehearsal, he made us sort of dig down. I don't recall a time when he said 'Use your own emotional experiences to gain something.' All I know is that when Parris recognized the horror that he had set up—I felt it, I felt every bit. When Parris runs off the stage at the end in terror at what he has done, it's probably the most exhilarating feeling I have ever felt—not that Parris is exhilarated, but that the work had gone off so well on stage."

At Auburn, Baker developed some of the directorial techniques that would serve him on *The Fantasticks* and many of his subsequent assignments. Rehearsals consisted of experimentation. He invited the participation of the actors, urged them to throw open the windows of their imaginations. He would test their suggestions and keep whatever worked.

For Baker, *The Crucible* would offer a chance to carry out an artistic vision supplied by one of his idols—Pulitzer-winning playwright Arthur Miller. When Baker was pursuing his aborted master's degree at Austin the previous year, he had traveled to Fayetteville, Arkansas, to attend a play festival. Miller was one of the guests, and Baker listened, rapt, as Miller delivered a post-mortem on what he saw as the failed 1953 Broadway production of *The Crucible*. "He spoke about how he thought *The Crucible* should have been done in the first place," Baker said, "which was 'no scenery.' He told us 'It's all there. You just need to do the play. No decorations or anything.' "

In bringing *The Crucible* to Alabama, Baker resolved to adhere to the minimalist credo Miller had laid out. Baker's personal stamp was to perform the play in the round, a technique borrowed from Margo Jones's in-the-round stagings at Theatre '53, which he saw as a daring extension of B. Iden Payne's open-stage concept. "I was very hot to trot for it," Baker said, "because it didn't need any scenery at all."

Alabama had seen nothing like it. But the compressed power of the drama combined with the fervor of Baker's young disciples overrode any qualms the local audiences might have had. *The Crucible* drew the same satisfying response that the two Austin musicals had.

"Theater is a lot of senses," Houston said. "It's the mind, it's the ears, it's the eyes. It's everything. That's what Charlie Baker was trying to show. He was our friend as well as a teacher and a mentor. He helped us to see more than we knew we could see. He gave us a larger canvas. He made us a lot richer. Those of us—I'm only one of many many people—who left there were never the same again."

* * *

While staging *The Crucible*, Baker continued his own writing through his round-robin correspondence with Jones and Schmidt as they continued to work on the nightclub act.

Rumor of the success of *The Crucible*—and of its director—traveled fast, and the little two-man drama department suddenly found itself with a star.

Which wasn't good. Students began to cluster around Baker to the exclusion of the head of the department. "He developed a whole new coterie of talent around him—people who were incredibly talented, very smart and good," Houston said. "They gave him everything they had."

Perhaps it was inevitable that a rivalry developed between Baker and Peete. "I think it scared him," Houston said.

Whatever the cause, it was announced that Baker's contract wasn't going to be renewed and that he would be leaving at the end of that school year, June 1955.

In retrospect, it looks like fate, because, with Jones biding his time on the turkey farm and Schmidt about to be discharged from the Army, all three suddenly found themselves at loose ends simultaneously. To a bunch of theater guys, it sounded an awful lot like a cue.

Their round-robin letters suddenly were filled with talk of going to New York. They'd need a portfolio of material to get in the doorway of agents and producers, and suddenly Jones's idea for a snappy nightclub show acquired a title: *Portfolio*.

Jones would write the skits and lyrics, Baker would direct, Schmidt would do the music, sets and costumes. They would support themselves by doing outside work, but they'd stick together on the revue until they got it right.

Noting that he still had a few more months of teaching left, Baker hatched a plan for a reunion for the trio. It also would serve as a warm-up before they attempted to scale the summit in New York. He would revive *Time Staggers On* at Auburn, using his adrenalized young Alabama disciples. When selling the idea to Peete, Baker had a good alibi: because Harvey couldn't write music, the whole score existed only in his head, and he would have to come in person to perform it or teach it.

It wasn't strictly true; a recording of the original Austin *Time Staggers On* had been made. But the excuse worked. Jones and Schmidt came as soon as they could say good-bye to their families and book Greyhound bus tickets.

Houston was cast as the loud-mouthed campus politico, Bennyboy Benson, and had a chance to observe the three in their first weeks of working side-by-side after nearly four years of airmail wartime collaboration.

"Tom was tall, lanky and extremely skinny," Houston said. "He must have some French in him because he waved his arms a lot, was very demonstrative and always talking. He was the word man. Harvey seemed more introspective; didn't talk a lot. But he really came alive at the piano. He still has the same energetic nervousness he had then."

Because Baker had fostered a closeness between teachers and students, Houston would spend time at Baker's house near campus, drinking beer and talking about the future.

"They were going to go to New York and become great theatrical people," Houston recalls. "They said they were going to do wonderful, great things on the stage. And I truly believed them. A lot of us love the memories and love the fantasies that were created back then. And we want those things to go on forever. They don't. People change, people die or get fat. But for two weeks in 1955, those three men brought to our little world a beauty that is like a legend."

Houston put his feelings into words in an editorial in the campus newspaper the final week of classes. "I wrote this glowing editorial about how 'next year at this time' their songs would become very famous and all that lah-de-dah . . . Well, I was wrong about that. It took four more years for that to happen, and certainly not with the play they had in mind to do."

After he cleaned out his desk and said his farewells, Baker loaded his pregnant wife and his two children into the gray 1954 Plymouth and embarked on an odyssey from Auburn, Alabama, to New York, New York. He followed Jones and Schmidt, who had gone on ahead by bus. Schmidt had his commercial art to fall back on; Baker hoped to teach or direct; and Jones hoped to direct or write.

With luck, their *Portfolio* revue would find producers, stars and a theater, and who knew what that might lead to?

But whatever else happened to them in New York, they knew that beyond the road lay an episode just waiting to be unzipped.

4

1955–57

"Who knows—maybe / All the visions that I see /
May be waiting just for me / to say—take me there."

THE three were well-enough acquainted with New York to know that the mayor would not be waiting for them at the George Washington Bridge with the key to the city.

The top item on their agenda was to find shelter, then "day jobs" to support them while they tried to break into show biz.

The apartment Jones had sublet with Tom Poston at 548 West Broadway in Greenwich Village was available, but it went to Baker and his burgeoning family. Baker made friends with UT graduate Valjean Axelrod Massey there, but soon had to move to Queens.

Baker's first summer in New York was made easier by the fact that he'd had a year contract at Auburn, so he still got a salary through September. But an Alabama salary didn't stretch very far at New York prices, so Baker took all sorts of jobs to make ends meet. He was a temporary typist and a drama teacher at Herbert Berghof's HB Studio.

Through Gerry Matthews he got a set-designing gig at the Montclair Summer Theatre in Montclair, New Jersey, that threw him together with two of the *Fantasticks* crew. One was press agent David Powers, with whom he would share bus rides from Manhattan several times a week.

Powers recalls there being no air conditioning, so big blocks of ice were piled in front of fans in the orchestra pit. Powers was impressed with the way "Word did these incredible sets overnight" for traveling stars including Gloria Vanderbilt, Jason Robards, Jr., and Arlene Francis.

While there, Baker got to know a young scene painter who aspired to be an actor—Jerry Orbach.

* * *

To save money, Jones and Schmidt decided to room together and spent their first summer in the city subletting a series of apartments owned by vacationing friends. They started in the Jackson Heights section of the outer borough of Queens with a tantalizing view of the Manhattan skyline, but wound up at one of Manhattan's most fashionable East Side addresses, between Park and Madison in the lower sixties. It was small, but elegant, and it had a piano.

To pay the rent, Jones took a job teaching and directing drama for the Community Club of St. Bartholomew's Church on Fifth Avenue, for $25 a week. The auditorium adjoining the church gained notoriety in the 1980s, when the parish split over whether to sell it to a real estate developer. In 1955, it was known as the low-key but high-class and beloved marble and brick parish hall. Jones taught there one night a week and directed amateur stage productions each spring and fall.

Though Schmidt had dreamed of becoming an illustrator at slick, sophisticated magazines like *Life, Esquire* and *Harper's Bazaar*, his showcase sketches so lovingly wrought at his parents' parsonage proved a hindrance on Madison Avenue.

"I had a very flashy, avant-garde portfolio which everybody loved but nobody knew what to do with," Schmidt said. "They'd tell me, 'This is wonderful, but we'll call you in six months.' " Schmidt recalls being down to his last $20 when his break came, though it didn't seem like such a great break at the time.

Ironically, it was his expertise in designing signs for the Army base that earned him his first job as a professional graphic artist. He was hired as part of a stable of ten artists creating title cards at NBC-TV's new art and scenic design studio housed in a former department store on 18th Street in Manhattan. His drawing, painting and lettering were used for the logos and credits of period TV shows such as *Peter Pan* and *NBC Opera Series*, both of which gave him contacts that would change the course of his career.

To help spur sales of sets using its newly-perfected color television format, NBC produced opulent shows which it dubbed Spectaculars, emphasizing stars of Hollywood and Broadway, with splashy sets and costumes in vivid colors. Esther Williams did a water ballet; a completely different tank was built to reenact *The Sinking of the Titanic*; the *Hallmark Hall of Fame* came in with another all-star special every few weeks. Almost nobody owned color sets in 1955—few enough owned black and white sets—but NBC was determined.

"It was like the early days of movies," Schmidt said. "Nobody quite knew what they were doing or where they were going with it. But everything was live, everything was in color, and they spent *fortunes* on it, even though no one had any color sets out there."

The NBC Peacock logo remained, for many years, the enduring emblem of this period.

"Color television was so gorgeous in the studio, as it is now in the home," Schmidt said. "If you have cable now, it's almost flawless. But at that time, it was that way in the studio only. For people who had the sets, the faces usually were green or orange."

Schmidt and the other designers worked on 18th Street where costumes and sets also were designed, built and painted. Most of the shooting, however, was done at the giant NBC studios in Brooklyn.

Arriving at the Brooklyn studio for the first time with an armload of titles for NBC's production of *Peter Pan*, Schmidt had his first brush with greatness since arriving from Texas. "I arrived out there one morning at ten o'clock," Schmidt said, "and opened the door of this huge sound stage, which had earlier been the old Biograph Film Studio. And there, coming at me, the whole length of a city block away, was Mary Martin, sailing through the air singing 'I'm Flying.'" For the timeless

TV musical, she was suspended by a cable from the ceiling and was rehearsing her flight through the midnight sky.

As the Texas-born star of Cole Porter's *Leave It to Me* and Rodgers and Hammerstein's *South Pacific* swung toward the dumbstruck Schmidt, she called out "Hello!" and waved down to him, and swung back again. "As I had been a fan since her movie days, I almost dropped everything I was carrying," Schmidt said. "Since I was the only person there, other than her rehearsal pianist, she started playing to me." The bottom-rung artist wouldn't forget her unpretentious greeting. In 1966, he and Jones would write *I Do! I Do!* for Martin and Robert Preston.

Unfortunately, the version of *Peter Pan* Schmidt worked on is not the version that was preserved later on tape and still occasionally shown, but one shot earlier and not preserved.

Another theater man who had found economic refuge in NBC's 1955 color scheme was Edwin Wittstein—"Ed" Wittstein professionally.

Then twenty-six, Wittstein had grown up quickly in the Westchester County suburb of Mount Vernon. At age seven, he was building sets for a puppet theater in his basement. When he was ten, he took a bus by himself to see the 1939 World's Fair in Queens, where he recalls being mesmerized by the fountains, dioramas and dramatic international pavilions of the "World of Tomorrow."

Parent-chaperoned trips to see Broadway shows like *Life With Father* and *Arsenic and Old Lace* were reinforced by a student trip backstage at the old Metropolitan Opera House on 39th Street. By age thirteen, he was designing sets for high school shows, at sixteen, was living in a half-room apartment on 9th Street in Greenwich Village, eventually to pursue studies at five different design schools. At age seventeen, the prodigy was accepted to the prestigious Parsons School of Design; the same year, he passed the test to enter the Broadway set builders union.

Voracious for knowledge of set, costume and lighting design, Wittstein took courses at the Art Students League, New York University, Irwin Piscator's Dramatic Workshop and privately from John McGrew. He began designing children's theater at the 92nd Street YM-YWHA, then at Equity Library Theater, then for an opera in Philadelphia.

He was hired by NBC in 1949 when he was nineteen and went on to become designer for the *Armstrong Circle Theater*, a major weekly program, while continuing his education and continuing to design sets for Off-Broadway shows, such as the American premiere of Gertrude Stein's *Yes Is For a Very Young Man*.

Later, Wittstein would design the films *Fame, Endless Love* and Woody Allen's *Play It Again, Sam* and *Bananas*. But in 1955, he was designing a full opera each week for NBC's classical music series, plus four sets daily for the wacky skits on Steve Allen's *The Tonight Show*. He welcomed the help of the network's newest graphic artist, Harvey Schmidt, who was given the cubicle next to his.

Their first project together was *La Boheme*, for which, Wittstein recalls, Schmidt did credits festooned with his own illustrations. "He did wonderful designs and drawings," Wittstein said. "We became very good friends, going to the theater a lot, having dinner a lot. And Harvey was a good critic. I'd show him my designs, like for *Cosi Fan Tutti*, and he'd say, 'Too many bows. It's better to be simple.' "

Wittstein said it came as a surprise when he learned that his colleague also wrote music. But he remembers Schmidt explaining that music was something he did on the side, "as a hobby."

While that may have been true *de facto*, Schmidt and Jones found that, like Harvey's first portfolio of artwork, their *Portfolio* revue of songs and comedy sketches wasn't in demand. Though it wasn't for lack of trying.

Willie Smith, an Army buddy of Baker's, worked in a shirt factory in South Carolina. Smith put Baker in touch with the owner of the factory, whose wife, Eunice Healey, was trying to build a career as a theatrical producer in New York. A former vaudeville dancer and big band-era singer, she had set up an office in the Plaza Hotel, one of New York's classiest landmarks, on Fifth Avenue at Central Park South.

Though essentially living hand-to-mouth, Jones kept house and office in one of the poshest sections of Manhattan. He would stroll over from Park Avenue, then go through the back door of the Plaza up to Healey's office where they would go over his material and plot to find backers and a theater. In between many other jobs, Baker worked there as well. Sometimes Jones would bring his lunch and sneak up to the roof of the hotel, where he'd look out over the park and the city and imagine what would happen once *Portfolio* was a hit.

"But it was all strange and illusionary, and nothing came of it," Jones said. The money and the bookings somehow never materialized, and Jones began to realize he was trading in pipe dreams.

One member of his amateur troupe at St. Bart's did have a big-time connection. She was secretary to Jo Mielziner, the set designer whose meticulous research and draftsmanship was complemented by his ability to create some of the most beautiful painted scenery on Broadway. He had been one of Broadway's top designers since the Gershwin era in the 1920s. In the previous ten years, Mielziner's assignments had included the original sets for Frank Loesser's *Guys and Dolls*, plus golden-age Rodgers and Hammerstein shows *Carousel*, *South Pacific* and *The King and I*.

The secretary was leaving, however, and offered to recommend Jones for the job. Confronted with an open back door to Broadway, Jones clutched. "I didn't think I would be capable of doing it," he said. "I don't know why." Perhaps being a part-time amateur director appealed to him more than being a full-time secretary. Whatever the reason, Jones turned around and told Baker of the opportunity. The father of two (soon three) jumped at it and quickly was promoted to Mielziner's assistant about the time when Mielziner was working on the Ethel Merman musical, *Happy Hunting*.

Mielziner maintained his office in the Dakota, a celebrity residence on Central Park West made infamous in 1980 when one of its inhabitants, Beatle John Lennon, was shot to death at its front door. Despite that black episode, there's still a great deal of white magic about the place owing to all the creative people who have lived or worked there, not least Mielziner and Baker, starting in 1955. Baker is still fond of bragging that his first job in New York was at the Plaza; his second at the Dakota.

* * *

For his part, Jones made valiant attempts to parlay his songs and sketches into a full-scale writing or directing job. He even tried television, with notably humiliating results. He was sent up as a possible writer for a rising TV child star named Danny Sharp who was a regular on Milton Berle's TV variety show. "I'll never forget it because it was in one of those old buildings, like the Brill Building, where they have rehearsal studios," Jones said. "I waited anxiously in the hall. I could hear the tap dancing going on. Then the piano stops, and Danny comes in—I think he was eleven years old—with tap shoes and a towel. And he says, 'OK, what have you done in New York?' There I am trying to impress him—me with my ambitions to be Shakespeare, my two college degrees and so forth—and Danny Sharp is telling me 'I don't want to do any more bed-wetting jokes.' "

Jones suggested a sketch in which the boy could play a Huckleberry Finn-type character, but that didn't go over very well.

"In the times of trying to survive," Jones said, "I would have done anything, just about. That was one of the many things I tried to do and was rejected for."

Jones said, with some irony, that his failure to tempt the child star wasn't a scarring experience. "I have had scarring experiences—that's where you get scars. This was too ludicrous to be a scarring experience. What's scarring is when people you know who are less talented than you suddenly become huge stars. That's when you start building the meanness we all get in the theater and the jealousy. It's the result of such a competitive business."

Luckily, Jones had a cushion in Schmidt, who was making "lots of money" and not only at NBC. His New York experience and amenable personality began to open doors for him at some of the New York magazines. His talent for simple, amusing sketches that had made him a successful poster designer at the University of Texas now started to land him magazine assignments.

Jones and Schmidt now entered something of an *A Star Is Born* period, in which the brilliant and respected upperclassman was pounding the pavement, knocking on locked doors, while his worshipful disciple was rising quickly in his chosen field, gaining professional respect and professional paychecks.

And yet, the dynamic of their college relationship remained. Schmidt continued to put Jones on a pedestal and willingly helped him financially while they continued to polish and augment *Portfolio* in hopes that someday they'd be "discovered."

Despite his penury, Jones dated prolifically, mostly actresses and artists, as he had in college when Baker remembers him "showing up with a different girl each semester." The shy Schmidt poured all his energy into his artwork. Their friendship and collaboration survived even the increasingly apparent stillbirth of *Portfolio*.

Schmidt blamed it as much on their material as on Eunice Healey. "She tried," he said, "but it was all sort of dreamlike and echoed Broadway on a high plane. It wasn't really coming to grips with how one might do a revue at that time."

That's why Schmidt described his songwriting as a "hobby" to Wittstein as he threw himself fully into his career as a graphic artist.

And that's why Jones ultimately returned to his collaboration with J. Donald Robb on their musical *Joy Comes to Dead Horse*. They had corresponded during Jones's retreat to Texas, and now that Jones was back in New York, he made regular trips to Robb's house on Shelter Island.

"He had a beautiful house overlooking the bay," Jones recalls. "They'd have string quartets and invite people over, and they'd be wearing bow ties—all these unbelievable things if you're from west Texas."

In expanding and updating *Les Romanesques*, Jones and Robb told the story of two Texan families and the finger-crossed love affair they concoct for their two unsuspecting children. To abet in this charade, the crafty fathers employ the services of a romantic bandit named El Gallo to stage an abduction so The Boy may seem to rescue The Girl and thereby seal the deal. But things don't go as planned. The road to reconciliation is longer than any of them imagine.

Written between autumn 1954 and the winter of 1955–56, the one hundred twenty-page script they produced is a fascinating hodgepodge of *The Cisco Kid*, *Our Town*, Shakespeare, *Zorro* and, unmistakably, *The Fantasticks*.

The version of *Joy Comes to Dead Horse* marked "#1" and copyrighted in 1955, opens with, "two burly bandits of the dirty sombrero and cartridge belt type" who "grab their rifles and move menacingly toward the footlights," only to be stopped by the suave "Don Enrique Curro de Gonzales y Pajarito-Sanchez de Azul," who breaks the fourth wall to tell the audience "that is my family name. My business name is El Gallo."

He introduces the orchestra and walks the audience around the small town of Dead Horse. He explains that any time he needs a musical effect or a piece of scenery, all he has to do is call for it, and a man with a clipboard, identified as the Stage Manager, will supply it.

El Gallo explains that he can even add ". . . an actor (spotlight flashes on an actor) and you can feel whatever you please. Happiness—(The actor smiles). Sorrow—(The actor frowns). Love—(The actor sighs). And even death. (The actor falls to the floor melodramatically.) All fake, of course, but very impressive."

There is no song until several minutes into the play, at which point El Gallo invites the audience to follow him deeper into the play with a song that anticipates "Try to Remember" in its mood, if not its substance.

Come along
Come with me
To the place where your dreams are free
Come along
Follow me—
Let's see how it used to be—
Down the chalky canyons of a dream
Beneath the rippling blueness of a phantom stream
Back beyond the smart of you
To the special childlike part of you
Where dreams are fancy free
Come along; come along
Come along to me.

Other numbers include a rootin'-tootin' choral title number (reminiscent of "This Time of the Year" from *Finian's Rainbow*) in which the hero, Matt Bellomy, returns home from college in Santa Fe. (The name "Bellomy" would transfer to The Girl's Father in *The Fantasticks*.)

> Matt Bellomy's comin' home today!
> We'll see did his education pay!
> He's gettin' near
> I hope he's here
> To stay!

That song did not survive the many drafts that led to *The Fantasticks*, but another, here in early draft form, did. In it, the fathers shake their heads over the contrariness of children:

Why did the children pour jam on the cat?
When the one thing we told them they shouldn't do was that?
And why did the children climb up in the tree
When the tree was the one place they knew not to be
When you know just as sure as the tree where they're found
If you told them to do it
They'd stay on the ground.*

Jones also wrote a monologue directly inspired by that scene Jones directed in B. Iden Payne's class some six years earlier:

> We've the obvious, open, schoolboy rape
> With little mandolins and perhaps a cape . . .
> The Comic Rape—perhaps it's too unique
> Romantic—in a boat: requires a creek.
> The Rape Alcoholic—in a dark saloon.
> The rape with moonlight, or without a moon;
> Moonlight is expensive, but always in demand.
> The Military Rape—requires a band . . .**

---

*From "Joy Comes to Dead Horse" © Tom Jones and J. Donald Robb. Used by Permission.
**© Tom Jones. Used by Permission.

Throughout the play, the music is more like operetta than musical theater. But in a nod to Agnes De Mille-style integrated ballets, the first act features a Mexican "Dance of the Matachinas" in which a male dancer representing a bull menaces a female dancer in white.

Jones's stage directions call for flamenco music and for the dance to "grow in intensity—with the Bull and the Virgin moving ever closer and closer together. Finally, as the music swells—the Bull grabs her and she falls rigidly into his arms—out of the spotlight circle—with only her extended right hand remaining in the light—stretched out—fingers wide—as if reaching for something in the air. The music stops, with only the tiny, unexpected percussive sound of the rattle carrying on the frantic struggle of the Virgin."

Just in time arrives Jones's Hero. "The ensuing battle between the Man and Bull is in the style of bullfighting. There is no brutal hand-to-hand battle, but the delicate placement of the fighter, aloof and cool—even haughty—against the ever oncoming rush of primitive force."

At last the Hero draws his sword. "There is a dramatic pause in the music. Then—the sudden plunge—the powerful last 'Ole!'—and the final slow throbbing of death as the Bull folds to his knees, and the proud Man [Hero] takes the Girl to his side."

According to *Bernstein*, Joan Peyser's 1987 biography of late composer Leonard Bernstein, choreographer Jerome Robbins had the idea to musicalize *Romeo and Juliet* in 1949 but conceived the new story as a kind of *Abie's Irish Rose*—about a Catholic and a Jew coming together over the objections of their parents. Bernstein and librettist Arthur Laurents worked on the project fruitlessly for several years.

Peyser reports that on August 25, 1955, in a poolside meeting in Beverly Hills, Bernstein suggested the story be relocated to Los Angeles and the milieu changed to that of Mexicans and Anglos. There is no way that they could have known of Jones's project or he of theirs. Reports of warfare among street gangs inspired Bernstein and Laurents, who made one last ethnic shift—to the Puerto Rican barrios of New York, before renaming the project *West Side Story*, which opened in New York in 1957.

Coincidentally, the ingenue in both *West Side Story* and *Joy Comes to Dead Horse* was named Maria.

In the spring of 1956, Robb arranged for the students and colleagues at the University of New Mexico at Albuquerque to mount a production of *Joy Comes to Dead Horse*. Jones traveled to Albuquerque but had mixed feelings about what he saw.

"It received pretty good press, and the academic community was reasonably warm to it; of course, Dr. Robb was the dean of the School of Fine Arts. And a wonderful man. A beloved man.

"But I felt it was a mess. Not so much his part, but just the whole thing. It wasn't clear. Part of it was so serious, and part of it was trying to be like the Rostand: light and airy and whimsical. It was a mishmash."

As for Dr. Robb, "I wouldn't say he thought we had a masterpiece," Jones said, "but he thought it was pretty near. We disagreed. And it was a terrible disillusionment for me because I admired him so much. He had become a surrogate father figure to me, and it was impossible for me to believe that a man this wonderful, this worldly, this sweet, this erudite, could believe the music was perfect. I just didn't believe it."

So they split, agreeing that each could keep anything he had done for the show. It was just a courtesy at the time, but it proved to be the foundation for *The Fantasticks*.

Robb's connections in the Southwest guaranteed that orchestral arrangements of his musical would be played fairly regularly for many years thereafter. Robb died in the mid-1980s.

"We agreed that I would be free to take my work—not any of his work—and to seek out somebody else to work on it."

He didn't seek far.

"Tom came to me one day and asked me if I would be interested in trying to work on this," Schmidt said, "and even though I was developing a career as a commercial artist, Tom would keep asking me. He was so brilliant and talented that I felt, well, if anybody that bright is going to ask me to collaborate, I should give it a whirl."

And for the next three years, they struggled with it, "as a huge Broadway musical in the Rodgers and Hammerstein mode," Schmidt said. "I always thought of it on the stage of the Winter Garden with people on horseback—real horses. 'The bigger the better,' I thought. We kept working on it and working on it, but this slight material wouldn't support all of that."

* * *

Thanks to Baker's connections through Mielziner's office, and Schmidt's income and connections through NBC, the three of them began the best master's degree in drama you can get: night after night wandering the creative garden of Broadway and Off-Broadway.

Finally, the trio from Texas was mainlining the good stuff. Though the high noon of Broadway's golden age had already turned into its late afternoon, and the upheaval of the 1960s lay ahead, they were breaking into show business at the very beginning of the Off-Broadway movement.

Off-Broadway's roots go back to the 1920s when the Provincetown Players and the Washington Square Players offered small-scale alternative theater in Greenwich Village. But it wasn't until landmark productions like Circle in the Square's revival of Tennessee Williams's *Summer and Smoke* in 1952 and the revival of Eugene O'Neill's *The Iceman Cometh* in 1956 that critics began to notice and name it.

Local audiences had found it much earlier. As its name suggests, Off-Broadway was founded in opposition to the scale and sensibility of Broadway. If Broadway was gaudy, commercial and pro-establishment, Off-Broadway would be intimate, experimental and revolutionary.

Though "Off-Broadway" in the 1990s is more of a contractual distinction—setting lower pay scales for smaller theaters—Off-Broadway in the 1950s was predominantly a Greenwich Village phenomenon, taking on the spirit of that neighborhood of laborers and artists.

Maybe it's the way the orderly grid of Manhattan shatters into unaccountable fragments. Maybe it's the fact that the towers of midtown give ground suddenly to idiosyncratic little buildings built by carpenters from Italy. Since the 1920s, the Village had been a place where the extraordinary was commonplace and where the forbidden was permitted. It was a place where Orwell's paradoxes sometimes ran in reverse: where war was peace, hate was love, rebellion was conformity.

It had always provided refuge to outcasts, including gays, minorities, the poor and those outcasts of the soul that all socio-economic groups spin off. But there was a joyfulness in this strange mixture. It was a place to meet young people with strange haircuts and daring clothes. It was a place to drink strange intoxicating brews with unpronounceable and mystic names.

To walk the Village's labyrinthine streets was to become a character in a mystery novel where every gesture, every face at a window, every folded slip of paper in the gutter, held potential significance. Around each corner was the chance for love or danger. In late-1950s Greenwich Village, you walked in light.

Some of its more rococo allures were alien to these middle-class kids from Texas, who still identified most strongly with midtown life. But as time went on, they found the greatest sympathy for their ideas downtown in the Village. As they moved deeper into the 1950s, their careers curved increasingly in its direction.

Off-Broadway was a symptom of Greenwich Village, and it was an indication of the cultural richness of the city as a whole that so many divergent strains of theater could take root and contend for sun there.

Jones, Schmidt and Baker became aware of fine distinctions only gradually. At first they simply absorbed as much as they could of everything.

They were just as happy to see the Kurt Weill/Bertolt Brecht *The Threepenny Opera* at the Theater De Lys (now the Lucille Lortel Theatre) on Christopher Street in the Village as they were to see the Leonard Bernstein/Lillian Hellman/Dorothy Parker operetta *Candide* on Broadway.

Both influenced them powerfully, though all cite *Candide* as a major influence on *The Fantasticks*.

"I've never been able to understand all these people who say it didn't work then and needed fixing," Schmidt said of *Candide*, which closed after a disappointingly short run of ninety-three performances. "It's never been as good since as it was in the original production. I thought it worked great. So did Tom. Things like "Happy Ending" [the Act I finale of *The Fantasticks*] are directly influenced by it. Take Luisa's obbligatos, which I've regretted ever since I wrote them because no one can sing them. Those are based on Barbara Cook's hysterical runs in "Glitter and Be Gay." The top of the second act is directly influenced [by "Quiet"]. It's probably in some ways the most stylish musical I've ever seen."

Jones's tastes ran more to drama. He frequented movie houses in Times Square and the upper West Side but said he was truly thunderstruck by a production of Goldoni's *Arlec-chino* by Giorgio Strehler's Piccolo Teatro di Milano, an experimental Italian company, which staged the work as if done by a road-weary itinerant troupe. It opened with the actors shaving, pulling their costumes on and generally looking like they were getting ready for work. With open stage techniques that would have warmed B. Iden Payne's heart, the production had a profound influence on *The Fantasticks*. Jones said Strehler became his new idol.

Gradually their sensibilities were honed. As they sized up New York's marketplace of ideas, their writing became more focused and sophisticated.

Important changes were taking place in Charlie Baker's life as well.

It seems that there was another Charles Baker in New York at that time, an agent with one of the city's biggest talent agencies. He also went by the nickname, Charlie. Mielziner had warned Baker that some confusion inevitably would result, but Baker was proud of his family name and was adamant about continuing with it.

The impasse came in 1956 when Baker was listed as casting director on the Ethel Merman vehicle *Happy Hunting*, which had sets by Mielziner. A story in *Variety* appeared to confuse the two men, citing the presence of Baker as the reason actors from a rival agency weren't hired.

Baker recalls reading the notice shortly after he had arrived for work at Mielziner's office in the Dakota, and finally agreeing with Mielziner that something had to be done. It was Mielziner who suggested that if Baker didn't want to change his last name, perhaps he would consider changing his first name. After rejecting several possibilities, he decided that not only would he continue the tradition of one family, but add another as well. He assumed his mother's maiden name, Word.

Settled in Elmhurst, Queens, the newly rechristened Word Baker spent three years (1955–58) as Mielziner's secretary (under a variety of "official" titles) on projects including Rodgers and Hammerstein's *Pipe Dream* and the film *Picnic* for which Mielziner shared an Oscar for best Art Direction/Set Decoration with William Flanner and Robert Priestly.

* * *

From their perch on 61st Street, Jones and Schmidt moved to a second-floor apartment in a brownstone on West 74th Street between West End Avenue and Riverside Drive with Robert Alan Gold, a painter who managed properties in the city and was co-owner of a former-nightclub-turned-theater on Sullivan Street in Greenwich Village; plus another UT alumnus, George Gilbreath. Gilbreath soon took a job as part of Mae West's Las Vegas act, and was succeeded in the 74th Street apartment by Robert Benton, Harvey's UT roommate.

Like Jones, Benton wanted to become a director and writer. He would get his wish in Hollywood, being nominated for the 1967 screenplay Oscar for *Bonnie and Clyde*, and winning the 1979 directing Oscar for *Kramer vs Kramer* and the 1984 screenplay Oscar for *Places in the Heart*, the last an evocation of the same Dustbowl Texas where he, Jones, Schmidt and Baker grew up.

In 1956, they were just a bunch of hungry, talented guys sharing a roof and a kitchen.

Benton was the first to change part of that, moving up from his job as assistant art director to art director of *Esquire* magazine, a valuable contact that enabled Schmidt to supplement his NBC money.

Jones earned his share of the rent by continuing to teach and direct at St. Bart's and by returning to reliable, if often frustrating, work at a book store.

When he first came to New York in 1954, he had worked at the tiny Lenox Hill Book Shop on the upper East Side. When he returned in 1955, he was hired at the Aberdeen Book Shop, a vast (half a city block long) and impersonal store just below Union Square. The manager, Jones recalls, was forever fearful of being robbed. Jones often was sent "racing out into the street to stop well-dressed people and say 'excuse me, but I think you have one of our books.' And they often did. It was an awful experience."

Jones continued living in the 74th Street apartment until 1963 when he married Elinor Wright. The place is full of memories for all who rested their heads there. Up a brownstone stoop, they entered a doorway that took them up a narrow staircase to the door, which opened into a small foyer. An archway to the right separated the foyer from the octagonal living room with its wide, south-facing windows that always poured light into the apartment. This is the window where the would-be *Fantasticks* producer would cry during the thunderstorm when he learned that the Mysterious Man in White was chosen to mount the musical.

From the foyer, two doorways led to the back of the apartment where there were two bedrooms, shared bunk-style by the four roommates.

"It worked amazingly well for an apartment that's not that big," Schmidt said. "When I started getting a lot of freelance work, I became Mr. Hotsy-Totsy. I was always out looking at penthouses. I was always going to move out, get out of 'this dump.' And now [1990] I'm like the old-maid spinster daughter that stayed at home. Everyone else has gone to opulent places like Tom's fabulous place in Connecticut and both of the Roberts's fabulous Hamptons places, but I'm still here."

Schmidt tried to do his early freelance assignments in the apartment but found too many distractions. So he rented a studio in a cheap hotel on West End Avenue, half a block away, which he outfitted with a drafting table and an easel. "It was very convenient because it was near the apartment. I'd run back and forth. It was also big, so I could spend the night if I wanted to. Once I started freelancing, I was so busy. These were all fabulous assignments, but you only got them if you did fabulous work. I'd often work around the clock and get very little sleep."

To help, he would drink endless cups of coffee and listen to the radio as he worked, just as he had as a child, though by the late '50s, "it all seemed to be turning into 'How Much Is That Doggie In the Window?' and I began to lose interest. I still feel that songs were only good until 1950." He soon switched to classical music stations.

Almost never cooking for themselves, the guys often ate out at the 72nd Street Automat. "It was wonderful, American, pre-microwave real food," Schmidt said. "The Automat was simply glorious. The poorest person could go in there and, for a nickel, get fabulous food, fresh vegetables. I've always loved to eat out. We never could afford to do it when I was small. I take great pride in the fact that my refrigerator in New York has never had any food in it. It once had a bottle of champagne that was in there like fourteen years. Every meal, I love to eat out. I look forward to it. Since I've had money, I can eat almost anywhere. And in New York, you never run out of places to eat."

In the winter, there were plays and movies and work. In the summer, there was stock theater, more work and on Sunday mornings, croquet on the Sheep Meadow in Central Park, just four blocks from the apartment, often with Benton's girlfriend of that time, Gloria Steinem. "We would meet at dawn—you could do that then," Schmidt said. "There weren't all the dangerous elements that you have around today. And it was wonderful, beautiful. Then we would go to the Edwardian Room at the Plaza and have breakfast."

Amid all their "day jobs" to pay the rent, however, Jones and Schmidt never lost sight of their goal to write musicals and, if possible, to fulfill their spiritual debt to B. Iden Payne and break new ground in doing so. Every once in a while, Eunice Healey would send them on an audition for the *Portfolio* revue, but for the time being, nothing seemed to come of it.

5

1957–59

"The story is not ended / And the play is never done /
Until we've all of us been burned a bit /
And burnished by—the sun!"

THOUGH their lives seemed to be moving in different directions, Baker said, the writers continued to get together with him on 74th Street to talk about what they hoped to accomplish artistically. "There was a certain affinity and belief in a theory of theater that was considered heresy: open stage, direct to the audience," Baker said. They all spoke the same language.

While Jones overhauled the libretto of *Joy Comes to Dead Horse*, Schmidt got to work writing a whole new score for the existing lyrics. To demonstrate his commitment to the project, Schmidt decided to take a year off from NBC and concentrate on writing the score. Schmidt's touch was far lighter than Robb's—less academic concert hall and more Hollywood pop. Owing to changes in the meter of Schmidt's music, Jones rewrote the fathers' lament into substantially its current form:

> Why did the kids pour jam on the cat?
> Raspberry jam all over the cat?
> Why should the kids do something like that,
> When all that we said was 'No'?

> . . . Your daughter brings a young man in,
> Says, 'Do you like him, Pa?'
> Just tell her she's a fool and then,
> You've got a son-in-law!*

Lacking a piano at either the apartment or Schmidt's office, the two of them sometimes worked after hours at a piano in St. Bart's auditorium, though they preferred working individually. Schmidt took Jones's lyrics and would fool around at the piano, trying on melodies until he found one that fit. Then he would embroider it.

One of Schmidt's first and most important tasks was finding a new melody to the show's opening number, in which El Gallo invites the audience into the show. For Schmidt's new music, Jones slightly rewrote the lyric:

> Come on along with me
> Follow along with me
> Back to a world that is easy and slow
> Follow along with me
> Follow the song with me
> Let's go see how it was long ago.
>
> . . . Let's go back beyond the smart of you
> Back to the special childlike part of you
> Back where your dreams are fancy free . . .
> Follow along
> Follow the song
> With me.**

"Certainly it had its questionable parts," Jones later told an audience at the "Lyrics and Lyricists" series at the 92nd Street YM-YWHA. He winced to recall writing "beyond the smart of you" and explained, "We thought we could do something more interesting, especially lyrically."

Schmidt was dissatisfied as well, saying "My music made it seem more pompous than it was intended to be."

When St. Bart's was unavailable, Schmidt booked a piano room at Nola Rehearsal Studios in the Steinway Building on 54th Street. "In the evenings after working at NBC, I would rent the studio so I could play the piano," Schmidt said. "One night I was working on something very jazzy, possibly for *Portfolio* or this early version of *Joy Comes to Dead Horse*. I was playing brute chords, real dissonant, pseudo-Leonard Bernstein-type things. I had been pounding cacaphonously for hours. I usually rented the studio for three hours, so this would have been about seven-thirty or eight. I was exhausted and so depressed that I wasn't playing anything good. I remember the next moment very well: I sat back in my chair and got ready to quit, but then I thought, well, I've paid for the piano, so I should keep playing.

"So, for a change of pace, I played 'Try to Remember,' I mean literally: there wasn't a hesitation, I went—" he hums the opening bar "—and it just kept playing itself. I have never felt like I wrote that song. And I remember thinking to myself: that's something."

At first, Schmidt didn't think of putting his sweetly spare waltz into *Joy Comes to Dead Horse*, but recalls, "Tom would hear me playing, and he'd say 'What is that song you're playing?' I'd say 'it's just a song that came to me.' And he said 'That's such a pretty melody, why don't we see about changing the song we have for El Gallo?' It's a very hard song to put lyrics to because, while the music is very simple, somehow the way the rhyme pattern falls is very tricky. But Tom worked very hard on it and, thank God, did a beautiful lyric for it. But it's funny how that melody was dropped in my lap. That happened several times throughout the show."

Taking a cue from his lyric for "Come on Along With Me," Jones expanded on the idea of inviting the audience to "follow" El Gallo, not only into the show but into an idyllic past:

> Try to remember the kind of September
> When life was slow and oh so mellow
> Try to remember the kind of September
> When grass was green and grain was yellow
> Try to remember the kind of September

When you were a tender and callow fellow
Try to remember
And if you remember, then follow . . .

The notion of metaphorical changing seasons was an appealing one, so Jones developed it in the song's final stanza. In doing so, he cast a figurative chill over the number, foreshadowing the drama to come:

Deep in December, it's nice to remember,
Although you know the snow will follow
Deep in December, it's nice to remember:
Without a hurt, the heart is hollow . . .
Deep in December, our hearts should remember,
And follow.*

Among their friends and associates in show business, the song was an immediate hit. Schmidt recalls an acquaintance, Broadway producer Max Gordon, calling them to say, " 'Boys, how does that song go?' and we had to hum it for him."

Encouraged, they forged ahead with their project, which seemed a lot like *Romeo and Juliet* crossed with *Oklahoma!* The 1957–58 versions called for a whole corral full of singing cowboys riding live horses on an enormous Texas ranch set.

But wherever they pitched it, people complimented them on the score but shook their heads over the physical production. Things were complicated even more by the September 1957 opening of Bernstein's own *West Side Story*, which told a star-crossed love story between a Puerto Rican girl and an Anglo boy. The settings and stories were by no means identical . . . but they were uncomfortably close.

But while Baker could tell that Jones's original idea had been "knocked into a cocked hat," he said, "Tom is very tenacious. He won't let go of a thing once he starts writing."

*   *   *

Schmidt had plenty of other projects cooking. His freelance assignments kept getting better and better. He was invited by

*From "Try to Remember" by Tom Jones and Harvey Schmidt. © 1960 Chappel & Co. (Rewewed). All Rights Reserved. Used by Permission.

Harper's Bazaar to do Hirschfeld-style caricatures of that year's theatrical season, as he had done for the *Houston Post* after college.

Schmidt's sketches appeared in *Life*, *Harper's Bazaar*, *Sports Illustrated* and *Fortune* magazines, and he even was invited to do easel paintings that were reproduced on the color pages.

In an era when the nation was building the interstate super-highway system, Schmidt was hired by Standard Oil, which essentially told him, as he recalls, "You can go anywhere in the country you want to and paint anything you want to having to do with the building of interstate highways."

"Well," he said, "there's no more dream assignment than that. I love to travel anyway, and I hadn't really been many places." He toured from New England to San Francisco, stopping for weeks to do nothing but paint. He also chose Texas, so he could visit his family. Wandering the beach in Galveston with Jones's lyrics to "Much More," Schmidt "heard" the melody and composed most of it on the spot.

Considering how hard he was working and how far from New York that work was taking him, it's ironic that his first high-visibility popular hit was a lark conceived in his living room—a project called *The IN and OUT Book*.

As part of his job at *Esquire*, Benton tried to keep track of the dizzying turnover in fads and fashions of trendy New Yorkers. He could be counted on to be familiar with the cutting edge in any creative field.

One rare night when all four bachelors were gathered around the apartment's long black table having dinner, they got into a discussion of why certain clothes, words, celebrities—even things to eat—go in and out of style from year to year. Groping to clarify his point, Benton began defining things by their quality of being "in" or "out."

Schmidt said, "Bob Gold and Tom and I all thought that sounded great, and soon all four of us were screaming with laughter as we started saying so-and-so was 'in,' and so-and-so was 'out.' "

Benton stewed about the idea the rest of the night, and the next morning asked Schmidt if he'd like to collaborate on an *Esquire* feature using the In and Out hook. The two men carried notebooks for the next few weeks, jotting down observations of things on their way In or Out. Both being artists, they also improvised pen sketches to accompany their planned piece.

The resulting *Esquire* feature became a fad of its own, with several sequels. In 1957, at the suggestion of Tom Ginsburg at Viking Press, Benton and Schmidt gathered them into a best-selling little tome, *The IN and OUT Book*.

"There are two kinds of things in this world:" it begins, "IN and OUT."

What follows is a highly subjective and (now) egregiously dated survey of pop culture. In some ways, it's also a survey of life on West 74th Street.

"A thing can be IN for three reasons: a. Because it is so classic and great. Example: the Plaza Hotel. b. Because it is so obscure. Example: Veda Ann Borg movies. c. Because it is so far OUT even the OUT people won't touch it. Example: Tchaikovsky."

The faceless figures in the illustrations are defined by simple clothes or props, like aggressively hep paper dolls. "Zen Buddhism is OUT," it asserts. "Southern Baptist is IN. All greeting cards are OUT, and if you send the bizarre sick kind you are OUT for life. Men who cook (especially with rice) are OUT. Fresh frozen food is OUT; canned food is IN. The most IN food is a Brownie Crumble Ball . . ."*

Though the *Portfolio* revue appeared to be a long-lost cause, Eunice Healey kept sending Jones and Schmidt to auditions, and, long after they'd effectively given up hope, they suddenly got a bite.

Julius Monk, a North Carolinian with a cultivated and sometimes opaque accent, remembered Jones from Le Ruban Bleu and offered to give them a hearing. He had the dashing good looks of a model, having appeared with an eyepatch in Arrow shirt ads. A former cabaret pianist, he had founded theater companies and cabarets in Bermuda and Provincetown, Massachusetts, and had worked for fifteen years as artistic director at Manhattan's Le Ruban Bleu nightclub. There, he presented entertainments that drew on the best elements of the witty sketches in the big Broadway revues like the *Ziegfeld Follies*

*From *The IN and OUT Book* © Robert Benton and Harvey Schmidt. Reprinted by Permission.

series and *Make Mine Manhattan*, the tart Greenwich Village nightclub acts like The Revuers at the Village Vanguard, as well as the more ribald skits of burlesque, though without what he calls "ladies' bazooms and tuckus."

He had an appetite for wit and preferred it fast and light. Among the talent he showcased were Ronny Graham, Dody Goodman, Imogene Coca, Jonathan Winters, Cy Coleman, and Bill Dana.

The year before he had moved to a basement-level club kitty-corner from Radio City Music Hall on 51st Street at Sixth Avenue (Avenue of the Americas) and presented a revue loaded with topical humor delivered by a quartet of performers. Its punning title was *Four Below*.

Julius Monk's Downstairs at the Upstairs revue was suddenly, as Benton and Schmidt might have put it, IN. And he needed high quality revue material fast.

Long-time *Portfolio* aspirant Gerry Matthews had performed in Monk's Le Ruban Bleu revues and was chosen as one of the "four below." He now acted as intermediary, urging Jones and Schmidt to play their material for Monk. The arbiters of IN and OUT would be just what Monk was looking for.

Monk invited them to his house in the East Fifties. Baker remembers it as "a teeny-tiny apartment decorated, I mean *filled*, with stuff, as was Julius's wont. He sat on a little love seat under an almost life-size portrait of himself. Harvey and Tom played their music on a little upright piano that had a great bouquet of peonies on it. Harvey hit some high note, as only Harvey can do, and one of the peonies shattered. Julius laughed, and we were in like Flynn from then on."

Baker supplemented his work for Mielziner by going to work for Monk as well. Billed as "associate," he fulfilled a number of administrative tasks, including maitre d' and "translator" of Monk's idiosyncratic style of speech for the performers.

When Monk moved his operations from the below-level club on 51st Street to larger quarters above-level on 56th Street between Fifth and Sixth Avenues, he somersaulted the name to help customers find it: Upstairs at the Downstairs. Under this new name, the club enjoyed its widest fame.

Four Below was followed by a remarkable series of fifteen more or less annual topical revues that set the standard for their kind. These included *Son of Four Below*, then *Take Five*, *Seven Come Eleven* and the most successful of the group, *Demi-Dozen* in 1958. The numerically-titled revues followed in sequence after that, *Pieces of Eight* and *Dressed to the Nines*, before surrendering the club to Ronny Graham and Ben Bagley and moving to a new stage at Plaza Nine.

When Stephen Sondheim was tracing the life story of a songwriter in his 1981 musical, *Merrily We Roll Along*, he includes a pivotal scene ("Bobbie and Jackie and Jack") at a topical revue clearly inspired by Upstairs at the Downstairs.

Jones's first two sketches appeared in *Son of Four Below* in 1956. One, titled "Gift From the Sea," was a parody of Anne Morrow Lindbergh's book of a similar title, in which she wrote poetically about lovely seashells and such. In Jones's sketch, performed by comedian Dody Goodman, the "gifts" were "kind of smellier," Jones said. Jones and Schmidt wrote more material for 1957's *Take Five* and wrote nearly half of 1958's *Demi-Dozen*.

Though Jones and Schmidt went on to write music for a number of the era's topical revues, including Ben Bagley's *Shoestring Revues* (an allusion to the budget), they considered Upstairs at the Downstairs their home base.

"It was a great thing for writers," Schmidt said. "It was a chance actually to get material heard, and lots of important people would come." Salaries were nominal (Schmidt said he got $7 a week while the shows were running), but the exposure was worth it.

It also, finally, gave Gerry Matthews a chance to deliver the revue material Jones and Schmidt had been preparing for him all those years. Monk's *Demi-Dozen* might also have been titled *Son of Portfolio*. Much of the score is preserved on an Offbeat Records disk that includes seven pieces by Jones and Schmidt, most of which were written or conceived back in Austin and Auburn.

Some were of newer vintage. "A Seasonal Sonatina" features four songs about life in New York City during each of the four seasons, including one that must have been dear to their hearts: "Autumn at the Automat." However lighthearted, it shows that *The Fantasticks* was not the first time Jones had explored a turning-of-the-seasons theme.

In a burst of enthusiasm about their new membership in New York's theater community—however far out on the fringe—they wrote a celebration of the seat-of-the-pants Village theater scene in "Mister Off-Broadway:"

Everybody calls me Mister Off-Broadway
Although they know that's really not my name
Still everybody calls me Mister Off-Broadway
'Cause it was many blocks off Broadway where I got my fame.

I've played in every kind of house, in every kind of hall
I once played "Cinderella" in an empty shower stall
The stage was kind of slippery, but I mean we had a ball!
Off-Broadway melody.

Give my regards to old Off-Broadway
Remember me to Sheridan Square
Tell all the gang at Jan Hus Auditorium
That I will soon be there!
Everybody calls me Mister Off-Broadway
Yes, everybody shouts it when we meet.
Although nobody knows me on the Great White Way
I'm very well respected south of 14th Street.

Over there, over there
I mean the Circle in the Square!
I played "The Iceman Cometh" there for almost a year
I never made much money but I drank a lot of beer.
That's why everybody calls me Mister Off-Broadway
Off-Broadway melody . . .*

The lyric goes on to offer a snapshot of their playgoing habits at the time, mentioning the Phoenix Theatre, *Pale Horse, Pale Rider*, *The Trial of Dmitri Karamazov* and plays by Machiavelli and Ionesco.

The accompaniment to "Mister Off-Broadway" reflects Schmidt's love of movie music. It contains quotes of "Over

*From *Demi-Dozen* © Tom Jones and Harvey Schmidt. Used by Pemission.

There," "Broadway Melody," "How You Gonna Keep 'Em Down on the Farm?" and "Give My Regards to Broadway."

One of the most memorable of their pieces in *Demi-Dozen* is "The Holy Man and the New Yorker," a rhymed parable with musical accompaniment. Introduced by Gerry Matthews, it tells the story of a Holy Man who dresses in rags and exhorts passing crowds from a Gristede's supermarket crate. It pleads for a regard for flowers that anticipates the flower children of a decade later. The Holy Man's entreaties to "Look up, look up . . . If you look up, you can see the sky" finally attract the attention of a jaded New Yorker to achieve enlightenment only long enough to exclaim, "Son of a bitch!" before he's mowed down by a speeding taxi.

The chords that answer the narrator's words echo Schmidt's underscoring of Jones's verses in *The Fantasticks*, particularly the dissonant chords in "This Plum Is Too Ripe," though it even more closely anticipates their work in the 1969 musical *Celebration*.

In *Demi-Dozen*'s "Grand Opening," the characters invoke festivity by exclaiming "Play, gypsy!" just as El Gallo would do in "Round and Round."

* * *

Several other future members of the original cast of *The Fantasticks* made their entrance at Upstairs at the Downstairs. Through Schmidt, Ed Wittstein and his companion, Robert Miller, were hired to design and build its sets. As Monk's assistant, Word Baker was on hand every night to oversee the operations and remained in close enough touch with the dark-eyed actor Jerry Orbach from his New Jersey theater days to introduce him to Monk backstage.

It was at Upstairs at the Downstairs that the songwriters also met a man whose jolly personal style recalls what Santa Claus might be like if he had a second job. He was George Curley, who served as Monk's production stage manager and lighting technician.

The son of an electrical contractor in Freeport, Long Island, Curley began running lights at Freeport High School and so entertained the school's drama teacher that he urged Curley to try out for a school play. That set him up for a life in show business. When he wasn't acting in regional theaters, he did tech work, and vice versa.

The jolly-old-elf air paid off for Curley. He made a name for himself after graduating Ithaca College by playing Rumplestiltskin in a touring children's theater that went on the road every summer during the early and mid-1950s. Curley also had a steady winter gig as Santa at a suburban A&S department store, which he performed as faithfully as his namesake from 1957 to 1977.

These attributes did not escape Jones and Schmidt's attention when they were casting for the lovable low comic Man Who Dies in *The Fantasticks*.

It was at the Automat in Times Square (now a Burger King) that one of Curley's techie friends told him of a job opening at Downstairs at the Upstairs. Curley helped build the lighting board for the club and eventually appeared onstage in small parts. He also taught Jones to operate the light board, much as Jones had done for the high school play contests back at the University of Texas. This time, it was not just for love, but for money.

* * *

Money sent Schmidt to Mexico City in the summer of 1958. Always fascinated with that region of the continent, Schmidt used his G.I. Bill scholarship to take the sabbatical from NBC and study painting at Mexico City College. There, he executed a series of tempera portraits and landscapes that he considers some of his best work. A selection of these paintings was published in *Look* magazine, September 2, 1958.

But the Mexico sojourn was a fertile time for Schmidt musically, as well. Hoping the atmosphere would provide inspiration for the Mexicans' songs in *Joy Comes to Dead Horse*, Schmidt resolved to write a song a day during his trip. Because he could not notate music, and because this predated portable tape recorders, he had to memorize the tunes or scribble diagrams indicating the rise and fall of the music in a way only he was able to translate. Many were simply pop tunes that wouldn't work in a specific show. But, inspired by the Mexican Halloween, the Day of the Dead, Schmidt conceived a full-length ballet. "I imagined Jerome Robbins doing it," Schmidt said.

"And while, musically, I think *Day of the Dead* was very good, that never happened. It was grandiose dreams of glory."

The resulting catalogue of sixty or so melodies included many seminal themes on which he continued to draw throughout his career. Schmidt used passages from *Day of the Dead* in the 1963 musical *110 in the Shade*. "Melisande" and "Lizzie, Stop Fiddling With Your Button" are two of the more pleasant. Some of its themes crop up in *The Fantasticks* as well, particularly in the Latin curlicues of "Never Say No" and, later, "It Depends on What You Pay."

While in Mexico City, Schmidt chose a hot, blustery afternoon to see Garcia Lorca's *House of Bernarda Alba* at Teatro del Bosque. He arrived early and strolled through the surrounding Chapultepec Park while waiting for the doors to open. As clouds grew darker and thicker and the humid wind gusted through the long branches of some willow trees, Schmidt remembers thinking to himself "Soon it's gonna rain." Under the self-imposed song-a-day regimen, he seized on the rhythm of those words to suggest a surging piano vamp.

As happened with "Much More" on the beach in Galveston, the rest of the melody composed itself in his head that afternoon while watching Lorca's play.

"I started playing it down in Mexico," Schmidt said, "and the kids at the college liked it. When I came back, I played [for Tom Jones] all the stuff I'd written down there. He heard 'Soon It's Gonna Rain' and thought it would make a good song for the boy and girl. He constructed lyrics for an introductory verse, which I then set to music. The first line, 'Hear how the wind begins to whisper,' is interesting because it is very much like the mood I felt in the park that day."

One of the first international productions of *The Fantasticks* took place in Mexico City, in the very theater where Schmidt had begun composing the melody. "It was spooky," he said.

* * *

Back in the States, Baker was deeply involved in theater as a teacher for Herbert Berghof and as assistant to both Jo Mielziner and Julius Monk. But despite the fun and the status, it still was at the periphery of creativity. He longed to move closer to the center.

One of Baker's protean duties under Mielziner was to act as script reader, screening the many plays, musicals and films that came to him for designing or producing. In 1958, Baker recommended a drama by Valjean Axelrod Massey, a playwright who had lived upstairs from Baker in his first New York apartment, on West Broadway.

"Valjean had written a very nice play, and Jo liked it too," Baker said. "We were having a meeting in Jo's studio, and I was taking notes. The only question was—who would direct? Jo had gone through a list of directors, all of whom had turned down the play. Valjean said 'Word's a director. Why don't you have him direct it?'

"And Jo very nicely said 'But he's not a director. He hasn't directed anything in New York.'

"Well, not at that moment, and not in anybody's sight, but by the time I got home I was furious. But my wife said, 'He's right. He's absolutely right. If you don't like it, shut up and get a job as a director.' "

Baker immediately thought of his successful Alabama production of Miller's *The Crucible* and decided that a great place to do it would be Off-Broadway.

"Major playwrights weren't letting their plays be done Off-Broadway then," Baker said, explaining that despite the success of Williams's *Summer and Smoke* and O'Neill's *The Iceman Cometh*, both were considered flukes. The downtown cachet was considered unworthy of writers of stature.

Recalling the speech Miller had given in Arkansas just four years earlier, Baker contacted the Pulitzer laureate and explained how profoundly the talk had influenced his career and his student production of the play.

To Baker's surprise, Miller invited him to a meeting at his agent's office. Baker brought photos of the Auburn production, explaining how carefully he had followed Miller's minimalist vision of the play. Miller responded with his blessing, and the revival which opened in the round at the Martinique Theatre in 1958 was widely praised. It starred Michael Higgins as John Proctor and Barbara Barrie as Elizabeth Proctor and wound up running a surprising 571 performances, still considered an enviable run for a serious drama. In the role of Reverend Parris that Sam Houston had claimed for his own back in Alabama,

Baker cast a member of the U of Texas "Mafia," Bill Larsen, who later would originate the role of Hucklebee, the Boy's father, in *The Fantasticks*.

Jones, who used his spare hours away from the bookstore and St. Bart's to help lay carpet and build sets at the Martinique for free, said he was deeply impressed with Baker's unusual vision. Completely surrounded by the audience and unencumbered by any but the most basic props, it was just the script and the actors' passions. "He did a very brilliant thing," Jones said with rare unqualified approbation. "After the original Broadway production, which was a failure, the play was published. In this published version, Miller interspersed the play with actual historical facts he had researched: 'This character actually lived' . . . 'So-and-so happened here.' In Word's production, he [added the role of] a reader with that manuscript. At certain key parts of the action, Word had the actors stop and freeze, and this reader would read Arthur Miller's words about the real people and how it all really happened. Then he would sit down, and the actors would continue."

The technique, which owes something to Thornton Wilder's Stage Manager in *Our Town*, was used again by Baker in *The Fantasticks*. This time, however, it would be El Gallo who would have the power to freeze the action and speak directly to the audience.

When the new Bantam Classic paperback edition of *The Crucible* came out in April 1959—the version toted by a generation of high school and college students—the cover illustration of Proctor standing tall over the prostrate and accusing Abigail was the poster designed for Baker's production. Its designer? Harvey Schmidt.

* * *

Thus, in the spring of 1959, Baker and Schmidt were on top of the world. Schmidt was a nationally famous illustrator; Baker a successful Off-Broadway director.

Jones was still writing material for Julius Monk while working in the book store and directing at St. Bart's, but he remembers feeling that his career was stagnating. Part of the problem was the lack of progress on his grand project, *Joy Comes to Dead Horse*, then nearly five years in the rewriting. Despite the charm of "Try to Remember" and the other new melodies, this enormous Western with a plot very similar to that of *West Side Story* seemed to have a very small chance of ever getting anywhere. Though the others were more than happy to work on it with him, it was Jones whose identity had melded with the musical. He persisted in probing at the problem.

"We still were trying to make it in the Rodgers and Hammerstein mode," Jones said. "That was the thing that musicals were at that point. And much as I would try to change it from that, I didn't know *how*. So eventually it collapsed. I mean it really was going nowhere. Life was going on year in, year out, but nothing was happening."

Jones's feeling of inertia broke that spring with the death of his father at age fifty-eight from a heart attack back at the turkey hatchery in Coleman, Texas.

"I went there and discovered what I hadn't realized," Jones said: "that his financial situation had been very bad. There was no question of selling the business. It was, in fact, bankrupt. That's what killed him, I'm sure. I stayed there in the spring for a couple of months trying to get things settled. I, with my job at $25 a week, was not able to help too much. My mother had never held a job other than faithful housewife. So there was a real crisis. Something had to be done. I knew that my drifting had to come to an end. When I came back to New York, it was with a renewed determination to *do something* or get out."

He was about to get his chance. Success with *The Crucible* brought Baker enough money to enable him to leave Mielziner's employ and set up shop as a full-time director. Its success also made him something of a hero in the tiny circle of Off-Broadway. Several offers came his way, but the one that interested him most was from Mildred Dunnock, an actress who had introduced characters by some of the most beautiful stage poets of the mid-twentieth century, including Big Mama in Tennessee Williams's *Cat on a Hot Tin Roof*, and most memorably, Linda Loman in Arthur Miller's *Death of a Salesman*. Her career reached its apex in the timeless "Attention must be paid" speech that ends that play.

Barnard's president Millicent McIntosh had come from the Bearley School, a private academy for girls where Dunnock had taught. Barnard hosted an annual summer stock theater series in its Minor Latham Auditorium on Broadway at West 119th Street. Looking for a prestigious name that would attract high-caliber young actors, McIntosh invited Dunnock to oversee the 1959 series. Shows changed weekly.

In early summer 1959, Dunnock came to Word Baker and invited him to direct a program of three one-act plays at the Minor Latham Playhouse. She could pay only about $100 for the student production, but it would be a chance to combine his two loves, teaching and directing. Dunnock told him he would be allowed to present the plays on a completely open stage, if he wished. Considering the budget, he would need to do it with a virtually bare stage as well, which was fine with Baker.

Just as he had recaptured the spartan beauty of the Auburn *Crucible* in New York, Baker saw the triple-bill as one more chance to conjure up the informal magic of his college productions. He scheduled premieres of *The Mall* by William Inge and *The Gay Apprentice* by Jack Dunphy but resolved to do a new musical as well.

Remembering the long-simmering *Joy Comes to Dead Horse*, Baker went to the 74th Street apartment and told Jones and Schmidt that if they could condense their musical to one act and figure out a way to do it with minimal scenery and costumes, he could get them a production.

6

June–August 1959

"Try to see it — / Not with your eyes, for
they are wise; / But see it with your ears . . ."

LOCATED on Broadway at
119th Street in Manhattan, the Minor Latham Playhouse is just
around the corner from Columbia University, where Allen
Ginsburg, Jack Kerouac, Gregory Corso and William S. Bur-
roughs had given birth to the Beat poetry movement less than a
decade earlier.

The howl of their writing still echoes there, however dimly.
But in the summer of 1959, when beatniks were emerging
from underground and becoming a phenomenon in the mass
media, the purity of their anger and the romance of their life-
styles were still fresh. The bohemianism had varying degrees
of effect on those who lived, worked or studied there, particularly their devotion to poetry, pleasure, soulfulness and simplicity.

Billed as "A Summer Theatre on Broadway," Mildred Dunnock's Barnard Summer Theatre harnessed the talent of these
theater students struggling for excellence and impeccability.
The atmosphere may have seemed odd for a cowboy musical,
but Jones, Schmidt and Baker couldn't have been more in tune
with their artistic goals.

Baker made his offer to Jones and Schmidt in early June,
telling them that if they could finish it in four weeks, it would

Pierre Laugier and Louis Leloir as the Fathers in the original
Comédie Française production of Edmond Rostand's *Les
Romanesques*.

The cast of the original one-act version of *The Fantasticks* at Mildred Dunnock's Barnard Summer Theatre, August 1959. From left: Dick Burnham, Susan Watson, Crayton Rowe, George Morgan, Bill Tost, and Jonathan Farwell.

The Fantasticks at Barnard in summer 1959. Jonathan Farwell (left) is El Gallo, George Morgan (center) is The Mute, and Lee Croghan and Ron Leibman are The Fathers.

The composers, Harvey
Schmidt (top) and Tom
Jones.

The
Fantasticks

THE
FANTASTICKS

THE
FANTASTICKS

THE
FANTASTICKS

THE
FANTASTICKS

THE
FANTASTICKS

The
Fantasticks

Various logo designs
submitted in spring 1960
by Harvey Schmidt at
producer Lore Noto's
request. The bottom one,
in Schmidt's own
handwriting, was
selected.

Hugh Thomas (left) as Bellomy and William Larsen as
Hucklebee in the original Sullivan Street Playhouse
production in 1960.

Jerry Orbach takes
a rehearsal break
among the con-
struction pieces of
the platform set
(1960).

Word Baker directs the two Fathers for the original production. Rita
Gardner is in the background.

Ed Wittstein's costume design drawing for Luisa (lower right) in *The Fantasticks*, and for several other costume and scenery design concepts.

Drawing of the Sullivan Street Playhouse by Leta
Anderson, who played Luisa in the early 1960s.

Harvey Schmidt's
drawings of the
original Fathers:
William Larsen (left) as
Hucklebee and Hugh
Thomas as Bellomy.

Harvey Schmidt (1960). (Photo by Duane Michaels)

Bert Lahr and Stanley
Holloway asThe Fathers
in the *Hallmark Hall of
Fame* television version of
The Fantasticks in October
1964.

The young lovers in the television production: John Davidson and Susan Watson as Matt and Luisa.

Harvey Schmidt (left) and Tom Jones (right) are joined by Charles Nelson Reilly at the fourth anniversary party for the show.

be produced a month after that—August 4 to 8, the second-to-last slot of the season, to be followed by Lynn Riggs's *Green Grow the Lilacs*.

After three years of drifting along with *Joy Comes to Dead Horse*—five for Jones—the fearsome deadline was invigorating.

"Without that," Schmidt said, "we might have gone on for years writing it as this big Broadway musical."

Jones moved out of the 74th Street apartment for the summer and sublet actress Barbara Barrie's 28th Street flat for $28 a month while she was doing Shakespeare in Stratford, Connecticut. It was on 28th Street that he did most of his rewriting each night after closing the Upstairs at the Downstairs, where he had begun working as stage manager.

When Schmidt decided to take a year off from NBC to work on *Joy Comes to Dead Horse*, he installed a piano in the 74th Street apartment and would begin composing early each morning. He had no air conditioner and would throw open the windows to catch whatever breeze was dawdling past. The open windows also brought in the street sounds, and Schmidt vividly recalls trying to compose with the 1959 Memorial Day parade thumping away in the background.

Jones and Schmidt did most of their writing separately, a regimen they still practice. Jones would write the lyrics then hand them over to Schmidt, who would noodle at the piano for hours trying different melodies for them. The two men would meet occasionally at St. Bart's or at the apartment to discuss broad outlines but did most of the actual work alone.

They knew form was going to dictate content to a great degree, and that meant they first had to cut anything that would cost, well, money. In creating the one-act version of their vision, Jones and Schmidt returned to its essence, to the words and the ideas.

"We were determined to start over," Jones said. "We kept a few songs, but not that many. Word and I knew now we could never do it in the Rodgers and Hammerstein way. So we decided to do all the things we always wanted to do, which had to do with an open stage, and had to do with presentational theater, celebrating the restrictions of the theater and the artificiality of it, rather than trying to disguise it in any way. We decided we'd just break all the rules and do what we liked."

Out went the horses, the western costumes, the ranch

houses and El Gallo's elaborate props. These compromises were tough for the trio from Texas, but Jones and Schmidt would have their chance to pay musical homage to the Southwest in their next big musical, *110 in the Shade*.

They went back to the one-act version of *Les Romanesques* Jones had been forced to watch so many times from the lighting booth at UT. It opens with a boy and girl—neighbors separated by a cruel wall—declaring their love for each other in extravagant poetic terms. They are kept apart by their mean fathers who are having a feud.

The fathers appear and call out insults to each other, ordering the children inside their respective houses. But once the children are out of earshot, the fathers reveal that they secretly are the best of friends, plotting to join their homes and fortunes by binding their children in matrimony. They fancy themselves experts in human nature and have built the wall to give their starry-eyed children an obstacle to overcome. But how to end the feud? The fathers plot to hire a bandit to fake an abduction of the girl so the boy may rescue her and appear a hero. The abduction comes off as planned, and the lovers unite.

Here the one-act version ends. But Jones decided to jump from there to the end of the full-length *Les Romanesques* to make the play something more than a skit. The young lovers discover their fathers' plot and immediately are repulsed by each other, just as the fathers feared. The boy runs off to see the world, and the girl permits herself to be wooed by the bandit—only to have her keepsake necklace stolen. The boy crawls back from his spree beaten and humbled, and the two newly sober lovers pick up their romance, though on a far more realistic basis.

With no time to dilly-dally in telling this story, Jones was forced to depend on things at hand—his Dust Bowl upbringing, the Toby shows, the medicine shows, all the wonderful toys of theatrical artifice, the grand theatricality of B. Iden Payne, the seemingly practical fathers who weren't really practical at all, the notion of going out into the world and having it hit you with slop pots, the notion of gambling and losing. The intense emotions concentrated in those four weeks left little time for intellectualizing. It all had to come from the heart.

To say that the show is autobiographical would be wrong. Jones had more worldly wisdom than he revealed in his script. But hasty choices often are telling choices.

Like the Jones and Schmidt song "Everybody Calls Me Mr. Off-Broadway," their score for *The Fantasticks* is a celebration of theater and an expression of joyful stretching and kicking in a long-sought new environment. Liberated from trying to squeeze their idea into an uncomfortable format, they gamboled in their newfound freedom. *The Fantasticks* is an expression of pure pleasure at finally being allowed to do all they ever dreamed of doing and being.

And it turned out to be easier than they thought. As they began to strip down *Joy Comes to Dead Horse*, they found that chunks of the old script virtually seemed to come away in their hands, like dry rot or old paint.

Removing the cowboy trappings meant removing cowboy references that wouldn't have made much sense out of context. Such excisions took an hour out of the script, but the result would have been too generic for such a stylized piece. To replace it, Jones and Baker cast about for some legitimate theatrical style that would lend itself to a simple love story while retaining dramatic legitimacy. That led them to the original travel-light itinerant performers: the *commedia dell'arte* of the sixteenth century. The ten-gallon hats and chaps crumbled away, and underneath they found the simple clown-like colors of the *commedia*.

For those reasons, lightening the load meant the old title had to be tossed out as well. Fate provided them with a new one. Running to the main branch of the New York Public Library to look up alternate translations of Rostand's *Les Romanesques*, Jones stumbled across George Fleming's 1900 version and was immediately seduced. It was the first time he'd seen the complete Fleming version of the play, which he'd encountered only in fragmentary form at UT.

"I decided to use that as a guidepost in terms of story," Jones said. He also liked Fleming's peculiar title: *The Fantasticks*.

Literally translated, a "romanesque" means one who is romantic, in the sense of being imbued not only with love but with adventure. Thus *The Romantics* would be an etymologically more correct translation but would lose a certain swashbuckling grace. The original programme for the Barnard production subtitles the show as *A parable about love based on "Les Romantiques" [sic] by Edmund Rostand*, though that title is an error Jones copied from Fleming.

The more commonly used title, *The Romancers*, is a more figurative translation but also a clumsier one, suggesting a Don Juan atmosphere that is absent in the play.

Rostand's enduring tragedy, *Cyrano de Bergerac*, contains another classic translator's headache. In its final line, Cyrano refers to the one thing his own folly cannot take from him, the one thing he will carry with him from Earth into heaven: his "panache" or "plume." What he means is the proud style the courage and the grandeur of his soul, but there is no way to sum this up as neatly in English as Rostand does with the expression "panache." Complicating the situation is the fact that the word has come over from the French into English with a slightly different meaning, which makes it sound almost blasphemous in context.

Fleming solves the similar *Romanesques* problem neatly. The word "fantastic" is an adjective derived from the same root as "fantasy," indicating a product of the imagination, or something that is odd, grotesque or wildly exaggerated. Fleming, however, had pounced on an archaic noun version of the word meaning "One who is fantastic in conduct or appearance." Certainly the affected characters in Rostand's satirical play are that.

Furthermore, Fleming applied some panache of her own by tacking on that extra "K" at the end. The extra flourish gave the word the whimsical curlicue it needed to communicate the play's spirit. Schmidt was so delighted with Jones's discovery that they agreed to adopt *The Fantasticks*—extra "K" and all—as the new title of their musical. The archaic meaning would help to explain the *commedia* costumes they were planning to add. Schmidt the graphic artist also simply liked the way it looked: the extra tall letter near the end acted to frame the word squarely instead of letting it slope away at the end.

Jones found the rest of Fleming's translation equally useful. It solved problems he'd been laboring over for five years. Its rhymed couplets mirrored Rostand's, which inspired Jones to render most of his libretto as verse. It also was intensely compact: just a boy, a girl, their respective fathers and the bandit Straforel.

It was straightforwardly realistic, with two literal gardens and a literal wall between them, but it was enough of a *tabula rasa* in the right spots to let Jones have fun.

In a new introduction to the libretto published on the musical's thirtieth anniversary, Jones wrote about the Fleming *Fantasticks*, "I determined to keep that little library book close by my side, and whenever I became hopelessly lost in my own verbiage and inventiveness, to turn back to the source to find my way out of the forest."

Part of the continuing charm of *The Fantasticks* lies in its lingering beatnik atmosphere. The Boy rejects his college education which taught him to dissect flowers. He contents himself with throwing whole flowers to the Girl, a.k.a. Luisa, over a wall built by their fathers. But Jones consistently has denied any influence from the then-contemporary Beats.

He says he was inspired in his writing by Shakespeare, particularly as interpreted by British playwright and critic Harley Granville-Barker (1877–1946) in his book *On Dramatic Method*. Its description of how Shakespeare used moonlight in *A Midsummer Night's Dream* and darkness in *Macbeth* prompted Jones to adopt themes of his own.

"The writing specifically follows his technique, his thematic imagery," Jones says. "It was a grab bag of presentational devices." The Shakespeare connection was a natural one for the show, considering that *Les Romanesques* was a parody of *Romeo and Juliet*. The script alludes to *Hamlet*: "Remember me in light" ("Remember me" I.v.91) and many other Shakespeare plays.

With this analysis in mind, Jones made a timely trip up to Stratford, Connecticut, to see his "landlady" Barbara Barrie in John Houseman's *A Winter's Tale*, which had a sunny Act II and a moonlit Act I. Moonlight was a favorite of Rostand's as well. Cyrano de Bergerac would claim the moon as his personal muse. Jones's *Fantasticks* began to fill with references to the moon and the sun as metaphors for romance and reality. When El Gallo presents the fathers with his bill, he charges them not only for his expenses ("Item—a silver piece for actor to portray Indian Raiding Party—body paint included"), and trouble ("Item—a piece of gold to the famous El Gallo for allowing himself to seem wounded by a beardless, callow boy"), but for the very moonlight ("Item—one moon").

Taking a cue from Rostand's two gardens, as reflected in the already completed "Try to Remember," Jones, who confesses to being "big on equinoxes," filled the show with images of the seasons; of plants and flowers; of the cycles of the sun, moon and planets.

For these he drew not only on Shakespeare but on his own love life. The song "Metaphor" was based on love letters he wrote to artist Maryanne McClean, whom he had dated in 1958. Fascinated with the subjects of nature, she had shown him how to appreciate the patterns in flowers, leaves and branches. "She liked to paint, study and think about natural things and how they were made," Jones said, "and what was the meaning of it."

Inspired, he wrote her love letters full of nature metaphors, comparing her to stars, fire, mountains, valleys, "the microscopic inside of a leaf."

Jones invested all this imagery in "Metaphor"—his expression of Matt's preliminary infatuation with Luisa.

McClean had given Jones a book full of botanical artwork inscribed "If you would be happy for a night, take a wife. If you would be happy for a week, kill a pig. If you would be happy all your life, plant a garden." In a late-night cocktail session during the early weeks of *The Fantasticks* Off-Broadway, Jones confessed that he used the book as a prop for Matt, who has returned from agricultural college in the play, hoping that McClean would see it and realize how much she had meant to him.

"The whole naturalist thing she was into had a great effect on me," Jones said. "There were many more naturalist things in the piece when it was at Barnard. The Boy came out and recited a naturalist poem."

Luisa's introductory aria, "Much More," has common roots, oddly enough, with *Oklahoma!* Jones had been a fan of Lynn Riggs since his UT days directing *Roadside*. When Jones got to St. Bart's, he had staged Riggs's *Green Grow the Lilacs*, on which *Oklahoma!* is based.

"*Oklahoma!* is a wonderful piece," Jones said, "but *Green Grow* is even more so. It has other levels. It's a true reflection of American poetry and rhythms. Laurie [the heroine] isn't as interesting in the musical. In the play, she has wonderful speeches full of images and the things she dreams about. That's what I was trying to capture in 'Much More.' "

Happy with the way the songs were working out, Jones resolved to extend the Shakespeare/Goldoni connection and write the entire play in verse: "to mix open verse with heavy rhyming and even, upon occasion, doggerel," he said. "I tried to let people end scenes with couplets, as a sort of [Shakespearean] flourish."

Jones claims another profound influence in Thornton Wilder, particularly Wilder's *Our Town*, from which he borrowed the idea of a narrator who has the ability to step out of time and address the audience. Partly separate in *Joy Comes to Dead Horse*, the bandit and the narrator are fused in *The Fantasticks*. This also is a convenient influence, since *Our Town* also made a virtue of minimal scenery.

The various protean scene-movers of *Dead Horse* were concentrated into one, billed at Barnard as The Property Man, but who emerged Off-Broadway as The Mute. The idea was borrowed from Japanese theater. *The Fantasticks* uses many East Asian theater conventions, which has helped make it perennially popular in Japan itself and with Japanese tourists in New York, who remain a core audience for the show.

Jones said he also was powerfully influenced by a City Center production of Goldoni's *The Servant of Two Masters* by the Piccolo Teatro di Milano, an experimental Italian company, which staged the work as if done by a road-weary itinerant troupe. *The Fantasticks* follows the classic structure outlined to him back at UT. Matt and Luisa are the *innamorati*, El Gallo is Harlequin, the two fathers are Gerontius split in two. *Commedia* is invoked by name more than once in Jones's script. When goaded by the children, Hucklebee protests "I'm no pantaloon!" referring to the *commedia* fool.

Rostand's play called for "bravos" to appear in the abduction scene. Further developing these characters as a subplot, Jones added his memories of the elderly Toby show actor Harley Sadler, crossing him with that glorious old man of the theater, B. Iden Payne, to create the character in *The Fantasticks* most wholly Jones's creation, The Old Actor, later christened Henry Albertson, a name Jones said he "pulled out of the air."

Word Baker said, "The Old Actor is totally B. Iden Payne. It's based on him and on things he always said. If you really want to know about B. Iden Payne, read carefully the Old Actor."

His sidekick, the Cockney "Indian" Mortimer, was inspired by Ronald Colman's 1947 Oscar-winning performance in *A Double Life*. In it, Colman plays an actor whose offstage life blurs with his onstage characters. As he's dying, he recalls a British actor who specialized in death scenes and became so adept at them that audiences would shout "Die again!" The idea of Britishness and the name Mortimer, suggesting "death," merged in Jones's mind to supply Henry with the last remaining fellow member of their lost theatrical troupe.

The Fantasticks reflects Jones's excitement at being a working poet at last. For someone who had drifted for six long years, his own moon had broken through the clouds. All the devices he'd absorbed came tumbling out, and his lyrics sing. Yet, like Rostand, he constantly pokes fun at "pretty poets" just like himself.

"The intention in the writing," Jones said, "is to celebrate romanticism and to mock it at the same time, and that's the reason it's so difficult to play. It's a fine line to walk, to be touching at one moment, and then to make fun of the thing that was just touching. It's always turning on itself, and then back and forth again, and that's true of each of the characters and of the whole piece."

*   *   *

For Schmidt's part, it's remarkable how little of Anglo Texas remains in the music. There is no country or western moment to be found anywhere in the score, though it remains rich in Spanish flavors: a tango ("Never Say No") and a flamenco ("It Depends on What You Pay"), along with smaller moments culled from his Mexican ballet, *The Day of the Dead*.

"We wanted it to be sort of Latin in feeling but evoking a *commedia* underpinning at the same time," he said.

That was the feeling Schmidt was striving for when he wrote the overture. "Tom wanted to create the sense of this little troupe of Italian actors arriving, running a flag up a pole and getting ready to do a show. So I wrote my impression of Italianate period music determined entirely by the spirit of Piccolo Teatro di Milano's *The Servant of Two Masters*."

Music copyist Ben Pickering transcribed the songs as Schmidt composed them.

The version of *The Fantasticks* presented at Barnard closely follows the plot of *Les Romanesques*—essentially Act I of the full-length *Fantasticks*. After The Boy runs away, The Girl is tempted by El Gallo into running away to the mystic East.

Their song, "Have You Ever Been to China?," has El Gallo painting pictures of faraway places and The Girl answering in operatic obbligatos:

Have you ever been to China? (No, no, no!)
Did you ever want to be there? (Yes, yes, yes!)
Well, honey, if you want to go to China
You can come away with me there. (Oh, how wonderful!)*

It was not Jones's most inspired work. "It was another *Day of the Dead* song, but it was just a song El Gallo sings to the girl. We realized it needed more scope than that to really make some kind of statement." It was cut after Barnard, to be replaced by "Round and Round."

After El Gallo steals The Girl's necklace, she meets The Boy returning from his scarring collision with the world, and they sing "I Have Acted Like a Fool," which Schmidt described as "a charming song but it wasn't emotional. It was just a back-and-forth exchange between the Boy and Girl, but there wasn't any real emotion in it." It later was replaced by "They Were You." A reprise of "Try to Remember" ended the Barnard version.

The last apparent vestige of the Western was a "sagging wagon" called for in the opening scene, though by now it was a *commedia* wagon much more than a Conestoga. The rest of the stage was an open space where anything could happen.

Though he was not a specialist in theater techniques as Jones and Baker were, the plan suited Schmidt just fine. "I had always loved theater," he said, "but I loved movies more, especially Vincente Minnelli movies like *Ziegfeld Follies* where he had used no realistic scenery at all in some places, and it looked very elegant to me. My sensibilities being visual, there was an instant connection when they talked about the open

*From *The Fantasticks* © Tom Jones and Harvey Schmidt. Unpublished early draft. Used by Permission.

stage, because to me it meant Vincente Minnelli space with little or no scenery. In a way, we all loved the same things about theater at the same time. So when we were ready to do *The Fantasticks*, we were ready to do a kind of theater that we all understood and wanted to see on stage."

* * *

Though they weren't quite finished with the script in late June, they traipsed to Barnard and met Dunnock and Baker in a rehearsal room with an old piano. They handed her the unfinished manuscript and played most of the score, which then consisted of "Try to Remember," "Much More," "Metaphor," "Never Say No," "Soon It's Gonna Rain," "Have You Ever Been to China?" and "I Have Acted Like a Fool."

Dunnock recalls feeling well-disposed toward the project for practical reasons—its simplicity, the number of characters and the fact that her students would be able to grasp and learn it quickly. But she recalls being struck by the "lovely" script at the audition and quickly gave it her blessing.

Though *The Fantasticks* was presented at an all-women's college, Baker wound up using none of its students. Male members of the *original* original cast were chosen from the corps of advanced theater students at Barnard's affiliated male college, Columbia University. They were cast for the diversity of their backgrounds, their flexibility and willingness to experiment and their ability to recite the poetry with freshness, forthrightness and seriousness, without being cloying.

The original cast consisted of Jonathan Farwell as The Balladeer (later changed back to El Gallo), Susan Watson as The Girl (later Luisa), Crayton Rowe as The Boy (later Matt), Ron Leibman and Lee Croghan as The Fathers, George Morgan as The Property Man (later The Mute), Dick Burnham as The Actor, Bill Tost as The Man Who Dies and Harvey Schmidt as The Pianist.

Several of these names are significant. Ron Leibman already was an accomplished mime and dancer. Working strictly as an actor, he later appeared on Broadway in Neil Simon's *I Oughta Be in Pictures* and *Rumors*; acted in the films *Slaughterhouse-Five*, *Norma Rae* and *Where's Poppa?* among others; and won an Emmy Award for his performance on the TV series *Kaz*.

Jones remembers Leibman as being one of the more trouble-some members of that first *Fantasticks*—constantly voicing his dissatisfaction with the fact that it was a musical and saying "This is not my kind of theater."

Tost was hired to play The Girl's Father Off-Broadway in the late 1980s and was performing the role at the show's thirtieth anniversary in May 1990.

Farwell worked extensively in regional theater, including engagements in California and Chicago, and for most of the 1970s, he was a familiar face at the Cleveland Play House. He returned to Broadway several times in the 1980s, most notably understudying Yul Brynner and playing the Kralahome in Brynner's final Broadway revival of *The King and I* in 1985.

Because Schmidt's *Candide*-inspired obbligatos were too chal-lenging for any of the resident actresses, they cast an outside professional, delicate-featured eighteen-year-old soprano Sus-an Watson, who had danced and understudied Maria in a British production of *West Side Story*. She did her audition for Jones in St. Bart's auditorium.

She would make her Broadway debut eight months later as the ingenue in the original *Bye Bye Birdie*. Watson also became part of Jones and Schmidt's informal repertory company of players. She played ingenue leads in their *Celebration* (1969) and *The Bone Room* (1975) and returned to *The Fantasticks* as Luisa in the *Hallmark Hall of Fame* TV version in 1964. Her sister, Janet, became Jones's second wife.

Working with Watson and with the students was natural and easy for Baker, who continued to teach acting and stagecraft throughout the 1950s at a number of studios, including Herbert Berghof's.

In addition to his Barnard responsibilities, Baker was still teaching at HB Studio the summer he did *The Fantasticks* at Barnard—and a lucky thing, too, as it turned out. He was so delighted with the material Jones and Schmidt were polishing that he brought The Boy's Act I dialogue with his father to the studio and had two of his students perform it as a class exer-cise.

Playing The Boy was a promising teenager named Gerome Ragni. A devoted student of the counter-culture, he'd later find his place in the pantheon of the Flower Power generation by writing *Hair* with James Rado and Galt MacDermot. Little surprise then that he put so much feeling into Jones's speech for The Boy who was rejecting the marriage his father has arranged for him:

> I will not go to wedding in a too-tight suit
> Nor be witnessed when I take my bride.
> No!
>
> I'll marry, when I marry
> In my own particular way;
> And my bride shall dress in sunlight,
> With rain for her wedding veil . . .
>
> . . . Without benefit of book!
> Except perhaps her handprint
> As she presses her hand in mine;
> Except perhaps her imprint
> As she gives me her golden hair;
> In a field while kneeling,
> Being joined by the joy of life! . . .*

There was something in the way Ragni stormed through Matt's rebellious speech that pierced one classmate to the soul. Here, at last, was the sort of material he'd been stalking secretly for years.

Auditing Baker's class that day was Lorenzo Noto, professionally Lore (pronounced "Lorrie") Noto, then thirty-six. He later told the *New York Post* that he instantly fell in love with "the lyricism and poetry in its writing."

It was a poetry he'd been denied in life. Noto was born in the Williamsburg section of Brooklyn in 1923, the same era and neighborhood as another theater notable, Joseph Papp. Noto's mother died when he was three. His Sicilian father, the owner of a poolroom, placed him and his older brother in the Brooklyn Home for Children where he was raised as an orphan, but where he also won a cherished gold medal as the brightest student.

*© Tom Jones. Used by Permission.

It might be reading too much into the situation to imagine that The Boy's speech of defiance to his dad had any but artistic appeal for Noto, but his relationship with his father was permanently marked by the next thirteen years he spent in the Home before being discharged at age sixteen and sent back to Brooklyn.

While attending the High School of Industrial Arts, he also worked at his father's pool hall, where he developed no small skill with the cue. It earned him enough money to pay for his primary vice—going to the movies, where Dick Tracy serials were his favorite. Already a good singer in church, Noto had a voice strong enough to land him a $2 per month job singing in an Episcopal church choir.

It fit in with his secret aspiration to become an actor. His father told him to forget that—he wanted Lore to become a lawyer. When Lore got a $5-a-month job as an actor in plays at the local library, he was beaten by his father who became enraged.

Threats of further beatings drove Noto out of the house and into the Merchant Marine in the early days of World War II, where his love of movies nearly cost him his life. While in an Antwerp cinema watching Gary Cooper in *The Plainsman*, Noto suffered a broken back when the theater was hit by a Nazi V2 rocket. He was buried in rubble for eight hours before being rescued.

The experience gave him a sense of mission in life: that he'd been spared for a purpose. After the war, he joined the Carroll Club, a proto-Off-Broadway theater on Madison Avenue, and quickly rose to become its star actor. He married company member Mary Luzzi, rented a three-room apartment on 211th Street in upper Manhattan and had four children with her: Thad, Anthony, Janice and Jody. He enjoyed the status of bohemian character while trying to make up for his father's mistakes by being a good father himself.

Believing that theater people had an obligation to invest in their business, Noto also decided to try his hand at producing. His first show, *The Failures*, was aptly named. It closed in a single performance in 1958, losing its entire investment.

Burned by that experience, Noto got a job as an artists' agent, eventually becoming a partner in Brownstone Inc., which did artwork for ad agencies and which counted Robert Sokol among its clients. Handling sales for the company, Noto did well enough to raise his family and continue acting lessons. The job also enabled him to put a little something aside each week. The money could have gone for anything, but Noto maintained his ambition to be a producer. He had a vision of theater that would be unusual in form but life-affirming in content. He had a sweet tooth for theater, but the experiences of his life had taught him to keep his feet on the ground as well.

He worked hard at his job, but he kept his antenna raised for talent and for just the right project that not only would compound his small savings—a total of $3,300 in August of 1959—but would give the world a special kind of theater as well.

He was scouting for an acting teacher when he audited Word Baker's class at HB Studio that summer. Noto later told *Dramatics* magazine that Baker "put two kids, a boy and a girl, on a bare stage and had them do a cold reading of some material he'd brought to class. The girl started out 'I'm sixteen years old, and every day something happens to me.' She went on with what today is one of the opening monologues of *The Fantasticks*. I was hooked, I was smitten, I fell in love. The language had flavor; it was charming. There was magic in it. There was a lot of depressing theater around in those days, kitchen sink drama, we called it, plays about little people with depressing problems. I was sick of it, I wanted something different."

Tingling with what he'd seen, he asked Baker for more details. Baker explained that he could see the rest of the musical at Barnard and judge for himself.

Baker warned Noto that Jones, Schmidt and himself had invited a number of potential producers—which today is standard practice at Manhattan theater tryout showcases. With the exception of Lucille Lortel, who had brought in the long-running revival of *The Threepenny Opera*, none of the invitees were major producers; just people Baker had met through his experience with *The Crucible*, and whom Schmidt and Jones had met through NBC and the Julius Monk revues.

In that context, Noto promised he'd be there.

* * *

Baker says, "It was quite a different show at Barnard. It was the cutesiest thing you ever saw—using a ladder and all the things we had been talking about doing in theater for ever. It was, quote unquote, darling. It's still pretty darling, but there it almost made you puke. Lots of things were changed. It was our trial run. We made all our mistakes at Barnard."

One Barnard touch that survived was Baker's use of confetti and colored paper squares to mark festive moments. Baker had seen a production of a now-forgotten play at UT in which one of the characters tore up her bills and flung the bits in the air. "I thought it was the most beautiful thing I have ever seen in my life," Baker said. At Barnard, however, this effect was almost too much of a good thing. Most of the speeches were punctuated with flying paper squares, and they were considerably larger at Barnard than they became Off-Broadway.

"At one point," Baker said, "the performers were throwing little flowers with weights on them, so they would stand up when they landed in both gardens. The flowers were silly and besides, those little colored squares were all over the floor."

Charles Lane, one of Jones's roommates at the University of Texas, was called in to design the clothes. (Lane changed his name to Charles Blackburn when he joined Actors Equity.) Following the mood of the script, Lane did very simple reductions of *commedia dell'arte* costumes. Though Lane later was replaced Off-Broadway, "he really helped establish very much the style of the costumes," Schmidt said. "The Girl's costume was absolutely beautiful. It was all white and Charlie worked in all these pieces of antique lace. It was just like a scrapheap of light."

Nevertheless, some of his costumes appeared almost clownish. The Mute, for instance, was in mime greasepaint. Ed Wittstein's costumes for the Greenwich Village production make the *commedia* point much more subtly.

The Barnard sets were even simpler than the ones that would be built for Off-Broadway. Even the lone wagon called for in Jones's script was too complicated and expensive for Barnard, so this last scenic vestige of *Joy Comes to Dead Horse* was eliminated that week. "Designed" by Geoffry Brown, the set consisted of a small wooden platform with little more for props than a sheet, a ladder, a bench and a cardboard disc—yellow on one side for the sun and white on the other side for the moon.

Brown later would become stage manager for the Off-Broadway *Fantasticks*.

Move mogul David O. Selznick's son Danny did the lighting. Choreography was by Lathan Sanford.

The Fantasticks would open the evening's triple-bill, followed by Inge's *The Mall* and Dunphy's *The Gay Apprentice*. Farwell, Morgan and Croghan appeared in *The Mall*; Leibman and Croghan appeared in *Apprentice*. Baker was supposed to direct all three, but most of his effort went into the musical, and to a lesser extent, the Inge play. A lot of the work on Dunphy's farce was left to stage manager Jerry Douglas (credited as "Associate Director" on that piece), but *The Gay Apprentice* would be cut after the first performance.

The Sunday before the show opened, *The New York Times* included Baker's triple-bill in "Along the Straw-Hat Trail," its roundup of summer theater offerings that week. The title was misspelled "The Fantastics" in the listing but was spelled correctly in a one-column-by-three-inch ad in the same issue. It advertised performances at 8:00 Tuesday through Thursday nights; 7:00 and 10:00 Friday and Saturday. Tickets cost $1.80.

The papers that week offer a wonderful snapshot of life in 1959. That same Sunday, Vice President Richard Nixon gave a speech on Soviet television, telling the Russian people that they would "continue to live in an era of fear, suspicion and tension" if Premier Nikita Khruschev tried to promote Communism in countries outside the USSR.

On the same day, however, there were ominous signs that this warning may have been too late. There was a story expressing U.S. "concern" about jungle fighting in the tiny Southeast Asian kingdom of Laos. Similarly there was a report about "Reds" in East Germany using teachers to inform on students. It was published right next to a story about President Dwight Eisenhower being satisfied with his golf game.

Blacks were "negroes," the ads were full of young women in pegged slacks and pleated skirts, Prof. Irwin Corey and the Kenny Burrell Trio were playing the Village Vanguard and *The Billy Barnes Revue* was transferring from Off-Broadway to Broadway's Golden Theatre under the headline "Beatniks on the Move."

While these things were percolating in the outside world,

Baker, Jones, Schmidt and their student cast were working so feverishly on run-throughs that Watson strained her vocal cords and slipped off the one ladder Charles Lane used for scenery during the wall scene, bruising her ribs. She could rasp and hobble, but she certainly couldn't sing or dance. To work through the blocking at dress rehearsal, it was decided that choreographer Lathan Sanford would do her dances and Schmidt would sing her numbers, so she could heal up in time for opening night.

The frenetic efforts of rehearsing three plays in one week made the Minor Latham Playhouse seem hot even though it was an air-conditioned oasis in the sweaty city. By the day before opening, August 3, 1959, there was chaos in the little theater.

And late on that hot afternoon, Lore Noto went to the closet at his apartment on 211th Street and began to dress for his visit to *The Fantasticks*. He had made his mistakes on *The Failures* and knew precisely what he was looking for. If the rest of the little musical turned out to be as sound as The Boy's speech, he'd give it his total commitment.

Though he knew the authors were nervous about his visit, he was nervous, too. He wasn't sure whether he hoped it would be a dud that he could pass by, or be the magical lozenge that would complicate his life and jeopardize his finances.

The heat required something light, and the occasion called for something theatrical. He pulled on the white pants, laced the white shoes and shrugged into the white jacket. To top it off, he chose the straw hat.

After he tapped it into place, the Mysterious Man in White was ready to go.

7

August–December 1959

"Moonlight is expensive, but it's in demand."

AMONG the many other people dressing for that night's performance were Don and Ann Farber. The Farbers had a little farther to go, living in the Long Island suburb of Merrick, more than an hour's drive to Manhattan's upper west side.

An independent lawyer with a tiny office on 42nd Street, Farber had served as Noto's attorney since 1957. When Noto was selling his interest in the Brownstone Inc. art agency, Farber had represented the buyer. Noto was sufficiently impressed with what he saw to call a few months later and ask Farber to represent him in his debut as a theatrical producer: *The Failures* at the Fourth Street Theatre in Greenwich Village.

Though Farber knew little about the specialized field of theatrical law, he was intrigued with Noto. He and Ann were long-time theatergoers, having gotten as a wedding present in 1947 tickets to ten of Broadway's biggest hits, including *A Streetcar Named Desire and Death of a Salesman*.

Farber also needed the money, so he hit the law library and tried to pick up as much as he could. Coproduced by David Ross and starring Albert Salmi, *The Failures* perhaps inevitably lived up to its title and closed after a single performance. Noto was checked but not discouraged. Less than a year later, he again called Farber and asked him to report to the Minor Latham Playhouse at Barnard College.

"He said he wanted me to come hear something he thought could be very special," Farber said.

Though accompanied by Ann, a Barnard alumna, Farber had trouble finding the theater, which had been built after she graduated.

"We saw this tall lanky guy in blue jeans and asked him where the theater was. He suggested we might be better off going to the movie down the street," Farber said. "It was Tom Jones."

Jones had heard from Baker that Noto was on his way and became livid. The last thing he wanted was his last shot in New York, his six-year brainchild, to be seen by a potential producer, with material still being written, a student cast and an incapacitated leading lady.

Upon Noto's arrival, he and Jones engaged in a lobby debate, consisting primarily of Jones insisting that the play was not ready for the pressure of an audience, and Noto clucking indulgently that he knew all about rehearsals and would make allowances.

"I was very impressed," said Schmidt, who hung back and let Jones try to repel this invader. "Lore's always played tennis, so he was very tan. And I was struck by his white linen single-breasted suit and white straw hat, like out of 1910. You only see that up here in the East, where people in the summer are tan and wear a lot of white. Down South they try to avoid the sun because it's so hot all the time. Lore had been an actor, which we didn't know at that time, so he was very articulate. Also very impressive was the fact that he had Don Farber with him. We knew no one who had a lawyer at that time. We immediately thought he was a fabulous New York millionaire because he looked so dapper."

Though Jones allows that Noto "looked every inch the impresario," he was adamant.

And though Jones was his potential author, Noto was even more adamant.

"I was to learn later that Lore's determination was not easily to be deflected," Jones later would write in an introduction to the play. "His obstinacy, which then, and later, infuriated me, has been a major factor in the survival of *The Fantasticks*."

Baker's arrival settled the matter. Noto was his guest and would have to be endured.

The Minor Latham Playhouse is on the north end of the Barnard campus, taking up part of the east wing of Milbank Hall, a four-story brick building. To get to it, Farber, Noto and the others passed through a courtyard full of plantings, then turned right up a short stone stair decorated with sinuous wrought iron railings. Inside was a tiny theater of one hundred and fifty to two hundred seats (since renovated) and a raked wooden thrust-type stage that projected several rows into the audience. As the audience came in, all they saw was a ladder and a bench, which served as the wall and everything else, respectively.

There were no good omens of the sort that constitutionally superstitious theater folk look for. In fact, considering the problems with the leading lady and the sudden arrival of Noto, the omens were all bad. His colleagues were in a panic, but Schmidt stayed calm. He was happy to be making his debut as a professional pianist in New York. The concentration needed to play the entire score from memory, plus recite the leading lady's entire part, kept him focused throughout the performance. "If I were sitting out front like they were, I might have been more panicked," he said.

The performance that evening was a thing of rags and patches. It opened with Jonathan Farwell pretending to strum a guitar and singing "Try to Remember." The Handyman juggled three oranges and tossed one to Watson, who caught it and then began to speak her monologue that builds to: "I'm sixteen years old,/ And every day something happens to me." But as her mouth moved, something odd happened. A baritone Texas twang was heard, coming, Oz-like, from that man who was sitting at the piano with his back to the audience.

Even more oddly, after that baritone began to sing that paean to adolescent girlish dreams, "Much More," another man appeared, muscular and clad in jeans, and began to caper around the stage, performing the choreography.

Thus Schmidt and choreographer Charles Lane performed

much of the part of The Girl as she trysted with The Boy next door. Noto and the Farbers sat in an audience consisting mostly of students and invited friends of the cast as the youthful cast introduced to the public "Metaphor," "Never Say No," "Soon It's Gonna Rain," "Try to Remember," "This Plum Is Too Ripe" and "Have You Ever Been to China?" Then they reprised verses of "Metaphor" and "Try to Remember."

Without "Rape," "I Can See It" or "Round and Round," there wasn't very much for El Gallo to do after the introduction. He participated in the sham abduction—the "Rape Ballet," which was all that remained of Jones's steamy Apache dance in *Joy Comes to Dead Horse*—and flirted with Luisa before stealing her necklace. But after "Have You Ever Been to China?" and her disappointment, Matt returned almost immediately for their reprise and the final curtain.

Though truncated, the one-act *Fantasticks* had all the essential elements of its full-length version. From the moment Matt and Luisa leaped up the ladder to hold hands and gaze into each other's eyes, the audience was ready to be enlisted as collaborators. Its collective imagination could be tapped again and again to supply walls, gardens, cavalry, clear-blue streams, ocean liners and a dragon. The audience was not only ready to believe a plywood moon was actually a cardboard moon, but that a cardboard moon could also have been a lover's moon, washing the stage with moonlight.

"We were absolutely enchanted," Farber said. "First there was the lovely music. But also, the simplicity of it. It was just a very lovely romantic little story."

"Lore instantly flipped over the show." Schmidt said. "I always tell people that he saw it as this very avant-garde thing, with disembodied voices and no scenery. But I say that in fun. He obviously saw through it and saw what was there."

Though the pre-curtain omens had been bad, many members of the audience crowded up to talk to the creators afterward, "always a good sign," Schmidt said.

Noto and Farber elbowed their way backstage and immediately wanted to talk about producing it. Because of its size and innovative staging, Noto proposed doing it Off-Broadway.

Noto immediately endeared himself to Schmidt by complimenting him on some of his commercial artwork, particularly a sketch of Senator Eugene McCarthy widely distributed and admired at the time.

They parted company agreeing to meet again after the end of the week's run.

Though Barnard is more than one hundred blocks north of Greenwich Village, the *Village Voice* sent a critic. Michael Smith, then, has the distinction of filing the first review of *The Fantasticks*. His one-paragraph piece captures the ambivalence that was to characterize most of the show's critical reception: "*The Fantasticks* is a musical parable which engagingly suggests that 'without a hurt the heart is hollow.' Harvey Schmidt's music is imaginative and prettily appropriate, but Tom Jones's words are conceived at such a high level of brilliance that the fantastick sometimes overreaches into the absurd."

During the brief run, three other producers came to look at the show. One was Lucille Lortel, one of the major figures of the Off-Broadway movement into the 1990s, and then best-known for her revival of Kurt Weill's *The Threepenny Opera* and for her championing of young playwrights. She had heard about *The Fantasticks* as Noto had, through Word Baker, but was unimpressed by the whimsy of what she saw.

Two other potential producers besides Noto *were*, however. Both were acquaintances of Schmidt's through NBC: Joseph Wishy, as assistant to the producer of *NBC Opera*, and another producer whose name has been lost.

"We didn't know how to choose between the three," Schmidt said.

Jones said the NBC producer wanted them to expand the show to a full evening, but was unwilling to offer any money in advance. That violated a pledge Jones and Schmidt had made between themselves not to surrender rights to the show for just a handshake and a promise.

Wishy liked the show just as it was and proposed presenting it on a double-bill with a selection of Jones-Schmidt revue material, fulfilling at last their dream of presenting *Portfolio*.

"We liked that idea because we had worked on this thing for years and it didn't work. Then, having thrown out this big elaborate two-act thing, we finally had it working as a one-act," Schmidt said. "Everybody seemed to like it and wanted to put it on. We were so exhilarated, we didn't want to tamper with it anymore. We loved the idea of using the Julius Monk material as the second act, because we knew that worked, too."

But Noto was adamant in his belief that the correct path was for Jones and Schmidt to expand the show back to two acts but keep its modest setting. "And thank God he did," Schmidt said, "because it would have disappeared as a one-act piece, I'm sure. One-act things don't have much of a life. Very few run for long."

Jones and Schmidt lay credit for the show's long-term survival squarely at Noto's feet. Schmidt said Noto's insistence on this point was the first of many times Noto exercised wisdom—and a peculiar kind of intuition—that enabled him to steer the fragile little show away from one reef after another.

"He believed in it with a religious fervor," Jones said.

The following spring when *The Fantasticks* opened and one of the more powerful critics said the show should have stayed a one-act, Wishy felt vindicated. "Thirty years later," he said, "it shows how stupid you can be when you're right."

In the next few weeks, Noto courted the pair, calling them and banging on their door in an effort to convince them that his way was the best way. At length, he figured out the magic words. He got Baker, Jones and Schmidt together and told them he didn't want to do the show unless the three of them made all future artistic decisions. He promised to step in only if they reached a stalemate. "Well," said Jones, "that's so unheard-of for a producer to say that. That's what really made us decide to go with him."

Why would someone as stubborn and cautious as Noto hand over that kind of power to his employees? Farber's theory is that "Lore recognized these guys had talent and, if he left them alone, they'd come up with something really good. He also knew that there were others who were interested, and the sure way to get the show was to offer to leave them alone."

Noto also came up with some cash. In a contract dated October 24, 1959, the three sold the rights to *The Fantasticks* to Lore Noto for the sum of $500; half in advance and half on delivery of the full-length version of the script. Jones and Schmidt agreed to accept three to six percent of the gross receipts, depending on whether the show was breaking even or not.

Noto reserved "full and final authority" but carefully wrote into the contract the agreement that made it all happen: "It is the desire of the parties that to the extent possible artistic decisions are to be left to the discretion of the Authors and Director."

It now was Schmidt's unhappy responsibility to break the news to his former coworker, Wishy. He called him to the 74th Street apartment. Jones was there as well.

There ensued the memorable scene in which a thunderstorm knocked out the lights, and Wishy, sitting in a window seat, wept in the dark with lightning flashing behind him as Schmidt broke the news. "There was something so insane about the scene," Schmidt said. "But all through it, I knew we had made the right decision."

* * *

Noto's contract for *The Fantasticks* ran for six months, with an opening targeted for late January or early February 1960, but with an option to extend for another six months for an additional consideration.

Noto wound up needing that option. Raising the money turned out to be more difficult than it seemed.

Assuming that Noto was a millionaire, Jones and Schmidt at first thought that he'd simply open his checkbook and underwrite the entire production. They hadn't reckoned with their new partner. Noto explained that he wanted to spread the risk around a little more and asked them to do a series of auditions, playing the score for potential investors, or "angels." If the investors liked what they heard, they'd write a check. If not, they'd be on their way.

In point of fact, however, Noto had decided to gamble everything on *The Fantasticks*. He told *The New York Times* in 1968 that he gave up his $17,000-a-year art consulting job to focus completely on producing the show. At first, Noto capitalized the show at $16,500, with the intention of forming a limited partnership of investors who could buy one percent of the profits for $330.

In time-honored theatrical fashion, then, Jones and Schmidt began playing what are known as backer auditions. Invited to these auditions were any people that any of them knew who might have some money to invest. In a prospectus, Farber and Noto described the "exciting musical comedy" as "a parable about love . . . about the funny pain of growing up. It is played by a small troupe of actors upon a simple platform stage. The style is light, effervescent, using song and dance and mime and imagery in words to create a hilarious and yet very human little world."

At first, the chance to invest was presented as a tantalizing opportunity for a lucky few. Many of the auditions were held at private get-togethers in the 74th Street apartment at which Jones would narrate the story and Schmidt would play the score and sing.

In a time when Off-Broadway was considered low-rent and marginal, the pools of Broadway capital were closed to them. Off-Broadway backers tended to be friends, fellow theater artists, visionaries or various combinations thereof. They indulged in small-time and uneasy capitalism with a broad streak of bohemian idealism. Lore Noto was typical of the breed; he needed to find others.

At first the auditions were fun, especially for Schmidt, not only because the project seemed to be flowering at last, but because he got to see a lot of his old friends and play the piano for them. Because so much of the music had been written so quickly, Schmidt got a chance to revel in it. He used the auditions to amplify and embellish his new creations.

Among those invited to those early auditions were Mildred Dunnock, from the Barnard series, and Tom Poston, from Jones and Schmidt's *Portfolio* days. But after several weeks, Schmidt and Jones found something disquieting happening. No one was investing. Dunnock turned them down; so did Poston; so did almost all their theater friends.

"People couldn't visualize the show," Schmidt said. "We could talk about long soliloquies and the moonlight and things, but it was hard for people to understand how it would play. For weeks we did the songs in our apartment with no success. We weren't getting anywhere."

As their connections with the potential backers grew more tenuous, there were some humiliating scenes. "One night, this couple dropped off this old lady and said, 'Well, Mama, we're going to the movies. We'll pick you up when we get through.

Enjoy the show.' She was the only person who showed up that night, and she dozed off after five minutes."

As they remember it, they were so eager to make a sale that they kept going, performing the whole score in hopes of impressing her, even in a fleeting moment of wakefulness. At length, they realized they were serving as free babysitters and weren't surprised when the couple declined to invest.

Even with all the problems raising money, Noto resisted the urge to simply write out a check for the $3,300 he had stashed in his bank account. At some point he might have to—but not yet.

The first break came when Don and Ann Farber invited Jones and Schmidt out to their house on Long Island to do a backer audition for their friends and relatives.

Rubin Blum recalls that his young son was invited by the Farber's son to come over and watch the show, and when Blum heard about it, he asked if he could come, too. Farber explained that it wasn't just for fun, that it was an audition to raise money. Blum came, was enchanted and bought a percent. Several of the other Merrick neighbors put up money as well, mostly as a favor to the Farbers. Several of the couples pooled cash to buy a percent, so they owned a half or even a quarter of a percent.

Such price-cutting seemed popular, so Noto agreed to sell shares as tiny as one-sixth of a percent, which cost $55. Farber went around to people he knew in buildings near his 42nd Street office and sold several of these quarter and one-sixth shares.

Farber recalls, "I took fifty-five bucks from one secretary who was working in the neighborhood. She brought her money up during her lunch hour and said, 'Look, this is all the money I've got. I just got paid, I want to give it to you before I spend it.' "

The money trickled in. Noto's mother-in-law bought a piece. Tom Jones walked through the kitchen of the Upstairs at the Downstairs and sold shares to waiters and kitchen staff. George Curley, the lighting man and sometime actor in children's theater, bought one percent. Alice Laprelle, a woman Jones had dated at UT, invested a Christmas gift check. Schmidt spoke to several of his friends from NBC and his former cubicle neighbor, designer Ed Wittstein, bought shares as well. Eventually it took twenty-seven auditions to get the fifty-seven backers, one by one, needed to raise the mere $16,500. Of the fifty-seven, forty-nine bought one percent or less. As it turned out, they were still selling bits of the show when it was in previews the following April.

These scraps, most of them gathered by the Farbers, eventually provided what Schmidt calls a "key block of the financing." And the trust and goodwill of these tiny investors did not go unrewarded. As of 1990, the show had repaid more than $45,000 for every $330 invested—more than a 13,500 percent return.

Not everyone was so lucky. Ann Farber's recently-divorced aunt was one of the investors from that first Merrick audition. She gave the Farbers a check but then asked them to tear it up when her brother, Ann's father, objected. He had lost $100 on Noto's *The Failures* and was determined that no other members of his family would blow their savings on a theatrical crapshoot.

* * *

Like Henry and Mortimer in *The Fantasticks*, Jones and Schmidt became a two-man traveling show, willing to go almost anywhere anytime to audition their show for potential backers. Though most of the auditions were done in the 74th Street apartment and at the Farbers' home in Merrick, the author and composer played *The Fantasticks* in several New York offices and halls as well.

When they needed an audition room in the Greenwich Village area, their roommate Robert Alan Gold offered to let them use a theater he was co-leasing just a few steps from the intersection with the Village's unofficial main thoroughfare, Bleecker Street. Jones and Schmidt's traveling show came to rest there for longer than any of them could have realized.

Gold operated the Sullivan Street Playhouse with a business associate, Jules Field. The son of a Second Avenue Yiddish theater singer and the brother of a three-sister vaudeville act billed as the Artificial Triplets, Field had made one fortune designing, manufacturing and selling corrugated shipping containers. Field made another fortune as cofounder of the Gaslight Club, a network of private clubs. He tried his hand at producing but had only modest success. A savvy businessman, Field noticed "the only ones making money were the theater owners. They had no responsibilities, they just collected rent."

In 1958, Field took a twenty-year lease on a four-story building at 181 Sullivan Street, which housed a small theater. Built in the late nineteenth century, it had a colorful history. At the turn of the twentieth century, it housed a blacksmith on the ground floor. Horse-drawn carriages would pull up in front, and the smith would lead the horses into what is now the basement to be shod. Two five-room apartments on the third and fourth floors are still in existence.

With the advent of automobiles and Prohibition, it was cleaned and renovated as one of New York's more colorful speakeasies. Under the name Jimmy Kelly's, it became a nightclub with tables and live music in what is now the theater space and somewhat shadier entertainment and libations up a flight of stairs in what is now the *Fantasticks* Museum. Mayor "Gentleman" Jimmy Walker was one of its patrons, along with the city's gangsters and their entourages. Even in the late 1980s, alleged underworld figure Vin "The Chin" Gigante still made his home on Sullivan Street, less than a block from the Playhouse.

It was this racy atmosphere that Field would try to capture in his Gaslight Clubs.

After repeal of the Eighteenth Amendment in 1933, Jimmy Kelly's became a simple nightclub. Minetta Tavern on Minetta Lane, a Greenwich Village landmark and later hangout for some of the *Fantasticks* crew, has a dining room decorated with a panaroma of Greenwich Village in the 1940s. The old Jimmy Kelly's can be seen in this mural, its distinctive T-shaped sign reading "Jimmy" across the top and "Kelly's" descending. The club's refrigerator vault still stands in the theater's basement, converted to a costume closet.

The club, whose entrance was a few steps below street level, was purchased and renovated as a theater by real estate man Phillip Edwards in the 1950s. It was operated briefly and unsuccessfully by a previous management who presented, among other attractions, the melodrama *Sweeney Todd*. The story of a murderous barber was adapted in 1979 by Stephen Sondheim and Hugh Wheeler as a Tony-winning musical.

After Field assumed the lease, he continued to act as producer from time to time, bringing in a variety of short-lived productions, including a children's theater run by Robert Walker, Jr., and some Ibsen plays including *John Gabriel Borkman* and *Hedda Gabler*, the latter starring Bela Jarrett. He toyed with the idea of starting a repertory troupe there, but his two other businesses left him little time for running a theater company.

Jones and Schmidt's roommate, Robert Alan Gold, had worked as Field's business manager for his theatrical productions but had stepped up to co-lessor of the Playhouse when Field became too busy with his other projects. Thanks to that connection, Jones and Schmidt got the Sullivan Street Playhouse for their backer audition. It presented an unusual sight.

Unlike other long, narrow Off-Broadway theaters such as the Cherry Lane and the Orpheum (both substantially larger as well), the Sullivan Street Playhouse has a stage that is not at one end with seats arranged in roughly parallel rows facing it. Instead, the Sullivan Street stage is set against a side wall, with the rows of seats curving around it on three sides. This thrust-stage arrangement recalls Greek amphitheater design, though on a much smaller scale.

The theater's dimensions have always been part of its appeal. At the Sullivan Street Playhouse, if you sit in the eighth row, you're also sitting in the back row. There were one hundred and forty-nine seats, since expanded to one hundred and fifty-three. These seats are arranged in three sections divided by aisles. There are no more than eight rows on the side sections, and no more than seven in the center. The theater is so narrow that Field could squeeze only three rows in the dead center of the center section.

Because there is no separate access to the dressing rooms, actors must make their entrances and exits down a passage next to the seats. Similarly, audience members must cross the stage to get to the seats on the right side of the house.

"It seemed to fit the play perfectly," said Field, who sat in on the backer audition and wound up becoming an investor himself. "I saw it and I loved it," he said. "It was heartwarming, just adorable. My wife (Mickie) didn't care for it, but it grew on her."

At the time of the backer audition, Jones and Schmidt had no inkling that their musical would open at that theater. They had their hearts set on the Theatre De Lys, Lucille Lortel's two hundred and ninety-nine seat gem at 121 Christopher Street. But Lortel's *The Threepenny Opera* revival was still going strong there.

As it happened, most of the other viable Off-Broadway theaters were occupied that winter as well. The Off-Broadway movement was growing faster than the number of theaters to accommodate its productions. By the winter of 1960, a booking jam had developed.

Field had an option on a thriller set in Africa. He hoped to open it at Sullivan Street but was persuaded by Gold and by his own instinct to offer the theater to *The Fantasticks*. After considering the alternatives, Noto agreed.

"We all hated it initially," said Schmidt, who had remembered the space as smelly, run-down, oddly shaped and gloomy. "I told them I'd rather not do the show than do it in this dump."

The theater's previous tenant had been *The Goose*, a personal project of 1950s health faddist J. J. Rodale. He achieved a bizarre notoriety by dying on *The Dick Cavett Show* moments after discoursing on how avoiding sugar had kept him healthy all his life. *The Goose* was a diatribe against sugar and used a refrigerator full of fresh food as part of the action. When the play closed after a short run, the refrigerator got left behind to smell up the little theater.

Baker was complaining about it to his wife one night when she snapped at him and woke him up. "My wife was indulgent to a point of all of us," he said, "but only to a point. She had heard so much about it that she'd tell me, 'Shut up about that damn show.' When I complained to her about the Sullivan Street Playhouse, she said 'You can do this goddamned show anywhere, that's what you've been saying for years. So take it.' "

Perhaps a larger or fancier theater would have been accessible if Noto had been willing to wait or wanted to spend more money. But it wasn't time to dip into that extra $3,300. Not yet.

Quieting Jones and Schmidt's objections, Noto booked the

Sullivan Street Playhouse at a rental of $350 a week for just six weeks, from May to June 1960, with options to renew for the run of the play. The option proved to be costly for Field. It was exercised again and again until 1978, when the going rate was more than ten times that amount, and Noto agreed to renegotiate.

Looking back, Schmidt said his dissatisfaction with the theater is ironic because "this theater helped us in so many ways. It helped freeze the minimalist style of the show which was already there, but which became even more minimal because of the inherent physical limitations there. The fact that latecomers walk across the stage, all that became part of the style of *The Fantasticks*. In a way, it contributed to the audience enjoyment, as did the fact that it's in a basement down in the Village. In the early days, people loved that. They had a sense of discovery about coming down the steps into this little space. Critics loved to describe in reviews how they walked into this dank basement and found a show."

* * *

But all that was in the future. Though they still didn't have all the money, they were confident enough to break the news of their plans to *The New York Times*. The show was trumpeted, if that's the word, in Sam Zolotow's column of December 10, 1959. Calling it "a graduate of Mildred Dunnock's summer theater at Barnard," he said, "Lore Noto will put it on at an Off-Broadway house in mid-February."

They also were confident enough to start looking for actors. There was no thought of bringing the Barnard cast to Off-Broadway, Schmidt said. "They were students. We decided we would try to get the best [professional] people we could."

They considered keeping Susan Watson as The Girl, but Watson had a chance to play Kim in *Bye Bye Birdie*, the new Charles Strouse and Lee Adams spoof of Elvis Presley mania, opening on Broadway that spring. Weighing the two projects, she chose *Birdie*.

"Over the years, a lot of actors have gotten ahead by appearing in *The Fantasticks*," Don Farber said. "Susie was the only person who got ahead by *not* appearing in *The Fantasticks*."

It was time for auditions.

8

December 1959– April 1960

"Time is rushing. And a major production to do. I need actors—extra actors—to stage my elaborate Rape."

For the Christmas holiday, Harvey Schmidt returned to his family in Texas, where he spent the last week of the 1950s.

The previous ten years had taken him from anonymous Texas art student to nationally famous illustrator. The new decade promised a new career and possibly even greater acclaim. But Schmidt doesn't remember facing New Year's with grand dreams of the future.

The calendar was carrying him farther and farther from his beloved 1930s and 1940s, with their glamour, luscious melodies and grand movie musicals, and into a decade where the music and cinema were a mystery. Judging from what he was hearing on the radio and seeing at the movies, things didn't seem too promising. The only way he could answer was with his piano, and as soon as he returned to New York, he resolved to do so.

The creative team reconvened in January and resumed back-

114

er auditions at the Sullivan Street Playhouse. The small investments gathered so far were fine, but at the rate they were going, it would take years to finance *The Fantasticks.*

To help potential backers visualize the show better, Baker staged scenes with volunteer actors, including their Barnard designer, Charles Blackburn, as one of the fathers. Singing El Gallo was actor Seth Riggs, later a successful Hollywood vocal coach. Schmidt played piano in the center of the stage, and Jones read—with increasing bravura—the two Old Actors and any spare roles for which they had no auxiliary personnel.

Cynthia Cohen helped with the backer auditions by singing the role of The Girl and was so impressed by what she was performing that she bought a share of the show herself.

Nevertheless, money came in very slowly.

Noto used some of his capital to place modest ads for actors in trade papers, but ultimately, most of the original cast members of *The Fantasticks* were chosen from among people Jones and Schmidt knew, had worked with, or who were steered their way by friends.

Still, when casting began, Baker imposed a utopian vision of auditioning every actor who came after a part. Auditions were held at the 74th Street apartment. The creators quickly found that even the weak signal they had put out had been heard. Actors formed a line almost every day during late January and February on the two flights of stairs to Schmidt's door.

Actors would wait in the apartment's foyer and, when called, would step through the tall sliding door into the living room. Facing them on a couch five feet away were a phalanx of Jones, Schmidt and Noto, sometimes augmented by Schmidt's two roommates, Robert Alan Gold and Robert Benton. Jones said the arrangement was uncomfortable for all involved, but eventually, it worked to the show's benefit, since it mirrored the intimate setting on Sullivan Street. They needed actors who could work nose-to-nose with the audience.

Auditioning in a living room virtually in the lap of a producer was irregular and slightly suspicious, even in those early days of Off-Broadway. Still, there was no shortage of applicants.

The most immediate and troublesome role to cast was that of El Gallo, the dashing and mysterious caballero who narrates the show and manipulates the young lovers' fate.

"We saw so many people, and nobody was right," Schmidt said. "El Gallo has been eternally difficult to cast. We needed a leading man type with real masculinity; someone who could sing, spout poetry effectively and yet have a sense of humor. We've found that you almost never get all that at once."

They came close to hiring an actor named Peter Lombard. Schmidt remembers, "He looked sort of like Jerry Orbach [the eventual choice]. He was more officially handsome but not as good, not as ballsy. He didn't have the humor, which wound up counting for a lot, though he had an interesting quality, and he was a nice El Gallo type. He was the only one of that initial group who seemed a second real possibility."

They decided to invite an actor they had seen and admired in *The Threepenny Opera*, Jerry Orbach, then twenty-four. He played the Streetsinger who opens the show with "Mack the Knife." Orbach also understudied and occasionally went on for the play's leading role.

Orbach was born in the Bronx but spent his childhood being moved around the country until his parents settled in Waukegan, Illinois. He went to college at Northwestern University. *Threepenny* was his first professional job in New York.

With deep-set eyes, a long face and a jutting chin, Orbach gave the impression of being older and more worldly-wise than he actually was. Slim-hipped, with graceful hands and a surprisingly forceful voice, he had a matinee-idol magnetism, though, as the cast's most prominent beatnik, he affected being too cool to acknowledge it. There was a counterculture danger about him, abetted by his fondness for spending all night smoking cigarettes in 42nd Street movie houses, which still showed mainstream films, then arguing passionately the next day about what he'd seen over espresso in coffee houses. These were located not far from his three-bedroom $77-a-month apartment on Perry Street in Greenwich Village, where he lived with his wife, Marta. Orbach also liked to gamble and had no small skill at billiards, which later helped endear him to Noto.

University contacts, friendships from HB Studio and the Mira-Rostova studio, plus four seasons of summer stock in New Jersey, had introduced him to lots of New York theater folk, including Word Baker. Orbach visited Baker at Upstairs at the Downstairs, where Baker was now billed as associate producer.

Orbach remembers, "Word said, 'I've got an interesting show, a great part for you.' I said, 'Yeah, that's nice.' "

Orbach could afford to be blasé. He'd just been cast in a Broadway-bound production of the London musical *Lock Up Your Daughters*, which paid $200 a week. (And which later closed out of town.)

His friendship with Baker spurred him to climb the stairs at 74th Street.

"Jerry had everything," Schmidt said. "And he looked like a Navajo prince or something. We all flipped over him."

The first thing they played for him was "Try to Remember." Orbach read and sang, then bowed and left. Jones remembers, "He walked out the door, and we said, 'Well, shall we see other people? No, let's grab him!' So we chased down the stairs and grabbed him before he got on the street and offered him the role."

That was fine with Orbach: "When I heard the score of *The Fantasticks* and read it, I said, 'I've got to do this.' It was so beautiful and funny. It was also $45 a week, but to me there was no decision to make. I had decided I wanted to do it, and that was it."

* * *

Next came the fathers. The Boy's Father (Hucklebee) was an easy choice. Baker wanted William Larsen, the University of Texas alumnus who had taken Sam Houston's role of Rev. Parris in Baker's Off-Broadway *The Crucible*. The Louisana native was a veteran of the Alley Theatre in Houston and had performed some supporting roles in New York.

Though he suppressed his drawl on stage, it sprawled comfortably at other times. He and the authors spoke the same language. His bushy eyebrows and roly-poly figure made him look older than he really was, which suited the father well. In good-old-boy fashion, he was quick with a joke or a song. Nevertheless, he rarely suffered foolishness not his own.

"He was just always around, and both Tom and Word felt comfortable with him in the acting department," Schmidt said. "He's not a great singer, but he's musical, so he was fine as far as I was concerned. He also helped us with some backer auditions."

They also were familiar with the man they eventually chose for The Girl's Father (Bellomy). He was Hugh Thomas, an actor who had played the juvenile lead in Broadway's long-running *Janie* and had appeared in John Huston's 1951 film of *The Red Badge of Courage*. A sometime English teacher, he had decided to turn his hand to writing musicals and actually completed the libretto for a musical version of *What Every Woman Knows*.

His collaborator was Billy Roy, the piano player at Upstairs at the Downstairs. The two of them did some work on another musical, set in a nightclub milieu. Thomas never appeared in any of the Julius Monk revues but got to know Word Baker through his association with Roy. Thomas was a spare man with a fastidious manner that contrasted well with Larsen's expansive exasperation. Larsen liked Thomas on sight and began to campaign for him. The chemistry was right, so the match was made.

The Upstairs at the Downstairs soon yielded another *Fantasticks* original cast member: Monk's lighting man, George Curley, who already owned one percent of the show. The perennial department store Santa and summer stock Rumplestiltskin was, by then, comfortably a citizen of the New York theater community. He wasn't a consort of stars. Rather, he spent his free hours at the Theater Bar, hobnobbing with stagehands, lighting men, wardrobe mistresses, hatcheck girls, set-builders, electricians, stage managers, ticket brokers and the other people who don't get on the marquees but nonetheless help keep those marquees lit. He'd have a few beers, swap stories, play a game of chess or checkers and generally talk shop. In this way, he got to know people on Broadway, Off-Broadway and nightclubs. He never became a star himself, but in an uncertain business, he also was almost never out of work.

Curley landed his role by keeping tabs on Jones to see how his investment was developing. Curley recalls, "Tom was downstairs one day in the locker room, and I said, 'Hey Tom, is there anything I can do in the show? Heh-heh.' He said, 'If we took you away from Julius, he'd kill us.' Then he just laughed and didn't say anything more."

Curley went about his business for a few days but then was approached by Word Baker. "He comes in and says, 'Were you serious about wanting to read for us in the show?' I said, 'Yeah.' He said 'You know what it pays?' I said, 'Yeah, $45 a week.' I was getting $90 at the club. He says, 'Well, we talked it over, and there is something that you might be right for. The hell with Julius, come and read.' So I went and I read."

When Curley showed up on 74th Street, he remembers an argument between Noto and the creative team. "I think a lot of it was, they looked at me as a technician, not as an actor."

At Baker's insistence, they let him read with Jones for the part of The Man Who Dies, a.k.a. Mortimer, the Indian. "They cracked up," Curley said.

Jones and Curley read the opening scene between the Old Actor (Henry) and Mortimer, his sidekick. Jones was having a great deal of fun playing the character he had modeled on B. Iden Payne—a characterization his colleagues richly appreciated (and a fragment of which is preserved on the original cast album, during the "Rape Ballet" sequence). Jones' orotund delivery and his tattered suggestion of faded but genuine theatrical glory was a fanciful bubble, and Curley saw that his task was to pop it.

Curley played the grubby, pudgy cockney Mortimer as the antithesis of Jones's high-flown but scarecrowish Old Actor. Playing Sancho to Jones's Quixote came easily to Curley. Jones had found a perfect foil.

"So they called me back to read again. I read with several people, and they were fairly good. Then they said, 'George, read with Tom,' and they all broke up again. So when I went back to the club and all the waiters said, 'How's it going?' I said, 'I don't know, but I know one thing: the Old Actor is going to be Tom Jones.' "

And Jones felt that The Man Who Dies was going to be Curley. He eventually worked out a deal with Julius Monk that allowed Curley to join *The Fantasticks* and miss the early show at the Upstairs Tuesday through Friday and both shows on Saturday. After each night's performances of *The Fantasticks*, Curley would rub off his makeup and zoom uptown just in time for the late show at Upstairs at the Downstairs.

* * *

The heart of *The Fantasticks* is its pair of young lovers, its Pierrot and Pierrette: Matt and Luisa, listed in the *Dramatis*

Personae as The Boy and The Girl. They needed to be young enough to convey their characters' freshness and callowness, yet experienced enough to handle the demands of Jones and Schmidt's score.

They chose the pair, Kenneth Nelson and Rita Gardner, separately, though, as it turns out, they had appeared together once before in *Nightcap*, a Greenwich Village nightclub show along the lines of Julius Monk's.

Nelson was born in Rocky Mount, North Carolina, but moved with his family to San Antonio when he was six months old. Yes, another Texan. A boy soprano in the church choir, Nelson said he wanted to be an actor from age eight. A disastrous year at Baylor University in Waco taught him only that a scholar's life was not for him. A small inheritance from his mother enabled him to settle in New York City. In one of those Hollywood movie twists of fate, he was tapped for the lead role in the 1951 Broadway musical adaptation of Booth Tarkington's *Seventeen* when he was twenty-one, simply by answering an open casting call. His wide-eyed winsomeness and clear tenor set a standard for male juveniles in the 1950s.

The show ran for eight months and seemed to establish Nelson as a rising star. He was contracted to play Henry Aldrich in the TV adaptation of radio's *The Aldrich Family* series, during the 1952 season. But after that, his skyrocket ride seemed to have ended.

"My career banged shut," he said. "I had very little training, and no background at all. I started at the top, and it was very difficult having to adjust to going down to the bottom and starting over again, which I more or less had to do. I couldn't go for chorus jobs; I wasn't well-trained enough. I *could* sing. I had to do what I could, which meant working in summer stock. I didn't do another Broadway show for years and years."

Though the bookings weren't impressive, he used the time to learn his craft, taking acting lessons from another of New York's gurus, Uta Hagen. He hit a low point in his acting career, appearing as a chorus boy in a Miami Beach hotel floor show, before returning to New York in 1959 to appear in *Nightcap*. The original cast consisted of four performers: himself, Charles Nelson Reilly, Estelle Parsons, and another actress who soon left the show and was replaced by Rita Gardner.

Nightcap is notable not just for its actors, but for its composer, the then-unknown Jerry Herman, who later would write *Hello, Dolly!* (which featured Reilly), *Mame* and *La Cage Aux Folles.* With Herman at one of two pianos, *Nightcap* contained several numbers that resurfaced with new lyrics in his hit Broadway shows.

Nelson's manager heard about *The Fantasticks* and set up an audition for his client. Schmidt was overjoyed to see Nelson come through the door. He had been a fan of Nelson's since he heard the original cast album of *Seventeen* while stationed in El Paso during the Korean War. "I was thrilled by the thought that he might do it [Matt] because I loved his voice on that record," Schmidt said. "When he auditioned for it, he was so fabulous and seemed so right for The Boy even though he was a little older."

At age thirty, he was scarcely younger than the composer or the man who was to play his father.

"In my opening speech," Nelson said, "I have to say 'I'm nearly twenty years old.' I said to Word and Tom, 'I don't think I can get away with this in a small theater. Can't I just say I'm young or something?' They laughed and said, 'No, you can get away with it.' But it worried me a lot till we actually opened. I've always looked about ten years younger than I really am."

Nelson said he walked into the audition with no clear idea what the show was about. "But," he said, "they gave me the script right away. I took it home and read it and thought, 'This is just the most delightful thing I have ever seen. I've got to get into this show.' "

Aside from her experience with Nelson in *Nightcap*, Rita Gardner had no connection with anyone associated with *The Fantasticks*. Born Rita Schier in Brooklyn, she was the cast's native New Yorker, an Arthur Godfrey Talent Scouts winner, who had studied opera. She had sung in a close-harmony quartet called The Honeybees on a musical TV show, *Ship Ahoy*, and also had sung and danced on Broadway in *The King and I* as one of the Siamese wives.

Though slender and exhibiting a girlish manner, there were certain things about Gardner that set her apart from other ingenues. First there were the wide-set almond eyes that made her believable as a Thai princess. Second, she was buxom for a girl of her petite frame and had a hip, feline way of moving.

Like Orbach, she considered herself a Greenwich Village

beatnik, with all the possibilities that seemed to imply to the Mr. Straights from uptown. Baker and the writers found her combination of provocativeness and innocence to be irresistible, though, as she made clear, she was recently married. Her husband was Herb Gardner, creator of the comic strip, "The Nebbishes," and later the author of the cult hit play, *A Thousand Clowns* (whose female lead was based on Gardner), and the Tony-winner *I'm Not Rappaport*.

"I didn't know Tom or Harvey or anybody," she said. "I came in, essentially, off the street. They didn't know me either. I came right after they had listed something in *Variety*, saying the last time you could audition for this was this date in February."

Mistakenly thinking *The Fantasticks* was a revue like *Nightcap*, Gardner phoned Lore Noto and told him she could do revue material. Gardner remembers, "He said, 'You can come down and sing but realize that we do have someone [Maureen Bailey] in mind. But I like you, I like the way you sound on the phone.' So I came down and auditioned."

She remembers dashing through a snowstorm on the way to her audition. "I dressed like a beatnik: black stockings and some crazy shoes that I had, a black sweater and big earrings. My hair was very long—long and light brown, and it was wet from the snow."

While she waited in Schmidt's anteroom at the top of the stairs, the first thing that struck her was a cacophony from the living room. "As I sat there I kept hearing people banging on bongos and singing, and I started to see these crazy people running around."

Word Baker emerged with Lore Noto and, as Gardner recalls it, a dialogue ensued.

"Word said to Lore, 'Who is that?' And Lore said, 'This is this girl I spoke to on the phone, Rita Gardner. I think she sounds great. I love her.' Word said, 'But you haven't heard her sing. She's weird. We don't want *that* for The Girl!'

"Lore said, 'Hear her. I just have a feeling.' I was ready to leave because I thought, 'These people are nuts here.' But then Lore came out of the room and said, 'Come in and sing.' "

Baker said she looked so bedraggled he was disinclined to listen to her. But he agreed because of his pledge to audition all comers, and because he felt bad that she'd come so far in the bad weather.

As her audition piece, Gardner sang "Over the Rainbow," the same number that had won her the prize from Arthur Godfrey. Gardner recalls Schmidt telling her, "That's very good. You want to take it up higher?"

Schmidt said he was immediately impressed. "I loved her voice because she's got no break in it. With a lot of singers you can tell when they go from head to chest voice; it's two different voices. With Rita it was all one voice. Rita was like a pop singer, yet she could do these obbligato things, and it didn't seem strange."

Jones also was looking for an actress who could handle the range but not sound like an opera singer. He wanted a technically superior voice with a disarmingly contemporary sound. Gardner had it.

The first of her songs she heard from the show was the new duet for the Act II finale, "They Were You." She recalls, when she went home that night, "I said, 'That's gorgeous. Wow! Maybe this is good.' Herb read the script and said, 'Don't do this, it's not good.' But I said, 'Yes it is. It's going to be a hit.' "

As much as Word Baker liked Nelson and Gardner, he did not hire them right away. It would be his first musical in New York, and it dealt with themes and theories that were close to his heart. He thought there were three ways to do the show: as a standard musical; as a Shakespearian joyous comedy; and as a darker, almost Brechtian tale of disillusionment in the style of *The Threepenny Opera*.

To those ends, he actually assembled three separate casts, one to suit each of these styles, and had them read together to see which sounded best.

The Shakespearian cast included people Baker knew from the Stratford Shakespeare Festival, including Kate Reid and Maureen Bailey, later in the Broadway cast of *The Sound of Music*. The Brechtian version included Chris Chase and Ken Kercheval, eventually to be one of the leads in TV's *Dallas*. They were very close to hiring Bailey before Gardner made her eleventh hour appearance.

"We read all three versions in my living room," Schmidt

said, "and then all decided on the one with Rita and Kenny because the Shakespearian one was too artsy-fartsy and the other one was too much in the gutter. Thank God, because the one with Rita and Kenny was the only one I really liked."

Before they made their final choice for actors, however, they had Rita learn her 'I-want' song, the fervent "Much More," in which she dreams of swimming "in a clear blue stream/ Where the water is icy-cold;/ Then go to town in a golden gown/ And have my fortune told./ Just once!/ Just once!/ Just once before I'm old!"

They also had Jerry and Ken learn the newly-written number "I Can See It," which the two of them rehearsed in Schmidt's bedroom, then wouldn't stop singing all over the apartment as they practiced its complicated overlapping of melodic lines to get them right.

Baker said his most vivid memories of the auditions were Orbach and Nelson helping each other learn "I Can See It," and Larsen helping Thomas learn "Never Say No," because they wanted to work together so strongly.

With all the technical demands of the role, The Girl was not the most difficult part to cast. That distinction belonged to a character who had no lines at all: The Mute—the black-clad, silent figure who would flit among the players, delivering them props and serving as an all-purpose piece of animated scenery.

"We saw quite a few people because we thought we wanted a dancer type," Schmidt said. "Well, it was embarrassing. I had no carpeting on the floors then. We would ask a Mute to improvise, and they would come right at us with these Marcel Marceau things. It was absolutely paralyzing behavior, and they kept skidding across the slick floor at us. So we finally stopped that."

Ultimately, it was Orbach who found the Mute, and he did it in true *Fantasticks* fashion: it was a classmate of his from college.

Richard Stauffer (who since changed his first name to Blair) was born in Terra Haute, Indiana, and attended Knox College before transferring to Northwestern University to study acting. Stauffer was a junior when he met Orbach, who was a sophomore.

His education prepared him in a very direct way for the Mute. He took part in a University Theatre production of *The*

Yellow Jacket, the Hazelton and Benrimo adaptation of a Chinese classic that contains a mute character called The Property Man. Dressed in black, he sits on the edge of the stage, jumping up to supply the actors with props and equipment out of a large box. "I was playing the juvenile, so I got to watch him," Stauffer said, recalling his fascination with the role.

That summer, he participated in a program of short Menotti operas, *The Telephone* and *The Medium,* the latter of which contains a role for a mute. This time, Stauffer took the role himself.

"Those were my two backgrounds," Stauffer said. "One was totally functional: the Property Man in the Chinese play. In the other, I played a character."

His first credits were technical. He went to California and worked on a movie, *The Hot Angel,* and then got a job as a grip at Desilu.

Stauffer arrived in New York hoping to become an actor. He got a job as a page at NBC, living an existence he compares to that of the narrator in the film *My Favorite Year.* He even took classes with Lee Strasberg, then reigning as king of the Method acting teachers. There he met Marta Curro, Orbach's wife, and thereby reestablished contact with his charismatic former classmate.

Stauffer decided at one point to change his goal to architecture and studied at Cooper Union for a time. He got a job at a 26th Street architectural firm as blueprint boy and was slowly rising to draftsman in the firm. But he found that the work bored him.

One night he happened to mention to Marta and Jerry that he was unhappy where he was and yearned for the theater. "I told them 'I'm really out of it. I'd love to get back into the theater. If you ever hear of anything, let me know.' A month later, Jerry called and said, 'I think I have something for you.' "

Orbach said he had bragged to Word Baker about his buddy from Northwestern who was an acrobat, a fencer and a mime. Because the previous finalist for the part had broken an ankle, Baker told Orbach to bring his buddy to a rehearsal at the Sullivan Street Playhouse.

Stauffer has the gentle voice of a Mister Rogers, but a sharp intelligence constantly pricks through it. He seems always to be examining the things and people around him. When he speaks, his lips seem to acquire a life of their own. When he's silent, his face is impassive. Perhaps from years of practice, he sits very still. And that's just the way he sat through the rehearsal on Sullivan Street, straight and still in his business suit.

"He looked like an Italian painting from the fifteenth century," Orbach said, "an incredible face. Word Baker went through the rehearsal for about an hour and a half, then he turned to Stauffer and said, 'If you want to play the mime, it's yours.' You see, Word had been watching him watching. And he just loved the way he was sitting there watching. He must have said to himself, 'This guy obviously is going to be perfect.' He didn't have to do anything."

Schmidt confirmed that reaction. "I saw this beautiful, smooth white face," Schmidt said. "We were searching for someone with an interesting look. We realized that's all we really cared about."

Aside from Jones, who would lay official claim to the Old Actor later, Stauffer was the last regular member to join the cast of *The Fantasticks*.

As he had in *The Crucible*, Baker had wrapped himself in a circle of eager adherents, ready to make magic under his baton. But while he was assembling this circle, a lot had been going on behind the scenes.

9

Winter 1959–60

"We know all the ropes!
And the ropes to skip as well!"

WHILE the actors were auditioning for Jones and Schmidt (and while Jones and Schmidt were auditioning for backers), the collaborators cadged time to fulfill their promise to Lore Noto to expand the little show to two acts.

Some of what had to be done was simply clarifying what they had and writing more. Some sections of Act I had to be rewritten. In her opening speech, Luisa said things like "I'm starving./ I haven't eaten anything for forty-two days,/ Except food." That line was cut.

At Barnard, she complained: "It's hard being a princess,/ Especially if you have to live in a house./ And if birds fly away when you say hello; Very hard."

At Sullivan Street, that image became a story about an omen: "This morning a bird woke me up./ It was a lark or a nightingale/ Or something like that,/ Some strange sort of bird that I'd never heard,/ So I said hello/ And it vanished: flew away."

Jones was determined to continue his Shakespearian theme of seasons and vegetation into Act II, but Baker was equally determined that the cutesy quality be soft-pedaled. With those two dynamics in mind, they set about creating a second act.

127

There was ample precedent. Rostand's *Les Romanesques* tells the story in three acts. But in looking for extra plot, Jones wisely decided to dispense with Rostand's Act III complication in which the Girl, Sylvette, arranges to have herself kidnapped again, this time by a revenge-seeking Straforel who hasn't been paid by the fathers for his first abduction.

Instead, Jones decided to spend the audience's time developing the story of Matt's journey through the wicked world and Luisa's parallel gaining of bitter wisdom.

"We had to justify The Boy going off," Schmidt said, "and their disillusionment, which had been hinted at in the one-act version, had to be really explored."

One of the first new songs they wrote was "I Can See It," in which Matt, having been spurned and slapped by Luisa for his callowness, imagines the wonders that await him in the world beyond the two gardens. In his duet with El Gallo, Matt sings: "I can see it!/ Shining somewhere!/ Bright lights somewhere invite me to come there/ And learn! And I'm ready!" For his part, El Gallo warns: "Those lights not only glitter, but once there—/ They burn." El Gallo calls on a higher, instructing power to "Make him see it!"

To emphasize the difference in their visions, Schmidt composed an uptempo canon, with optimism overlapping cynicism and wisdom overlapping naïveté. It has the most *brio* of any song in the show up to that point, coming to an even bigger ending than Act I's "Metaphor," but having none of the earlier song's fey quality. "I Can See It" added the dark, threatening edge that Baker had called for and showed a muscle that hadn't been seen before.

This song was written early enough in 1960 that Orbach and Nelson learned it at the 74th Street apartment to help convince Noto and the others to hire Nelson.

And though they sang it well enough to clinch that deal, Schmidt said Noto was not happy with the song. "He thought it was too big for the show and felt like we were going off from the mainstream," Schmidt said. "And in a way I think that's true. I know what he means by that. And yet, the nice thing about the show is that it does dare to be that big in places. It's bigger than you can possibly play with just a piano, harp and two singers. But then the rest of us liked it so much, we talked Lore into it."

As Matt goes off to seek those lights, El Gallo performs a feat of white magic by freezing the two lovers and discussing their plight with the audience. He observes that Luisa has a tear quivering on her cheek, so he scoops it up and stores it away. "This tear is enough," Jones had him say, "this tiny tear—/To save the entire world."

Everyone melted at the last part of line, but as Schmidt observes, "No one actually knew what it meant. We finally cut it because Word thought it was pompous, and I guess he's right. But it was so poetic and so full of mystery and meaning. Every time I see the show, and it comes to the part where he says, 'This tear is enough. This tiny tear,' I always go [whispers] '. . . to save the entire world.' I hear that inside my head."

Jones, who said he took the image from the 1946 film, *Stairway to Heaven*, made the cut because he felt the line was "too cute." It leaves El Gallo's thought hanging. That bends its significance back to suggest that the Matt/Luisa romance has been ruptured only temporarily. Baker's judicious editing continually kept the show in focus at a time when conflicting demands constantly pulled Jones and Schmidt's attention.

At Barnard, Matt wandered off to points unknown while El Gallo dallied with Luisa, then stole her keepsake necklace and abandoned her in order to shatter her romantic notions. Afterward, Matt crawled back from a nameless fate having undergone his coming-of-age offstage. Showing the audience his evolution was a natural addition to the action, since demonstrating is always better than describing.

In a show that already had a preponderance of Spanish musical influences, "Have You Ever Been to China?" was one Latin number too many. Jones, Baker and Schmidt collaborated closely on its replacement, "Round and Round," which became the equivalent of the show's closest approximation of a "production number." Jones and Schmidt weren't enthusiastic about the idea of such a number, but Noto insisted on it to give Act II some splash.

They could have shown Matt's adventure and Luisa's adventure separately and in sequence, but "Round and Round" enabled them to do both. As at Barnard, El Gallo appears to the abandoned Luisa and offers to show her the world. Luisa is all too happy to accede. As El Gallo describes their intinerary—

Venice, Athens, "Indja"—these destinations appear in her imagination. There is a twist, however. Every scene includes a vision of Matt undergoing some misfortune in these romantic places: being beaten, tortured or burned in some exotic way. These scenes provide Baker's antidote for the sweet icing in Act I, though they obeyed Jones's stylistic rule (borrowed from Houseman's *A Winter's Tale*) of harsh daylight for Act II to balance the idealized moonlight for Act I.

El Gallo protects Luisa from the horror of these visions by supplying her with a magic mask, a stylized pair of rose-colored glasses, that makes the scenes "look pretty." But the mask's magic is not a perfect screen. No one who looks upon cruelty with delight can ever be innocent again.

Not only is Matt learning the hard way; so is Luisa. The song provides the play with its symbolic death, as the idealistic lovers have their highfalutin notions literally burned out of them. The scene has no equivalent in Rostand.

Still, Jones found room for some saving humor. Matt is put through his paces by a pair of scoundrels who happen to be Henry and Mortimer in disguise (renamed Lodevigo and Socrates, respectively). Jones said he based the two characters on the cat and fox in the Disney film *Pinocchio*, who lure the ambitious puppet into becoming an actor.

No matter where they take Matt, the two always greet Luisa with a cheerful "*arriverderci.*" Schmidt explained that the idea popped onto the page one day. "It was just Tom being light-hearted," Schmidt said. "It's the wrong word in the wrong place, but it never fails to get a laugh."

The reappearance of the Old Actors not only brought these two favorite characters back to the stage, it also gave Jones a further chance to play B. Iden Payne while beefing up Act II. But Baker made sure the song wasn't just stuffing. No longer mere catalysts of the Fathers' scheme, the Old Actors seem to be working for a higher power, becoming agents of Matt and Luisa's real education in the ways of the world.

That moonlight/daylight balance was applied to the Fathers themselves, who also got a second song. "Plant a Radish" is simply an expansion of a speech Bellomy has in Act I. It's the most dispensable (plotwise) piece of business in *The Fantasticks*, yet it never gets cut. The explanation lies in Baker's savvy about the rhythm of a play and audience emotions. First of all, it's a typical vaudeville turn, which unbilled choreographer Lathan Sanford filled with buck-and-wings and other show biz touches. It's one of the most entertaining numbers in the show. Second, it's peppered with some of Jones's most creative rhymes as he weighs the benefits of raising vegetables against the benefits of raising children.

> But if your issue
> Doesn't kiss you
> Then I wish you luck.
> For once you've planted children,
> You're absolutely stuck!

Though its content is redundant within the show, "Plant a Radish" fulfills an emotional need to see the two feuding fathers restore their friendship. Like their children, they've learned a lesson. Once again they take up common cause, and while they're still railing at their perverse children, they no longer are scheming to manipulate those children's lives.

The extra dialogue and songs had added close to forty-five minutes to the show, which was enough to satisfy Noto. But Jones and Schmidt still had some loose ends to tie up. Matt and Luisa's sadder-but-wiser reconciliation song, "I Have Acted Like a Fool," written after Barnard and sung at backer auditions, fulfilled the dramatic requirement that the two of them realize their folly. But the lyric makes them sound like they're reciting a moral that they might as well be writing two hundred times on the blackboard:

> It's a tragedy.
> I mean it really is a tragedy.
> If someone were to write it in a book or play,
> I think you may agree
> We'd say it was a tragedy, we
> Have acted like a fool!*

There was a better and more satisfying lesson to be learned, and it could be found in Rostand.

*From *The Fantasticks* © Tom Jones and Harvey Schmidt. Unpublished early draft. Used by permission.

To use George Fleming's translation of Sylvette's speech:

> Oh, not in distant lands, in untrod ways
> In wild adventure or in unsung lays,
> But *here* lives Poetry.
> > [*She falls into his arms.*]

Or, as in Henderson Norman's 1921 translation:

> Poetry, love, but we were crazy, dear,
> To seek it elsewhere. It was always here.

In short, rather than taking the negative approach and making them beat their breasts about being fools, Jones took the positive approach and wrote a new song about how Matt and Luisa truly had love—now a mature love—for each other.

> When the moon was young,
> When the month was May,
> When the stage was hung for my holiday,
> I saw shining lights, but I never knew
> They were you
> They were you
> They were you.

> When the dance was done
> When I went my way,
> When I tried to find rainbows far away,
> All the lovely lights seemed to fade from view—
> They were you
> They were you
> They were you . . .*

Jones found a couch for these sentiments in a sparkling waltz Schmidt had written at the urging of their publisher Dr. Albert Sirmay, at Chappell Music, who felt "Try to Remember" and "Soon It's Gonna Rain" weren't really ballads.

The music came to Schmidt while he was visiting Houston for his sister's wedding that spring. He was standing outside Sakowitz Brothers, the department store where he had worked briefly between college and the Army. "I was waiting for the light to change," he said, "and suddenly I started hearing this very simple melody. Like 'Try to Remember,' it came to me all at once. It was so simple, it was easy to remember. We were already looking for something for the ['I Have Acted Like a Fool'] spot, so when I came back to New York and suggested we try it, Tom liked it, too."

With Act I and Act II now separate entities, Schmidt and Jones had to write finales for each act. The Act I finaletto, titled "Happy Ending," turned the music of the overture into laughter and merged it with lines from "Metaphor," climaxing in a tableaux of family happiness. The Act II ending presented a more complex problem. Jones tried to find the answer in Rostand, and this time went astray.

Seeing Matt and Luisa reconciled, Bellomy suggests the wall be torn down again. But El Gallo stops him, saying, "No. Leave the wall. Remember—/You must always leave the wall," then segues into a reprise of "Try to Remember."

The line parallels one near the end of Fleming's *Fantasticks*: "No; keep your walls. Without them naught had been." Jones said, "After due consideration, I decided that was not a good line to end with. That wasn't the point being made. We were making a different point: 'Without a hurt, the heart is hollow.' But Lore adored the line and insisted that we keep it."

But the line continued to niggle at Jones, and sure enough, it eventually got him in trouble. Three decades later, when *The Fantasticks* made its USSR debut shortly after the Berlin Wall was demolished, it was the only line the Soviets excised from the show.

The very last song written for *The Fantasticks* was "It Depends on What You Pay," also known as the Rape song. It completed a circle, since it finally set to music the Straforel/El Gallo monologue that had first attracted Jones's attention to the piece in B. Iden Payne's class in long-ago Texas. Through all the many versions he worked on, it remained a spoken passage, though one that provided a stylistic anchor for the comic bandit El Gallo, as distinct from the narrator who sang "Try to Remember."

Their reason for writing "It Depends on What You Pay" was pure show biz: they wanted to give Jerry Orbach another song. Schmidt said, "We had this magnificent talent, and he sang so well and was so comedic that we realized we weren't using his talent enough." Jones's rendering of the speech was already in verse, like much of the rest of the play, so it was just a matter of tailoring it to fit a melody.

That song marked a departure for the Jones/Schmidt collaboration. "We wrote that at the piano together, which we don't do too often."

It gave Schmidt a chance to reflect on his relationship with his former upperclassman, who had not achieved nearly as much materially as he, but who had tenaciously stuck with his dream. "A partnership is like a marriage," Schmidt said. "You sometimes have disagreements while you're married, which we did, though I've never thought they were serious. But I realized that, working with Tom, I had always felt like I was a guest in Tom's 'house' [the theater]. I hadn't set out to do this as a career. I was so impressed that he even wanted to work with me. Even now, I certainly wasn't coming on very strong, except to do the best I could."

In writing Act II, Jones was working more as a technician than a poet, though many of the passages are beautiful. He wasn't writing in the headlong, illuminating, thunderstruck rush of the previous summer. He was writing methodically to satisfy dramatic necessities. He had an advantage, however. The previous summer, it was just him wrestling with his muse. Working with the cast on Sullivan Street in late winter 1960, suddenly there were all these new people to be excited about the show.

10

April 1960

"Anything else that's needed /
We can get from out this box.

EVEN as Jones and Schmidt
were polishing the new material, Baker was hard at work on
the old material, trying it on his cast and beginning to shape it.
Rehearsals began the first week in April 1960.

"The atmosphere of creativity was extraordinary," Orbach
said, "because Word Baker told us that we should think of
ourselves as a family, as a troupe of *commedia dell'arte* players
who live together and pull into somebody's back yard and play
this show on the back of a wagon. So that's how we began to
work. We had the freedom to say, 'Hey, I've got an idea: How
about this?' and Word was wide open to anything. That was
very unusual at that time. As I've gotten older and gotten a
little more self-assurance and power in the theater, I could walk
up to a Gower Champion and say, 'Hey what if we changed
this?' But at that time, you were supposed to just sit there and
do what the director told you."

Openness was Baker's directorial style. He functioned less as
a sergeant and more as an editor, allowing his actors to improvise different approaches to the material, then exercising his
authority to say which would be used.

135

It worked well for "Metaphor," in which the two young lovers declare their love over the wall built by their fathers. Baker started with Matt and Luisa simply holding hands over the wall and singing it straight, then gradually adding business. The song calls for Luisa to swoon, and Gardner tried more than a dozen different swoons before she found one that would neither be painful nor difficult to rebound from, since her swoons are followed quickly by new lyrics. She finally hit upon one in which she would slump to the floor histrionically with a high-pitched sigh, only to pop up unscathed and fully alert when she hears a new flattering metaphor. The swoon served as a comment on the seriousness of her romance-inspired condition and on her girlish vanity. It had the additional practical value of getting her back on her feet quickly and believably. It also got a laugh.

Similarly, Baker had two fathers who were virtually interchangeable, except for one's preference for watering his garden lightly versus the other's preference for pruning it. But from that toehold, the two original actors climbed into distinct characters based on themselves. The fussy and sensitive Hugh Thomas loaned that color to Bellomy, who reacts with initial horror at the idea of the expensive abduction. The extroverted Larsen, on the other hand, pumped up the shears-snapping Hucklebee with brashness.

Baker may have waited for his players to invent business, but that didn't mean he was effectless or passive. Baker was searching for very specific stylistic touches. The B. Iden Payne influence was consecrated in his determination to recreate an Elizabethan open stage, one where Jones's poetry would act as a clapper on the bell of the audience's imagination.

Though there is neither garden nor wall to be found anywhere on the stage at Sullivan Street, both are integral parts of the drama, thanks to Jones's script and Baker's staging. When the fathers threaten to reinforce the wall, saying "I'll lime that wall with bottles! I'll jag it up with glass!" the barrier veritably glitters laceratingly in the moonlight—though there's neither wall, glass nor moon anywhere in the theater. And when Hucklebee and Bellomy gaze with pride upon their invisible magnolia, pepper and kumquat, carefully tilting an (empty) watering can over them or snapping a shears in midair, the root and branch begin to take shape, supplied by Payne's favorite set designer: the mind's eye of the beholder.

Schmidt analyzed Baker's directorial style, saying, "He's wonderful at creating an atmosphere in which people can really flower. He always encourages people's natural artistic bent . . . and makes you feel like you're really hot stuff. And that's very invigorating because, as a result, you try to do your very best and please him."

Baker pulled his influences from wherever he or Jones found them. He lifted the opening of *The Fantasticks* directly from Strehler's Piccolo Teatro di Milano production of *The Servant of Two Masters:* as the overture plays, the actors came on as themselves, still shaving or pulling on their costumes. But as they take their places, finish with their buttons and take up their hats or flower, they begin to change, assuming their stage personae, until the moment El Gallo whisks the curtain away to reveal them fully in character.

Baker and Jones wanted the show to be a primal theater experience, a ritual, a gathering around the campfire to hear a story. Jones and Schmidt returned to this theme in greater depth (though with less success) in their 1969 musical *Celebration.* But for *The Fantasticks,* El Gallo functions as a storyteller who can step out of the action, manipulate it or stop it entirely, like the Stage Manager in Jones's revered *Our Town.*

There was another handy tool that Baker used to move the little musical: the device of White Magic.

Though El Gallo and the Mute are able to control everything from the weather to the movements of the sun and moon in their efforts to teach Matt and Luisa about life, nowhere is the White Magic more graphically in evidence than in the supernatural Prop Box.

With the bare stage and no access to wings, there was no place to stash the many minor props the script called for. The fathers' clippers and watering can could be placed unobtrusively alongside or beneath the wooden platform, but what of plums, drums, masks, mirrors, dowels and scarves? One of the few presentational devices surviving from *Joy Comes to Dead Horse* was El Gallo's address to the audience, pointing to the story's artifices. Showing the source of the props would fit in perfectly.

Schmidt remembers a backstage debate over how to introduce the Old Actors, Henry and Mortimer. At Barnard, they had simply wandered in from the wings, but Baker wanted to make it more magical. "We were all sort of battling over where this Old Actor would come from, and Tom was sort of sketching some ideas," Schmidt said.

One idea was inspired by Goldoni: an actor hiding in a box. He sketched Henry emerging from the box, thinking perhaps such a box could be worked into the play somehow. "It's a very seminal drawing," Schmidt said, because the sketch made them consider that Henry and Mortimer were, in a sense, props too. They were pulled out like hats or scarves, then put away when not needed. Why not make an extra-big prop box and let the two Old Actors make their entrance from there? It was intensely theatrical and used the sort of rabbit-out-of-a-hat magic that Baker gloried in.

"It's the oldest theater device there is," Stauffer said. "What's in the box?"

Wittstein eventually opted for *two* prop boxes: a smaller operational one that could be carried around the stage as needed; and a larger, stationary one with a secret entrance in the back and room for two actors to crawl in shortly before their cue.

"It's funny," Schmidt said. "After the fact, things like that seem so simple and logical. But when you are starting with a blank page or the blank space or the blank whatever, sometimes you don't have any ideas at all."

In keeping with an almost postmodern notion of theater drawing attention to its own theatricality, Baker also wanted to bring in elements of vaudeville. Aside from the fathers' "Plant a Radish," the cockney Indian, Mortimer, a.k.a. The Man Who Dies, gave Baker ample opportunity to work clowning into the show. Though it's the shortest role in the show in terms of number of lines, it is full of rolling, falling, snatching and other hijinks. To prove to El Gallo that their credentials for the abduction are in order, Henry bids Mortimer to "Die for the man," and Mortimer must oblige. "I wish Word had given me a little bit more on the death scene," Curley said. "He told me, 'Just die,' so I just [keeled over]. He said, 'We have to give you more than that.' "

Curley said first he just kicked at the end, then he began flipping over. The death gradually became more and more elaborate until Curley had concocted an elaborate pantomime of pretending to mix a glass of poison, mixing it with his finger, then tasting the mixture on his fingertip and doing an elaborate pratfall.

A year into the show's run, he continued to improvise, eventually developing a whole repertoire of exotic deaths: fiddling with a gun that suddenly comes unjammed, cutting down a tree that falls on him, blowing himself up with dynamite, throwing himself on a sword and stringing himself up from an imaginary rafter.

For all his invention, Curley owns up that he did not invent the piece of business that finally became standard. A subsequent Mortimer in Boston came up with the idea of a bow and arrow that somehow gets out of control, burying its shaft in the Indian instead of his intended target.

Curley does, however, take credit for a line change. Mortimer originally bragged, "It's not easy dying like that. But I like it. I've been dying for twenty years. Why, I could die backwards off a twenty-foot cliff!"

Curley thought he'd get a better laugh by changing the last line to "Why, I could die off a twenty-foot cliff—backwards!" Baker and Jones saw that he was right and let him keep it that way.

For all that, Baker said he was determined to make *The Fantasticks* less cutesy than it had been at Barnard. Schmidt said, "Word always very strongly stressed he wanted it realer and he wanted it more American because Tom and I were in love with *commedia* and we would have sent it much more in that direction if he'd let us. So it ended up a nice blend because it hints at *commedia* origins without being too strong about it. People, especially kids, can relate to it. If it were too stylized it would make them think it was not about them."

Orbach said he welcomed the way the play was becoming somewhat more down-to-earth. "My big thing was realism," he said. "I hated anything fake or phony. My goal was naturalistic, realistic acting. I was working in musicals because I could sing, and because I could sing I was getting jobs while other friends of mine who didn't sing were stuck. Still, I wanted no hokeyness, except when it's really called for, like in the 'Rape Ballet.' But as far as everything else—talking to the audience and the poetry—I wanted truth. That was very, very important to me, much more important to me, I think, than even the writers or the director. I think that was my particular contribution to the structure of that play: you have to have the reality when you're doing the little poetic speeches, leading to 'Soon It's Gonna Rain' or whatever, otherwise the high flying poetry and comedy have nothing to bounce off of."

Baker could see that in Orbach he had found his charcoal stick for sketching in the shadows around the brightly-colored bauble. He saw that Orbach was stretching his acting muscles and allowed him to have his head. "In *Threepenny*, I had learned the power of the pause," he said. "The way an actor can focus the audience's attention almost like a director with a camera. He can bring them into a close-up if he wants to. There was a pause in *Threepenny* where Macheath says, as he's about to be hanged, 'Which is worse—to rob a bank or to own a bank? And which is worse—a man dead lying on his back or a man alive on his knees?' I could hold that beat for as long as I wanted to. Then I'd let them go, and I would go up the stairs to be hanged. I loved that feeling of taking them by the throats, holding them and then letting them go, and I think I used it just before 'Soon It's Gonna Rain'—the lines 'You wonder how these things begin. . . . It is September, Before a rainfall,/ A perfect time to be in love.' I'd just grab them . . . then let them go."

Baker's communal improvisational style worked well in *The Fantasticks* because he knew precisely what he wanted stylistically, and because he was blessed with an enthusiastic and creative cast to give him the kind of feedback he needed. In later years, that style sometimes would fail him. There would be times in Baker's career when he'd wait in vain for that kind of feedback, and other times when he couldn't harness it. That's part of the reason Baker had no real stage success again until 1970's *The Last Sweet Days of Isaac*, and no major hit until 1978's *I'm Getting My Act Together and Taking It on the Road*, which became the fifth longest running musical in Off-Broadway history. The style failed him perhaps most notably in late 1961 when he was removed as director of *A Family Affair*, in

Philadelphia, and replaced with Harold Prince (though Prince later saluted Baker's work, in his book *Contradictions*).

But in spring 1960, with the glow of *The Crucible* behind him, Baker seemed to have the Midas touch. It inspired those who worked around him.

Despite the spartan setting, low pay, money worries and the time crunch, there was a carefree spirit at the Sullivan Street Playhouse. They had fun.

"For the first week-and-a-half," Orbach said, "I could never get through the entire 'Rape' song without falling down laughing. I couldn't say 'I play Valkyrie on a bass bassoon.' It was just too funny for me to even finish the words. But that's how much I liked it anyway."

Actors were balancing on pianos, dancing flamencos on benches and swinging on poles, and these flights of fancy often made their way into the show.

To balance the humor and menace of El Gallo, Orbach conjured up John Barrymore, whose grandiose acting style was anathema to much he was learning from Lee Strasberg and Herbert Berghof, but whose theatricality Orbach felt was right for the piece.

"I specifically thought of Barrymore," he said, "in the 'Rape Ballet' when The Boy stabbed me, and I had to clutch at this fake wound and point at him as if to say, 'You did it.' I remembered a picture of Barrymore doing a sort of broken-wristed point. So when Kenny stabbed me, I went like that, and suddenly it was a big laugh. It was just a little outrageous, a little bit over the top, and it worked."

Baker began by staging the musical numbers like "Rape Ballet" and moved into the poetry and connective tissue later. Part of that would be the Mute, whose job is to pull the show together and keep it snapping along.

When Stauffer, who was cast after rehearsals began, first saw the show, several songs had already been staged. He remembered, "They'd say, 'OK, let's go to the 'Singin' in the Rain' number,' " which is how the movie fans in the cast referred to "Soon It's Gonna Rain." Stauffer said, "Everybody would assemble, and they'd go into the number. It was like watching a production for some kind of movie musical. I thought, 'Gee, this is pretty good, except that these are all separate numbers.'

It was almost like revue material in that sense, except there were characters."

After Stauffer's arrival, that began to change. The Mute provides more than his share of White Magic. After all, it is the Mute who stands in for the wall itself. It would be an exercise for any actor to embody the impassivity of a wall, and Stauffer accomplished that with as blank a look and as immobile a stance as he could muster. But when the fathers need to step over the wall, all they do is push his arm down. He must seem to yield, then vanish.

"Originally we had him do a lot more," Schmidt said. "In 'Soon It's Gonna Rain,' he at one point had a stuffed dove on a string and a stick that he would fly through the air. But his part got simpler and simpler. And as a result, stronger and bolder."

The best White Magic of all is the way the Mute marks celebrations by flinging colored squares around the stage, and suggests rain by standing on the piano and sprinkling blue and green confetti over the lovers; using white confetti to suggest snow.

Baker had introduced the colored squares at Barnard, but they were larger there, four by four inches, and made of construction paper. Baker and Stauffer soon discovered that they simply did not flutter. They sort of fell. The idea was good, but the squares weren't. As a result, Stauffer had plenty of chance to experiment with the aerodynamics of confetti. The final choice: fireproof colored tissue cut in squares two and three-eighths inches on a side.

Stauffer said he discovered that throwing them in handfuls didn't work, either. They wouldn't go very far. They had to be packed patiently each day by stage manager Geoffrey Brown and flung at the high point of the ceiling where they would strike and burst open, showering the stage evenly. "There was the odd night when they went up in a clump and came down in a clump," Stauffer said. "But that was good too. It kept you on your toes. Sometimes they'd stick in the lights, and they'd come down at the oddest times. It would be right during the last scene or something like that, and everybody would go 'Ohh.'"

The frivolity and lightheartedness of *The Fantasticks* took a lot of work to perfect. But for Baker, the effort was necessary.

Whimsy is a difficult thing to construct and maintain. Timing and grace are important components, but above all, he said, the secret of *The Fantasticks* is, "It has to be real. It has to happen every night with nothing faked. The magic has to be real."

As they reported to work each day for a new round of the nuts and bolts of making magic, the actors would converge on the theater by bus or subway, walking the last few blocks on Bleecker Street. The Italian ambience of the neighborhood was still strong. Fruit sellers, fishmongers and knife sharpeners still plied their trade from curbside pushcarts. As the actors left the theater in the evening, the aroma of garlic and tomato sauce hung in the air from the area's numerous southern Italian restaurants. A little later and the tart smell of espresso would loiter by the coffeehouse doors. It was the generation that believed, as Henri Michaux did, that "men with caffeined thoughts will change the world." A decade later, the streets would be full of flower children. But the beatniks, while a presence, tended to stay indoors.

"I don't know that Greenwich Village was full of beatniks," Nelson said. "It was just full of people who were young and full of enthusiasm for life and freedom."

Sullivan Street itself was mostly residential. Two doors south of the theater was the house where New York mayor Fiorello La Guardia had been born. The long block that stretches south to Houston Street was flanked mainly by old but well-kept three- and four-story townhouses.

On the north side of the theater was a hotel at the corner of Bleecker and Sullivan with shops facing the street on the ground floor. The shops were pleasant enough, but the hotel had a rowdy clientele who sometimes tossed things at unwary passersby. Once the actors got to be recognized they were spared, however. The actors came to be accepted not just by each other but by the neighborhood.

"From the first day of rehearsal," Kenneth Nelson said, "we realized that this was something quite extraordinary. It was an atmosphere of total family happiness. We had fun during rehearsals. There was never any tension or fighting or squabbling. Nothing. Never. A lot of that had to do with Word. He picked the right people at the right time, and it just jelled."

Other members of the original cast had much the same to report. That was doubly remarkable considering their accommodations backstage. Most actors are used to doubling or tripling in dressing rooms, particularly members of the chorus. But the Sullivan Street Playhouse represented a new low. There was one giant dressing room that everyone had to share, including Rita Gardner.

The room was arranged in a lopsided U-shape separated by a low bank of shelves and cabinets. Orbach, Larsen, Thomas, Stauffer and Nelson changed in the larger side closer to the stage; and Jones and Curley (the two Old Actors who had the least stage time) shared the smaller side, with Gardner in the far corner. She had privacy only when Jones and Curley turned their backs.

Gardner said she had no problem with that. "It was just a very *gemütlich* group, and I never worried about that. Tom and George were very polite so I never had any trouble. They were great to have around to help button the back of my dress."

"Everybody respected the fact that she was a girl," Stauffer said.

The actors even had to share a common rest room in the theater's dingy basement.

Nelson said, "The first time I saw the theater I thought, 'Well, it's tiny, but it's what we need.' It was a bit shabby. Our dressing rooms were so communal that most of the sounds one remembers is just everybody talking. But I don't remember anyone complaining about it. I can't remember anyone ever getting cross about it or beginning to sulk. If anybody did, it probably would have been me."

Nelson had the biggest credits, having had the lead in a Broadway musical, so he was treated with the deference of the top-billed (his name came first in the Who's Who section of the programme).

But Orbach clearly was the dominating presence. His talent was obvious, his opinions were strong and well-reasoned and his dark good looks would have stood out in any crowd, though, in fact, he was the youngest in the cast.

"He never had a boyish quality," Nelson said, "not even a youthful one. A lot of that had to do with his size and that kind of brooding look he had always. I liked the fact that he had a sense of humor about himself. He was very good at putting himself down and making jokes at his own expense."

Orbach's interest in billiards endeared him immediately to Lore Noto, who had spent his teenage years helping his father run their pool hall. The two of them would spend evenings after rehearsals and later, after performances, shooting pool and drinking beer.

A weekly poker game soon developed, in which Noto would try to win back their salaries, but just as often would wind up augmenting them, particularly Orbach's, according to Stauffer.

Oddly enough, Stauffer's coworkers remember their Mute for his speaking voice, which is soft and melodious. He was devoted to Orbach (later taking time away from his acting career to become Orbach's dresser), but, Nelson said, "He was much tougher and more streetwise than he looked and sounded." He also was a sports fan, and whenever he could, he would dial the backstage table radio to that day's game.

The actors tended to keep to themselves and shut out the musicians and writers, with the exception of Jones, who worked among them. Everyone took an immediate liking to Schmidt, though they felt he was quiet and withdrawn next to his more flamboyant collaborator.

"I really frankly think Tom wanted to be backstage so he could hear if we didn't say the lines correctly," Gardner said. "Then we would get notes from him. He was so cute. He was very influenced by the classics. He loved Shakespeare and was always quoting."

Most of the *Fantasticks* crew fell into two groups: the beatniks/New Yorkers (mainly Orbach, Gardner and Noto, plus Stauffer, Curley and Thomas), and the expatriate Texans (the writers, Larsen, Nelson and, later, Jay Hampton). But there was no friction between the two groups. The show drew on the best of each.

The most outspoken member of the Texas mafia was Bill Larsen. There was something sturdy about him, as well. Stauffer said that whenever someone in the company needed sound advice in the ways of the world, they'd turn to Larsen.

Curley remembers Larsen's jokes and how he would begin philosophical statements by saying "I always say to myself, 'Myself.' "

Nelson remembers Larsen with affection. "If people come in the categories of dogs, horses and birds, he was a great big puppydog."

For his part, Curley was always ready with a joke that he'd bring back from nights at the Theatre Bar. These were not the best jokes, and sometimes his colleagues had to drive him off to get relief from the barrage of dubious humor. "He was a bit of a chatterer but was always terribly friendly and well-meaning," Nelson said. The fact that Curley had the smallest part guaranteed that he'd spend the most time backstage. He never hung around after curtain calls. He'd always leave just in time to get uptown to Julius Monk's to run the lights at the late show.

As the only female, Gardner got plenty of affectionate attention, though most kept their distance, owing to her wedding band and the fact that her husband, then-cartoonist Herb Gardner, sometimes would meet her backstage after work.

Hugh Thomas, who played Gardner's father, assumed something of that role backstage as well. She remembers him watching over her, offering fatherly advice and bringing her occasional small gifts from an antique shop he helped run in New Jersey. She still cherishes antique perfume bottles that date from rehearsals.

When prompted, Thomas would share stories of his adventures in Hollywood, where he had appeared as a soldier in *The Red Badge of Courage*. Stauffer vividly recalls Thomas telling "wonderful stories about how they used to line them up at five in the morning and the makeup people would throw mud at them. And how John Huston was an absolute madman who would ride around on a white horse at the several-hundred-acre ranch where they filmed the thing."

For all his past, Thomas was the frailest of the cast members, neater and more delicate than the others, but ready to join in fun when there was any to be had.

Their coworkers sensed that there was a positive tension between their leading man and lady, an innocent flirtation. Things quickly got too busy for anything more to develop.

Most of the time they spent socializing was at mealtime. Toward the end of rehearsals in mid April, Baker would work the cast long hours, sometimes running from morning to near midnight. Under Actors Equity rules, Noto had to provide meals on these days, and he often would order food from

At the ninth anniversary party, (from left) Tom Jones, Harvey
Schmidt, Word Baker, and Lore Noto.

The Fantasticks company, appearing in 1970 at the newly-revamped
Ford's Theatre in Washington, was invited to perform at the White
House. Joining Mrs. Richard Nixon (third from right) are (from left)
Glen Clugston, Karen Goldberg, Gwyllum Evans, Peggy Clark,
Larry Small, Stephen Douglass, Guy Grasso, and William Larsen.

Full-page announcement in *The New York Times* of the show's tenth anniversary.

Richard Chamberlain and Indira Danks in the 1973 Chicago
production at Arlington Park Theatre.

George Chakiris as El Gallo,
rehearsing for the Dallas
Summer Musicals production.

芸術座7月公演
製作一菊田一夫
東宝ミュージカル特別公演

The Fantasticks
ファンタスティックス ————愛についての寓話————

エドモン・ロスタン作〈レ・ロマネスク〉より
脚本ートム・ジョーンズ
音楽ーハーベイ・シュミット
訳ー渡辺浩子
訳詞ー小池一子

Tokyo

Buenos Aires

MÜZİKAL KOMEDİ
2 Bölüm
EDMOND ROSTAND'IN «LES ROMANESQUES»
PİYESİNDEN
Mülhem Olarak Yazan
TOM JONES
Müzik
HARVEY SCHMIDT
TÜRKÇEYE ÇEVİREN
ORHAN AZİZOĞLU
KOREOGRAFİ
TRAVIS KEMP

Ankara

Stockholm

Mexico City

The Fantasticks around the world.

Detail of a wall hanging in the upstairs lounge of the Sullivan Street Playhouse depicting the Act I tableau in a brilliant fabric interpretation by noted artist Norman La Liberte.

Rita Gardner (left), the original Luisa, and Sarah Rice, then the current one, at the show's sixteenth anniversary celebration.

Glenn Close, who played Luisa in a college production, joins Tom Jones (left) and Harvey Schmidt at an American Theatre Wing party at Sardi's in New York in 1984.

BARNARD CENTENNIAL ARTS FESTIVAL

presents

the 30th Anniversary celebration of

The Fantasticks

Tuesday, March 21, 1989
Barnard Hall Gymnasium

by special arrangement with the producers
of the Sullivan Street Playhouse Production
and Actors Equity Association.

This special presentation of THE FANTASTICKS
has been made possible through
the generous sponsorship of the
Cynthia Sue Green Visiting Artist Program.

The Fantasticks plays a special commemorative return engagement at Barnard three decades after its premiere there.

Ron Hudd (left) as Hucklebee and Anthony O'Donnell as Bellomy
in the New Shakespeare Company's production of *The Fantasticks*,
performed at the Regent's Park Open Air Theatre in London,
summer 1990.

Robert Goulet,
joined by (from left)
Gerry Vichi, Neil
Nash, Glory
Crampton, and
Ralston Hill, in the
thirtieth anniversary
national tour in
1990.

Covers from assorted programs through the years as *The Fantasticks* begins its fourth decade at the Sullivan Street Playhouse.

Punjab's, an ostensibly Indian restaurant at the corner of Bleecker, across Sullivan Street from the Playhouse. It was run by Peter Mengrone, known to most of the cast members as Peter Punjab. Despite the restaurant's name, it served mostly Italian food with a curry or two thrown in.

Noto would set up a table in the second floor lounge of the Playhouse and the actors would dine buffet-style, then sit on the banquette and talk, or slip out the theater's rear fire exit to smoke a cigarette in the tiny backyard.

What did they talk about? Despite the impending presidential election that year and all the ferment going on during Eisenhower's last months, they mostly talked about the theater—sometimes prospects for the future but mostly the minutiae of making their little show work. "It seemed tremendously interesting, whatever it was we were talking about," Stauffer said: "How I slipped off the bench but caught myself without bending my ankle, how Luisa caught her fringe in one of the pipes that goes up the stage. 'Did you see the way I made that last entrance? I tripped over the stage.' Because we were all living so totally in our own world there, the slightest thing that happens on stage is suddenly elevated to a major event. Once George complained about Tom farting, or Tom about George, while they were waiting to make their entrance from that Prop Box—things like that."

In general, the original cast of *The Fantasticks* was not a close-knit *Our Gang*. They were working professional artists. After work, they tended to go their own ways. But as they got to know each other better, they inquired more frequently about one another's private lives and even grew protective of one another, but that was waiting for them in the future.

Most important of all at this point, however, was their optimism, innocence and complete faith in the show. "We were young," Gardner said, "and everything lay ahead of us."

* * *

Through it all, the cast grew accustomed to Jones's rolling "r's" and rolling eyes in the role of the Old Actor. They assumed that he would perform the role in the actual production. Baker and Noto accepted the fact as well— but the decision wasn't quite that simple.

Jones was not a member of Actors Equity Association, the

actors' union, and therefore risked pickets by performing the role. But in 1959, the rules governing Off-Broadway were still liquid enough to allow a compromise. The union agreed that as long as the production paid eight actors, all would be square. The non-union Jones would be permitted to play the part as long as a ninth, union, actor were placed on the payroll.

Noto agreed, but it was not in his nature to pay somebody to put his feet up. He asked Jones to figure out a way to add another part to *The Fantasticks* and give the new actor something to do. Jones responded by creating the role of the Handyman, whose job eventually would consist of coming out during intermission, setting up a ladder and changing gels, the thin squares of tinted plastic clipped to the front of the lamps to give the lighting designer a palette of colored light.

To play the minimal role, Jones and Schmidt urged Noto to hire Jay Hampton, a classmate of theirs from the University of Texas, who had been saluted by Margo Jones as the best actor in Texas back in 1950, and who had worked on Broadway and in Hollywood. Hampton proved to be handy in another way as well. During the first months of the run, Hampton (and for a short time, actor Laurence Luckinbill) would serve as general understudy for the male roles.

Jones wound up playing the Old Actor until autumn 1960. Nevertheless, Hampton's Handyman role continued to exist until 1961, after which Hampton assumed one of the speaking parts, and the Handyman was eliminated. Hampton went on to play all the male roles in the show.

Partly to keep a low profile vis-à-vis the union, partly to downplay the incestuousness of an author on stage—and partly just to have some fun—Jones decided to play the part under an assumed name. He used his first full name and appended the name of a cousin. When the *Playgram* programme went to press, one "Thomas Bruce" was listed as playing the Old Actor. Alert playgoers could have noticed that there was no separate listing for him in the "Who's Who in the Cast" section.

Meanwhile, something had to be done about the Sullivan Street Playhouse, which Schmidt described as "a shambles." The upstairs room still had residue of its speakeasy days: an ugly banquette running around three walls and garish mirrored ceilings. All that came out. To fill the suddenly empty and dingy space, Jones and Schmidt convinced their roommate Robert Alan Gold, co-owner of the theater, to display his student paintings of Mexico City there. Many rehearsals were held in this room, which later became the *Fantasticks* museum, and Gold's paintings are visible in rehearsal photos.

A far worse mess had to be dealt with in the performing space itself. The refrigerator that had been left onstage from *The Goose* loomed pungently. "God knows how long it had been sitting there," George Curley remembers thinking on the cast's first day in the theater. "Somebody opened the door and— phew! They'd left the food in there. Boom! We slammed that door."

For the time being, then, rehearsals were confined to the 74th Street apartment and the second floor lounge at Sullivan Street while cleaning and renovation of the auditorium was carried out by carpenter Richard Thayer under the supervision of production stage manager Geoffry Brown. Thayer improved sight lines by reinstalling the seats on plywood risers. There also was the problem of the prominent pipes on the north wall behind the stage. Noto almost had these removed until it was discovered that they were attached to the boiler in the neighboring hotel and had the effect of delivering free heat to the playhouse. Noto decided the pipes would stay.

Before Thayer could install the wooden *commedia* platform, the stage itself had to be rebuilt. The linoleum floor was torn up and replaced with plywood, which seemed to be an improvement until Baker noticed that it squeaked. The creaky floor was a factor in *The Fantasticks* for several years until it was relaid in the late 1960s.

The problem might have been fixed sooner if Thayer hadn't covered the plywood with white ceramic tiles. For a week or so, Curley recalls, Thayer or Brown invited actors rehearsing in the lounge to spend their free time downstairs, standing on freshly-glued tiles, to help them set properly.

Superficial repairs also were made to the dressing rooms and lobby area, particularly the concession stand, but the backstage areas remained spartan for many years.

11

March–April 1960

*"Don't forget, Mortimer — dress the stage,
dress the stage."*

Most musicals have a music director, a conductor, an orchestrator/arranger and a rehearsal pianist. For *The Fantasticks,* all four jobs were telescoped into one and handed over to Julian Stein, who also would serve as half the orchestra.

Born in New Haven, Connecticut, and introduced to touring musicals at that city's legendary Shubert Theatre, Stein nevertheless headed into a career as a classical pianist and composer. He earned his B.A. from Yale, his M.A. from Columbia, and did further graduate work at the Paris Conservatory before returning to the States in the early 1950s and launching a concert tour under the auspices of Community Concerts, a division of Columbia Concerts.

Unhappy with life on the road, he settled in New York, taking a job as staff musician for ABC, then becoming musical director for a dance company organized by José Limon and Doris Humphrey.

In 1954, he got his first job on Broadway, playing piano in the orchestra of *The Golden Apple.* "I fell in love with the theater," said Stein, who went on to work on other shows, including *The Teahouse of the August Moon* and a revival of Cole Porter's

Anything Goes, sometimes just playing in the pit, sometimes orchestrating. Between legitimate stage ventures, he worked at nightclubs and in industrial shows for companies including Kodak, Nabisco and General Motors.

He married dancer Tao Strong and composed music for her troupe, the Tao Strong Dance Company, in the one-room loft apartment they shared on West 10th Street in the Village. One corner was designated the kitchen; the rest was wide open except for his piano, so he could play as she danced.

There was a tenuous connection between Stein and Lore Noto: Noto had invested some money in *The Golden Apple* and was acquainted with Stein's work. But Stein was only one of several musical directors interviewed for the *Fantasticks* job. Another was Jack Lee, who went on to conduct many musicals, including *Sweet Charity, My One and Only* and *Grand Hotel.* Most were people like Jones and Schmidt, who had come out of the club scene, or Word Baker's acquaintances from Off-Broadway.

Because the musical director would need to be as proficient a pianist as a director, Stein auditioned for the job by playing for Baker and Schmidt. Although Schmidt's score already had been transcribed by Ben Pickering, Schmidt envisioned a two-piano version accompanying the show, and he would need an arranger who would be flexible enough to help create that while working alongside a composer who could neither read nor write music.

Stein was intrigued by the miniature size of the show—a musical comedy on nightclub scale—but really began to covet the job after he heard Schmidt play the one-piano version of the score.

Stein's first suggestion, and one that had a profound impact on the way the show sounds, was to forget about the second piano and use a harp instead.

"When Harvey played the score for me the first time, there were a lot of harplike configurations—arpeggios, glissandos, things like that. A harp was suited to the whole sound of the score and the size of the show, the color of it. I had read the script, and the lightness of it, too, suggested the instrument. The harp just leaped out at me like a light bulb going on."

Jones said he was torn between Lee and Stein until Stein came to him with the harp idea. "I had wanted to use two pianos," Schmidt said, "because I love two pianos and I think they imply an orchestra when you don't have one. But I felt the harp was such a brilliant and right idea. It never would have occurred to me, but I love harps too, and it's dead right for the show. So that's what made me decide to go with Julian, and I never regretted it. It was an enormous contribution."

The harp is one of the distinctive components of *The Fantasticks*, providing the ornamentation and richness that Schmidt hoped to capture with duo pianos, but giving the musical a classical ethereality that matched the script. Also, in performance, it's fascinating to watch.

Nevertheless, Stein was unable to begin work on his harp-piano arrangement for several weeks.

"Learning to play the show was like learning a concerto," Stein said. "You would fake your way through most shows I'd played, to maximum effect. *The Fantasticks*, I had to learn note for note, like a Beethoven sonata. You can't improvise. I found that intensely difficult. Poor Harvey had to play rehearsals for a long time while I was learning the score. He'd been playing most of it for years and years and had it down pretty well. It took me several weeks before I'd try anything."

Stein's sincere admiration for the score caused him to suggest few changes in Schmidt's underlying ideas or effects. When those suggestions came, Schmidt's admiration for the harp suggestion enabled him to trust Stein's instincts. Though they sometimes disagreed on tempos—Stein tending to slow things down and Schmidt to snap them along more quickly— their collaboration interlocked smoothly. As a result, Stein's fingerprints are evident throughout the score, yet there is nothing that was not rooted in either Baker's overall concept or Schmidt's piano style.

In the disillusioned Act II opener, "This Plum Is Too Ripe," Stein suggested that the mood of tension could be heightened by moving up a half-step every sixteen bars. This unsettling trick complements Schmidt's effect at the song's outset, in which a pair of dissonant chords mirror the "Sorrys" used to illustrate the characters' newfound annoyance with one another.

Schmidt trusted his musical director enough to let him tamper with "Try to Remember," which up to this point was a solo for El Gallo. Stein pointed out that the rest of the cast might be introduced subtly by using them as a chorus before the second verse and in the bridge. Instead of singing "Follow follow follow" himself, El Gallo sings the word once, then hears it echoed first by Luisa, then Matt, then the Fathers, before the song changes key for the last verse. Stein said he wanted the song to build to a dramatic point more cleanly, then ebb.

Once Stein felt completely comfortable with every corner of the score, he began auditioning harpists. It was his plan to work directly with the harpist, improvising and experimenting until he achieved the effects he wanted.

The "community" of professional harpists in New York was small but well organized and mutually supportive. Word of new job opportunities would spread quickly, and if one harpist couldn't take a gig, he or she would have a half-dozen friends to recommend. Stein's inquiries quickly led him to the Bronx-born Beverly Mann (now Beverly Statter), a music teacher on West 93rd Street, who occasionally played small clubs, restaurants and hotels, or private parties. She had attended the High School of Music and Art and earned a degree in music from The Juilliard School. She was proficient in harp, though her primary instrument was piano.

Mann never had performed in professional musical theater. Ironically, her theater experience was limited to a college production of another Rostand play, *Cyrano de Bergerac*.

Her teaching load was unusually light that spring, so she jumped at the chance to play *The Fantasticks*, not only for the union minimum of about $100 a week (more than twice what the actors were getting) but for the fun of seizing an opportunity to stretch and do something new.

She was hired over the telephone. A few days later, her apartment buzzer rang. "I opened the door, and I saw a pile of music almost as high as my head. Looking further, I saw there were legs under it. It was Julian. He came in and said 'Let's see what a harp can do.' He didn't know, and I didn't know; we were groping around. We began by trying random passages and experimenting. That was the beginning."

She did have some initial reservations: "When I saw the music," Mann said, "I opened a page at random, and it said, 'Plant a radish, get a radish,' and I thought, 'That's lyrics?' So I told myself, 'Well, I'll get two weeks of work out of it.' That was exactly my reaction to the whole idea."

As an indication of how long it took Stein to learn the piano part, and under how much pressure the score was arranged, Mann first laid eyes on Stein on April 11, 1960, just twelve days before the first preview and about three weeks before the opening night.

"Julian once said to me, 'Let's use this next thirty seconds'— he meant that literally—'to work out this passage.' He wasn't needed for thirty seconds elsewhere, so he decided to use that to work with the harpist."

Still, they got a lot done in that short time.

Part of the folklore of *The Fantasticks*—especially among harpists, as might be expected—is that Mann wrote the harp part herself. "That's not accurate," she said. "What happened was that Julian would say things like 'Play eighth notes in this passage' or 'Play chords over there'; 'Play the melody here' or 'Play the part as originally written for the piano in this spot'; and I would supply the actual notes that fit under the hand of the harpist, or at least under *my* hand. So it was a collaboration in that sense."

Stein and Mann did much of their work at her apartment, though Baker and Schmidt urged them to get down to Sullivan Street as quickly as possible. Stein would play the bare piano part at rehearsals, experimenting with different effects under Baker's direction, then he'd scoot uptown to continue developing the harp part with Mann.

"I had never written so specifically for harp," he said. "Usually you can just indicate a gliss' or an arpeggio. Mostly you use a harp to sweep up to an accent, so I expanded on that. I sat with her for days, saying 'Try this, try that. Let's see what this sounds like.' "

In many cases, the harp indeed is used in this way, shimmering and surging its way through the score. But Stein used it even more abstractly during Jones's flights of poetry. The original cast album includes several brief examples of these, though one entire spoken passage, "You Wonder How These Things Begin," was recorded like a song, largely to preserve the sparkle of Mann's harp.

Though clearly indicated in Schmidt's original piano score, the lush, wistful passage was transferred to harp because the angelic instrument "evokes so much more poetic effect," Stein said.

Hampering the process was the fact that Schmidt's score had been copied onto a slick paper that did not take either pencil or pen. As a result, Mann was forced to memorize her entire part Schmidt-style, or indicate it in words, e.g., "play two octaves higher than written," scribbled on scraps of paper. For most of the first year's run, she was the only one who knew the harp part. She would have to teach her successor from memory, but she eventually transcribed it for posterity.

In the meantime, Stein was watching rehearsals and doing his best to integrate his arrangements with Baker's staging. As with the acting, Baker was editor to improvisation, letting his musicians follow their heads but steering them where necessary. For his part, Stein tried to invent musical effects that would underline or affirm the emotional points Baker was trying to make. "The confetti, the streamers and all the props contributed a great deal, in the way of inspiration," Stein said.

For the moonlit Act I glen scene, in which Matt and Luisa sing "Soon It's Gonna Rain," the orchestrations indicate a dreamy nocturne with the piano, or the patter of raindrops with the harp. In the opening of Act II, El Gallo reverses the plywood crescent moon to reveal a bright yellow sun, accompanied by a flourish which Stein promptly handed to Mann. "The music was there," he said. "I adjusted the dynamics to match the flareup. But without seeing the lights (designed by Ed Wittstein), I never would have conceived of doing that."

Just before previews began, disaster nearly struck. A new union contract provided a raise for Off-Broadway musicians. Stein remembers a glum Lore Noto coming to him and explaining gently that the production could not afford the raise and that Mann would have to be let go.

"I was so in love with the idea of the harp that the idea of reducing it to one piano appalled me," Stein said. Instead, he agreed to pay Mann's salary out of his own wage. "I've always felt in my heart that without that concession on my part, we might not have made it," Stein said.

Why would someone with his experience make such a concession? "It wasn't just a job," he said. "I liked the show, I liked all the people, I wanted it to succeed."

It wasn't until April 20, three days before the first preview, that Mann came down to Sullivan Street and began to work in concert with the actors. The show was being polished rapidly now, but a few adjustments still had to be made.

For one, Stein had to get used to playing piano in the narrow space between the piano and the theater's north wall. Because the piano is built into the stage (the Mute stands on it during the glen sequence) and because the stage couldn't be pushed very close to the seats, something had to give—and it was Stein's arm room. The space between the stone wall and the keyboard was a fraction less than his arm from elbow to fingertip. Also, because the theater space is below ground level, there was earth behind the wall at Stein's back. Pipes from the neighboring hotel ran along the top of the wall and helped deliver heat to the theater, but the section of wall behind Stein was chilly in summer and almost unbearably icy in winter. To this day, he blames that wall for bringing on bursitis in his back and shoulder.

During those few brief days working with the actors, several changes were made. Stein urged Nelson and Orbach to pounce on their vocal entrances in "I Can See It." He said, "I wanted them to get the climax at the right time, not building too fast, and saving a little of the volume and intensity for later."

In return, Nelson asked Stein for some changes. In "Metaphor," Stein had asked him not to pause for breath between the lines ". . . microscopic inside of a leaf" and "My joy." Nelson felt it was too much of a calculated effect. Stein capitulated because "for him to feel right about it was more important than the little thing I was after."

Overall, Stein said, "I remember spending a lot of time trying to get a certain intensity, but soft: that's when the volume is down, but you're still having it very fiery. That's a difficult thing to get, because when singers go soft they tend to relax, and it sort of goes into crooning. I remember telling them about the intensity of a whisper—how a whisper can be very intense, but very soft. I did a lot of work on words, too. Good singers tend to go for melody. I persuaded them that they had an acting opportunity while they were singing these songs, and that that opportunity comes from the words."

The Greenwich Village neighborhood was a familiar one for another of the *Fantasticks* team as well: designer Ed Wittstein. Schmidt had remembered Wittstein from his days at NBC, a time when the designer lived in an apartment on Bleecker Street at McDougal Street, just around the corner and down one block from the Sullivan Street Playhouse. It was one of the most famous intersections in the Village, with landmark watering holes on three of its corners: Cafe Borgia on the northeast, Figaro Cafe on the southeast and, most famous of all, the Beat hangout San Remo on the northwest.

"It was like a cafe in Paris," said Wittstein, who recalls the bar as a place where the original Italian neighborhood people mingled with poets, playwrights, musicians and theater people like Wittstein who had colonized the area. He remembers meeting Edward Albee there and singer Jimmy Ray.

Though it was not primarily a gay bar in the sense they've come to be known, the San Remo was one of the few places where gays were not just tolerated but accepted and treated as just folks. It was an open and tolerant headquarters for a tolerant enclave in an otherwise repressive time. Wittstein and his companion, Bob Miller, felt at home there. "People just sat around and drank and talked," he said.

Though he had lived above a liquor store just a half-block east at 178 Bleecker, Wittstein rarely had time to go. As in the mid 1950s when he had worked beside Schmidt designing at NBC and later at Upstairs at the Downstairs, he still worked sixteen-hour days, putting in a full day at NBC working on *The Steve Allen Show*, then sitting down to do sketches for an opera, a stage show or a club act. Schmidt visited him at NBC and convinced him to put *The Fantasticks* on his roster.

Owing to the size of the show, Wittstein agreed to serve as costumer, set designer, prop master and lighting designer, four jobs for which he would receive a total of $480, plus $24.48 a week. As of summer 1990, Wittstein said his $24.48 was still coming in the mail, as regular as clockwork.

"I'd done a lot of good Off-Broadway stuff in my career, and in some rather small spaces," he said. "I always enjoyed the challenge."

Wittstein sat down with Baker, Jones and Schmidt and discussed the intentions of the show: it's *commedia dell'arte* overtones, the open-stage concept, its imagery of gardens, of seasons, of day and night and above all, its simplicity. He reviewed some simple sketches Schmidt had made to help sell the show at backer auditions. Owing to his background as a designer and as Jo Mielziner's assistant, Baker said he took special interest in the show's look.

Wittstein began by making sketches, dozens of them and quickly, experimenting with different looks, different styles. Though many later were modified or changed completely, these early dashed-off sketches capture the mood of the eventual show: stylized but anchored in reality; *commedia*-like but clearly American. Compared to Charles Lane's (Blackburn's) designs for Barnard, Wittstein's costumes were less self-consciously whimsical, and his sets were slightly more deliberately designed.

Sets

Wittstein had a total of $900 to spend on the set, so, like Blackburn, he decided to forego the traveling players' wagon (à la *Cavalleria Rusticana*) that Jones's script called for. (*Variety* reported in June 1990 that big musicals typically spent $1–2 million on sets and props and nearly as much on costumes.) In the course of his sketch pad experiments, he designed a raised stationary platform anchored by six poles, with a piano built into the back on which the Mute could sit or stand. This minimalist performing "frame" was a stylized evolution of Blackburn's bare stage at Barnard, but it also was a vestigial version of B. Iden Payne's beloved Elizabethan open abstract playing space. His design called for simple pine or spruce roofing planks. Wittstein helped carpenter Richard Thayer nail them together and anchor them, with steel pipes for the surrounding poles.

There was a practical as well as an esthetic reason for the sturdy and unadorned little platform. "I wanted the scenery to last forever," Baker said, "because I had seen several Off-Broadway productions that had gotten good notices and run a long time but became very tatty because there was no money for maintaining or reproducing. Our theory was that the pipes and the boards would last."

What came next proved to be the single most pervasive design element in *The Fantasticks*, and, coincidentally, one which also had its origin in Shakespeare, though it traveled a far less philosophical route into the show.

Wittstein, too, had worked at Barnard the previous season, doing a student production of *Pericles* that included a navy with billowing sails of white China silk. Wittstein had become so enamored of the cloth that he used it throughout the production for drapes, dressings and anything else he could think of. *Pericles* was awash in yards and yards of brightly colored raw China silk, and when it closed, Wittstein arranged to take the cloth with him, thinking it might someday come in handy.

That someday arrived in spring of 1960. Because the audience surrounded the Sullivan Street stage on three sides, there would be no way to raise and lower a curtain in the traditional sense. But since part of Baker and Jones's concept was a Strehler-like actor's troupe, Wittstein decided to hang a small false curtain across the wooden platform. Trying to save pennies any way he could, Wittstein pulled out mighty Pericles's white China silk sail and cut a piece just big enough to stretch between the two center poles.

The effect delighted everyone, and Wittstein realized he'd found a textural theme for the show. "*Pericles* was hung in sea colors—greens and blues," he said, "so I dragged all this China silk downtown and began to cut it up."

The shredded greens and blues are most obvious in the glen sequence, when Matt and Luisa sing "Soon It's Gonna Rain" in front of a drop consisting of shreds of silk, to suggest mysterious undergrowth. But Wittstein soon found plenty of other uses: El Gallo's flamboyant cravat, Luisa's shawl (later replaced with chiffon), Henry and Mortimer's scourges in "Round and Round," the piece of cloth the Mute folds and refolds to suggest his rebuilding of the wall. A thin strip of red serves even for the ribbon Luisa ties around her wrist, to mark the spot where El Gallo seizes her and leaves a tiny bruise.

Wittstein's recycled Shakespearian curtains also helped enhance the magical prop box. He stapled rags of China silk to the inside of the lid to give an impression, when opened, of being loaded with tattered but brightly-colored old costumes. The secret entrance was covered with a curtain of black silk, and a final hunk of silk was hung across the passage at stage right that leads to the dressing rooms. Henry and Mortimer would crawl behind this low barrier during Act I when they'd enter the prop box.

One prominent piece of China silk vanished in a happy accident. Hoping to eliminate the ladder Blackburn had used to suggest the all-important wall, Wittstein decided to let the Mute create a wall by simply standing and holding up a silk banner on a dowel. Baker already had instructed him to use dowels to suggest swords in the Rape scene. Wittstein designed the banner to be light enough for the Mute to hold in his outstretched hand for minutes at a time, yet be able to slip easily on and off the dowel.

Baker invited director Michael Kahn (later artistic director of The Acting Company) and some potential backers to a run-through of the show in the Sullivan Street lounge. The cast was a little nervous, having incorporated some of the staging relatively recently, but Baker told them to relax. If mistakes occurred, they were simply to ignore them and keep going.

Sure enough, when the moment came for Blair Stauffer to pull out the dowel and banner for the wall, the silk accidentally slipped off. The stoic and obedient Stauffer played the scene holding up a bare dowel. "It was just a matter of concentration," Stauffer said. "You feel responsible somehow. You think, it wasn't your fault that it wasn't there. But after all, it is *supposed* to be there, so maybe if you think real hard and look like you're not there, nobody will notice that the wall isn't there, that the drape isn't there. It's all make-believe anyway."

So it was. Afterward, some audience members commented to Baker that the dowel-wall was a stroke of genius. True to form, Baker contentedly told Stauffer to bag the silk banner and incorporate the bare dowel permanently.

This blooper remains one of the show's most charming and *useful* effects, since it neatly solves the problem of the play's most important prop cutting the stage in two and blocking views from the sides of the theater.

The loss of the banner may have been a timely one. George Curley remembers Jones and Baker having an argument over Wittstein's design choices, with Jones's side consisting primarily of: "I didn't write a show about China silk!" Baker relented and decided enough was enough. The silk is pervasive in the show but doesn't draw undue attention.

To complete the stage's meager scenery, Wittstein designed and built a low bench for El Gallo to stand on while singing "Rape," and he bought a ladder-back chair at an unfinished furniture store.

And one last item—one moon. Schmidt cut a disk of cardboard, painting one side bright yellow and the other side black with a crescent of white. This moon was frail and apt to fray, so Schmidt made another, this time out of plywood. With a hole drilled near the top edge, it was hung by a nail from one of the poles.

Costumes

Wittstein and Noto batted estimates back and forth and came up with a costume budget of $541, which, at a little over three percent of the capitalization, was low even for a project the size of *The Fantasticks*.

Wittstein was undeterred. He had a plan. As a costume designer for NBC, he often had hunted down obscure items of clothing for various productions and had paid for them himself, figuring it would all work out in the end. As a result, he came to think of the NBC costume shops as extensions of his own closets. Many of the original props and accessories for *The Fantasticks* were dug by Wittstein out of NBC's archives. These include El Gallo's gaucho hat, the fathers' mufflers, Luisa's paste necklace and other items.

He borrowed just as liberally from his own household. The Mute's stovepipe hat was a genuine, Lincoln-era antique discovered by Wittstein in a shop in Pennsylvania's Bucks County, on one of his earlier prop-hunting jaunts. He had given it as a gift to his friend Bob Miller, but took it back to give the Mute a jaunty but somehow eldritch look. Children's author Dr. Seuss gave a similar hat to the Cat in *The Cat in the Hat*, to similar effect. The Mute's eventually fell apart and had to be replaced with a reinforced copy.

Wittstein began by sketching Henry and Mortimer with capes and hats but eventually settled on a seemingly odd choice—sneakers and tinted thermal underwear—which wound up suiting the play-within-a-play concept, since, like paper dolls, the Old Actors could then be dressed in any other costume that seemed appropriate to the moment, whether bald-wigged thespian, Indian, brigand or devil.

For Henry's comically threadbare Shakespearian doublet, Wittstein went to Louis Guttenberg's Sons, a costume rental shop at 12 West 45th Street that specialized in leasing whole operas-worth of period costumes to second-class opera companies and stock theaters around the country. It had been doing so for many decades and would offer worn pieces for sale cheap. With the NBC operas to outfit, Wittstein had become a steady customer and had gotten to know this "wonderful attic of ancient costumes" very well. He picked the gaudiest and most timeworn war veteran he could find and, with some creative augmentation of its tatters, transformed the old *shmatte* into something strangely beautiful under light. The same one was still being used at Sullivan Street thirty years later, largely because the more ragged it gets, the funnier it gets.

Wittstein returned to Guttenberg's more than once, particularly on the fathers' and Old Actors' costumes. For less idiosyncratic things, he turned to the Village Squire, a men's haberdasher at 59 West 8th Street.

But time was short. Most of the costumes were designed in March or April (at least one was registered with the union on April 11, less than two weeks before the first preview). Working with an assistant, James Bidgood, and seamstresses Susan Sweetzer and Anthea Giannakouros, he designed and executed Luisa's dress, based on Degas bronzes of dancers in tulle skirts. Wittstein's was executed in a white and yellow gingham plaid with a princess cut and a dropped waist. He put her in white stockings and white shoes to help the delicate but thirtyish Gardner look more like Luisa's age—sixteen.

To emphasize the link between Luisa and Matt, Wittstein

gave them the same color scheme, yellow and white, with Matt wearing a clown's athletic shirt under his bourgeois street clothes. Nelson also had a nubbly sweater knitted for him. It was so striking that he once was stopped on the street by a passerby who had seen him in the show. But instead of complimenting his performance, the buttonholer wanted to know where he'd gotten the sweater.

Realizing that the rest of the cast comes in pairs, Wittstein color-coded them the same way as he had the two lovers: the fathers are done in variations on brown; the Old Actors are in pastel shades, lavender for Henry, peach for Mortimer; the fourth-wall-breaking narrators El Gallo and the Mute are in black. All the characters wear headgear of some kind except the two lovers.

Another designer might have felt straitjacketed by a $541 estimated budget for eight costumes (nine when the role of the Handyman was added), but not Wittstein. His total actual costs came to $309.57.

For several very hectic weeks, Wittstein remembers arriving at the theater after dinner, working until after midnight, then getting four or five hours sleep before dragging himself out of bed to be at NBC by 8:00 A.M. "I was so busy living my life, I couldn't be bohemian; I couldn't be anything. I was just designing and doing extra projects. I was very serious."

Lighting

With just weeks left to go, Wittstein turned to lighting the show. Today's Broadway extravaganzas can use up to a thousand computer-coordinated lamps with dimmers, color wheels, strobes, lasers and other special effects. To illuminate the tiny Sullivan Street Playhouse, Wittstein used forty rented lamps whose gels had to be changed at intermission by the stage manager (later the Handyman) on a ladder.

"In that small space, I could do with one light what they need twenty lights to do," Wittstein said.

"Also," he said, "I think an awful lot of theater is overlit. I've always loved to see shows from backstage—it's so beautiful. You get these edges of lights, backlights, and sometimes a face is in shadow. But I believe that you don't have to see everything all the time."

That philosophy enabled him to make a virtue of necessity in *The Fantasticks*. With audiences on both sides of the stage, some would be facing into the lights on the other side. "One person on stage left of the house will see a character fully lit while the people across the way only see them as a silhouette surrounded by a glow. *The Fantasticks* is lit like that partially because we didn't have the equipment, but partially because I thought it was beautiful. And it is beautiful. We have one light coming down the aisle [for when Matt leaves on his adventure]. When The Boy turns and looks back, he's wonderfully lit" whether you see him from in front or behind.

By 1960, Wittstein had moved to East 82nd Street near Madison Avenue. *The Fantasticks* gave him an opportunity to reestablish his ties to the Village. Each day, he'd pass the fruit peddlers lined up on Bleecker Street or drop into the San Remo or Minetta Tavern for good southern Italian food, which was a chic cuisine in the age of meatloaf: pastas with tomato sauce, scallopini, white clam sauce, rum cake and custards.

*   *   *

Though all the artistic elements of the show were falling together, one crucial component was not: financing. Throughout the rehearsal period, Jones and Schmidt continued to play backer's auditions and continued to sell fragments of the show in $55 to $330 increments. Even set builder Rick Thayer bought shares. But by late March, the show was still short more than $7,000 of its $16,500 cost. Jones and Schmidt were happy to negotiate an extension of Noto's option, and the new opening was set for May 3.

That just gave him a little more time to be desperate. Noto began hitting up the members of the production to invest in it. Among those who bought shares were Kenneth Nelson and Ed Wittstein. Nelson bought one percent, Wittstein two. But both could have afforded more, and both said they have spent the ensuing three decades kicking themselves for not buying more.

But they didn't, and with less than six weeks to go before the planned opening, *The Fantasticks* was far short of the total needed to pay its bills.

"I went through every dime of my savings," Noto would tell *The New York Times.* "When we went into rehearsal I had no money and no income."

As producer, Noto already owned 50 percent of the show. Reluctantly, he withdrew his hoarded $3,300 from the bank and bought an additional 10 percent, figuring he could sell off this extra as new investors came along. But that still left the show $4,000 in the hole. A more cautious producer might have suspended operations, but Noto was absurdly confident that the cash would come from somewhere.

And sure enough, it did.

Sheldon Miles Baron read a squib in the trade newspaper *Show Business* mentioning Noto's name and saying he was preparing a show for Off-Broadway. "It didn't say anything about auditions," Baron said, "but that doesn't mean anything to an actor. An actor grasps at any straws. I immediately called Lore and said, 'I'm Sheldon Miles Baron. I'd like to audition.'

"He said, 'Audition! I don't even have the money for this thing!'

"I said, 'Oh. Well. As it happens, I'm also a producer. My partner and I have a summer theater.' "

He was referring to the Saranac Lake Comedy and Mystery Theater, an upstate New York stock company, which he had run since 1955 with Dorothy Olim, a friend from his days at Columbia University's School of Dramatic Arts, and Richard Edelman. Olim later would become president of ATPAM, the press agents and managers union, and Baron would give up theater for sculpting under the name S. Miles Baron. But in spring of 1960, he was Shelly Baron, the actor, who had family money to invest in ventures like upstate stock companies and struggling Off-Broadway musicals.

"Mr. Big Shot," Baron calls himself. "Big Shot had a cockamamie summer theater, and all of a sudden, I was this big time producer. So I went to see it [*The Fantasticks*] at Schmidt's apartment, and all of a sudden, I was in love with it. It was so simple, so pretty, so gentle. . . . And a point comes where something strikes you, and you say, 'Oh yes, this I like.' "

As Olim remembers it, "One day, I got a phone call from Shelly, and he said, 'Listen, I just heard this marvelous musical. I think we should get involved in it.' At that time, we thought of ourselves as managers and producers. 'They need $4,000 to complete the banking.'

"I said, 'Four thousand dollars!? What's the deal?'

"He said, 'Let's go listen to it.' So we went over to Harvey's apartment, and they played the score for us. I have a tendency to listen to scores very coldly. Harvey was, at that time, not a master piano technician, not in my estimation anyway. He played very simply. At the end, they turned to us, very excited, and said, 'What do you think?' I said, 'We'll let you know.' We walked out of the brownstone, and I turned to Shelly and said, 'What kind of score is that? Plunk plunk plunk plunk—it doesn't have any melody to it.'

"He said, 'It's the way he's playing it.'

"I said, 'It's really simple. "Try to Remember"? "Deep in December"? What kind of sophisticated rhyme is that?'

"And he said, 'Trust me, it's terrific.'

"I said, 'And, God, it's got rape—who's going to buy that?'

"He said, 'Trust me, it'll sell.' "

Part of the chemistry of collaboration is trusting your partner's instincts. In this case, Olim remembers, she decided to lean on Baron's judgement: "I said, 'Listen, you want to do it? OK.' "

Baron explained, "I've learned this as a sculptor: either I'm right or I'm dead. When you're doing something creative, you either have right vision or get out. A lot of people will tell you 'You can't do this and you can't do that.' But that's bullshit, because the dreamers always win out in the end. So I'll go out on a limb. So maybe it will snap off under me, but maybe not."

In return for completing financing on *The Fantasticks*, Olim and Baron negotiated for billing and became associate producers. "I don't think Lore wanted to do it," Olim said, "but he realized he had to get four grand and there was no other choice. Part of the arrangement was that we could say whatever we wanted to say, but his word was final."

With the financing in place, the show was at last ready to begin tooting its own horn. To do that, it needed a press agent to handle theatrical reporters and critics, and it needed an advertising agency.

For both delicate jobs, members of the creative team turned

to people they'd worked with before and trusted.

In 1990, one advertising agency handled most Broadway advertising: Serino Coyne Inc. In 1960, another company had an even more powerful clamp on that position, the Blaine Thompson Agency. For all practical purposes, there was no one else to go to, and Noto didn't. But Schmidt urged him to seek out one of the brighter associates there, Fred Golden. He had hired Schmidt from time to time to do sketch work, and now Schmidt was in a position to return the favor.

Noto visited Golden in his office in the Sardi building at 234 West 44th Street. "Lore came up and told me, 'Harvey said you're the only one to handle this,' " Golden said. "Lore was a very nice guy. I liked him very much. He had very little money to spend, but we figured, OK, fine, the show will become a big hit and he'll spend more money."

In those days, there were few radio ads for Broadway and none on TV. Advertising a show consisted mainly of ABC listings in the daily newspapers, maybe a display ad with quotes in the *Herald Tribune* or *New York Times* and possibly posters in railway stations. Golden later founded his own agency, The Golden Group, which handled *Driving Miss Daisy* and the Los Angeles company of the musical *The Phantom of the Opera*.

For a man used to advertising the top talent and most glittering extravaganzas on Broadway, Golden took on the tiny show as much to continue his relationship with Schmidt as to make money. As far as he knew, the show was a hobby being indulged by a commercial artist. Golden came to see it. His first impression? "I liked it, let's put it that way. If someone had told me then it would run thirty years, I don't know . . ."

More closely involved with the show would be the press agent. Their choice was David Powers, who had worked with both Lore Noto and Word Baker. When he was just starting out in the business, Powers had worked at the same New Jersey stock company that had employed Baker as designer and Jerry Orbach as scenery painter. Later, when he began working in Manhattan for legendary press agent Harvey Sabinson (later a partner in Solters, Sabinson and Roskin), Powers had helped promote David Ross's Fourth Street Theatre, where Noto did

The Failures.

"I like working with Lore because he is a wholly complete original," Powers said. "Lore is capable of astonishing feats."

In order to begin designing ads and posters, Golden needed a symbol for the show, a logo. Ordinarily he would farm out such a task to a commercial artist, but Schmidt volunteered to handle that delicate task himself. As he always did, Schmidt ordered several typefaces from a printing shop, but he found that few of them captured precisely the right mood of the show.

After he eliminated those he didn't like, only four were left. He incorporated them into poster designs with illustrations of a boy and a girl in various poses. "But I didn't think four [designs] was enough," Schmidt said. "I always like to give a variety of choices, and five seemed like a better number."

As he was about to go out the door to show the logos down at Sullivan Street, and just to provide that one extra choice, Schmidt took pen in hand and in purple ink scrawled the play's title in his idiosyncratically spiky handwriting.

There's nothing particularly festive about the result; in fact, at first glance, it's a little hard to read if you don't already know what you're looking at. But in a subtle way, it suits the show well. It looks like precisely what it is: something scrawled quickly. But by whom? Perhaps by the barker of an itinerant troupe? While it's obviously handwriting, it's like no other handwriting you've ever seen, so there's a mystery to it. Yet there's nothing slick about it. It doesn't look like it was designed by an ad agency. It's more like a piece of primitive folk art. The F, two T's and the K anchor the word like the poles on Ed Wittstein's little *commedia* platform. Those consonants not only burst above the rest of the letters like outspread arms, but they stretch below them like roots.

"When I lined up the five logos along the upstairs banquette to show to Lore," Schmidt said, "he instantly said 'I like that one,' " pointing to the handwritten logo. "As it turned out, it was perfect for the show."

Wittstein liked it, too, and suggested Schmidt paint it in big letters on the stark white China silk curtain that the audience sees hung across the stage as it takes its seats. The logo's artlessness worked even better there, strongly conveying the sense of a just-passing-through *commedia* troupe. Nobody who has entered the Sullivan Street Playhouse and seen that name dancing across the curtain has failed to sense at least the promise that something odd and wonderful was about to transpire behind it.

When Schmidt delivered it to the advertising agency, Golden said he at first tried to talk Schmidt and Noto into "something bolder." Golden said, "I wanted the word to look more like it sounded. When you say something is 'fantastic,' you don't do it lightly or with a thin pen; you take a big brush in hand, and you say 'Fan-*tastic*.' But Harvey said, and he was right, 'Our show isn't like that. It's a light, frothy little musical.' I was looking at it from the viewpoint of advertising. Now, maybe he was right and maybe he wasn't, but who can argue with thirty years?"

The first ads for *The Fantasticks* ran in early April. On April 23, Jones and Schmidt's dream musical was ready to open the doors and invite Off-Broadway inside.

12

April 23–May 3, 1960

"Children! Lovers! Fantasticks!"

W̲ORD BAKER was determined to have the first preview of *The Fantasticks* at midnight.

Rita Gardner said it was more than just a histrionic gesture on Baker's part. True, it let uptown audiences experience a tickle of danger and mystery, descending, as they were, into the depths of after-hours Greenwich Village. But it also showed Baker's savvy about the ways of theater. In an era when theater curtains went up at 8:40 and didn't come down until after 11:00, a late show like the one Baker envisioned would give actors working in other shows enough time to change out of their costumes and wash up before settling in on the other side of the footlights.

"Word said, 'Let's have a midnight show for all the people doing shows on Broadway,' " Gardner said. " 'Invite your friends.' " Baker knew that insider audiences don't sit on their hands.

It paid off. "They just shook the rafters," Orbach said. "They stood and gave us a wild ovation. I could not believe the reaction. I thought the show was going to charm people and that they would leave feeling good and happy and entertained and amused. But I never expected such a spontaneous outburst. Of course that gave everybody a tremendous boost. We

170

left there that night feeling we had a hit. Until then, I don't think anybody really knew except maybe the composer, writers and the producer, who always had great faith in it."

That first preview on April 23, 1960, also helped augment the show's financing in an unexpected way. Earlier that evening, Don Farber, the show's attorney, was attending his wife's birthday party in the Bronx when a call came from Sullivan Street.

"The fire department had come in and found some problem with the number of seats, and could I come to the theater and settle the matter?" Farber said. "I told the crowd I had to go, explaining about the midnight preview. I asked if anybody wanted to come and see this wonderful little show, and quite a few said yes."

Having quaffed a considerable amount of champagne, they were in a party mood. They got sitters for their children, piled into two cars and drove through a pounding rainstorm to lower Manhattan. But by the time Farber had straightened things out with the fire inspector, the champagne had begun to take its toll, and the partygoers promptly fell asleep, napping their way through the show and being awakened only by the clapping and shouting at the curtain call.

"They came out afterward feeling embarrassed that they'd fallen asleep," Farber said, "and to make us feel better, they said 'It's a shame the show's all sold out because we'd love to invest.' They thought because it was a preview it was all sold out. They didn't realize that Lore was still trying to sell that extra 10 percent he'd bought with his life savings. I told them, 'As a matter of fact, we still have a couple of units left!' So, begrudgingly, they bought the shares, figuring they needed a tax loss anyhow."

* * *

The original cast members look back on the ensuing week-and-a-half of previews as a sweet time. Though the first-preview reaction wasn't repeated as strongly, nor were as many seats filled, the actors felt confident that the show would charm the critics on the official opening the following week. They concentrated on perfecting their performances.

For harpist Beverly Mann, it was her first theater audience.

"Watching their collective reaction," she said, "you could tap their wavelength very closely—whether they liked it or not, whether they were cold or warm. That was very interesting to me because I had never really experienced that before."

Although Mann's job, when she wasn't playing, was simply to sit and look composed, George Curley recalls her laughing each night spontaneously in all the right places. "She was a great audience," he said.

The show acquired another set of regular fans as well, three little girls, ages five, seven and nine, who lived next door to the theater. The entrance to the Sullivan Street Playhouse is a step below sidewalk level, a throwback to the days when teamsters walked their horses to the basement blacksmith. Prettied up and surrounded by a brass railing, the recessed area made a little playground for the cute youngsters, who soon were invited inside and adopted by the cast as mascots.

"They got to know all the parts in the play," Kenneth Nelson said. "We came in one afternoon between shows to find them on the stage doing the whole show, playing all the parts."

Though Noto was not one to give tickets away, he allowed the girls to attend performances free whenever there were available seats, which was almost every night at that point. Schmidt recalls, "They'd get all dressed up in pretty dresses with bows in their hair. And they'd sit in one of the empty rows and help fill up the house. They were there just night after night after night."

One week on the boards, and *The Fantasticks* already was doing repeat business. Sort of.

The show they saw continued to change ever so slightly. In front of an audience, any weak spots in a play jump out glaringly. Baker sat in the back during previews and noted what needed to be trimmed. Still, decisions weren't easy. Schmidt said The Boy's speech just before "Metaphor" used to be longer. "There was a wonderful little poetic chunk right at the end when he's getting excited about what he's going to do. It's beautifully written, but it made the speech too long. We cut it, then we missed it and put it back, but then had to cut it again."

Still, the mood was buoyant. As if in answer, rain vanished, and the days started to turn warm. Jones, who had moved back into the 74th Street apartment with Schmidt, would ride to work with him on the West Side subway. They'd get off at the 4th Street station and come up in front of the Waverly Theatre, a cinema that would be immortalized in the *Hair* song "Frank Mills" as the spot where the singer met the title character of that song.

Schmidt and Jones then would walk southeast to where Sixth Avenue intersects Bleecker Street, and they'd head east past the peddlers and coffeehouses. "It was very pleasant being down there at that time of year," said Schmidt. "It was balmy, and we were able to open the windows upstairs" in the second floor lounge. "That's when I started liking the theater."

The first posters for the show appeared, printed in light purple on a black background, with the names of the creative team in white. To continue this theme, Schmidt bought purple and white flowers and planted them in boxes around the railing in front of the theater. "At that time, I just did it to make the theater look a little nicer," he said, "but I wound up doing it for the first ten years or so because I felt, God, we have a show that's running. It was like paying tribute."

But while the actors were confident of the show's success, no one imagined it would run ten months, let alone ten years. Schmidt recalls that even after a winter of hard work, he had no great expectations for *The Fantasticks*. He said he just wanted it to run long enough for his illustrator friends to come see it.

As the old man of the company, George Curley was philosophical. "I'd done years of summer stock and all the openings at the Upstairs at the Downstairs," he said, "so opening night was just another night to me. Everybody was uptight, but I thought, 'What the heck, it'll either go or not go.' "

Fred Golden and David Powers were hard at work banging the drum for the show. Ads started appearing about two weeks before the opening, showing Schmidt's simple logo and listing the credits. Performances were scheduled Tuesday through Friday at 8:40 P.M.; Saturday at 7:30 and 10:30; Sunday at 3:00 and 8:40. Ticket prices Tuesday, Wednesday, Thursday and Sunday evening were $2.90, $3.90 and $4.20. On Friday and Saturday evenings, they scaled upward slightly higher—$2.90,

$3.90 and $4.90. But you could save a buck on the front seats at the Sunday matinee, when the prices were $2.90, $3.45 and $3.90.

There was a flurry of advance publicity on Sunday, May 1, two days before the opening. Nelson and Gardner snuggle bravely as Stauffer sprinkles confetti in their faces in a staged Friedman-Abeles photo that ran on the cover of *The New York Times* drama section. Orbach gestures to a singing Gardner and Nelson in an odd caricature in the *New York Post* amusement section.

The prominent placement in the *Times* probably was due as much to the compositional appeal of the photo as it was to any clairvoyance on the part of the editor. There were no other portents of success. Broadway was occupied with Ethel Merman in *Gypsy*, Carol Burnett in *Once Upon a Mattress*, and long-running hits like *The Music Man, My Fair Lady* and *A Raisin in the Sun*. With competition like that, scarce notice was given to a nine-character musical opening far from Broadway in a basement theater. It caused scarcely a blip on the radar.

The Fantasticks opened May 3, 1960, and again, it was scarcely noticed. A lot of other things were going on that day.

At 2:15 P.M. precisely, sirens blared all over the country in a nationwide civil defense drill. TV and radio stations were handed over to the military in a dress rehearsal for Armageddon. All citizens were required to take cover, but a total of thirty-five were arrested in Manhattan and Brooklyn for defiantly staying on the street. At New York City Hall, twenty-six were arrested for protesting the drill, which they charged would be useless in the event of a real war with the Russians.

The half-hour duck-and-cover exercise didn't seem to deter voters in the Indiana presidential primary held that day. The two winners were Vice President Richard Nixon on the Republican side and Massachusetts Senator John F. Kennedy for the Democrats. It was noted ominously that Nixon managed to outpoll Kennedy overall, some 339,000 votes to 261,000.

There even was other Sullivan Street news that overshadowed *The Fantasticks*. The Pulitzer Prize for drama was bestowed on Jerry Bock and Sheldon Harnick's *Fiorello!*, a musical biography of the fondly-remembered reformist mayor—who happened to have been born two doors from the Playhouse at 177 Sullivan Street. A plaque marked the building until it collapsed November 11, 1987.

Harvey Schmidt paid no mind either to the air raid drill or the Pulitzer. "I was very busy doing opening night gifts for everybody," he said. He painted stars for each of them, each in a different color, and inscribed them "To my favorite new star" followed by their name. He spent the late afternoon putting them in frames, then he wrapped them individually, packed them up and headed downtown.

The Farbers drove in from Long Island, parked, had dinner in the Village. With some late spring light still in the clear sky, they strolled over to the theater.

Fred Golden's ad for *The Fantasticks* that ran in the *Times* that day contained a typo. It said "Opens tonight at" and didn't list the time.

The time was 7:30 P.M. It was earlier than usual so the critics for the morning papers would have time to get back to their offices and write their reviews before deadline.

There were a half-dozen major dailies in New York at that time, each with its own critic, but the two most important were Walter Kerr on the *Herald Tribune* and Brooks Atkinson at *The New York Times*.

David Powers, whose job it was to greet the critics at the door and escort them inside, noticed that Atkinson and Kerr arrived together in the same limousine. Between them was Kerr's wife, Jean Kerr, perhaps best known for her book, *Please Don't Eat the Daisies*, about the suburban family of a prominent theater critic.

"Brooks Atkinson was a celebrity then," Schmidt said. "It was like when we had Roosevelt for President. We'd had Brook Atkinson for decades as critic, and he was highly thought of by everybody. People took him seriously. When you read his reviews, you felt that you were given the essence of a show. I just loved that he was reviewing our show. Walter Kerr too, although he wasn't as big a presence. I wasn't really afraid. I don't know why. My whole life, whenever I've done something, I'd just do it."

New York Arts magazine reported in 1982 that the front row was occupied by Tom Poston (from Jones's "Movie Matador" days), Dody Goodman (a Julius Monk alumna) and movie doyenne Lillian Gish. Because all one hundred and forty-nine seats were occupied by press, friends and investors, Schmidt had to stand in the back with Powers, Powers's boss Harvey Sabinson and the ushers, though Schmidt does recall his excitement at seeing Gish in person.

Stein and Mann came out and took their places behind the *commedia* platform. As they began to play the overture, *The Fantasticks* began its long run.

Things immediately began to go wrong. Though Jones's eyes were blinded by the stage lights, his actor's instincts told him that something was amiss. Things were too quiet. There was no give-and-take that is the essence of live performance. On the opening night of his dream project, the audience wasn't responding. Unluckily for him, that soon changed.

Stein remembers that one audience member fell asleep shortly after "Try to Remember" and began to snore. Critic Charles McHarry of the *Daily News* was sitting on the side of the theater farthest from the exit door, and his female companion began to complain in a voice clearly audible not only to the cast but to the entire audience.

"She was talking very loudly," Schmidt said, "and started slurring her words, saying, 'I don't understand this show,' maybe five minutes into it."

McHarry tried to help her out, but because of the way the theater is laid out, the only way out is straight across the stage. The first performance of Act I was punctuated by sighs, whines, snores and disparaging commentary. It was impossible for the actors not to be aware of the problem, but they were professionals used to the rigors of the live theater and ignored it.

When intermission at last arrived, Sabinson was waiting. He pulled McHarry aside and asked him to leave. Gentlemanly and apologetic, McHarry complied.

But that wasn't the end of opening night woes. Still standing in the back, Schmidt noticed other things as well: "Jean Kerr took the programme and just ripped off one whole third of the cover where it said *The Fantasticks*. She put her chewing gum in it and rolled it up. I thought to myself, that doesn't look too promising."

Curley remembers an usher coming backstage and reporting

this desecration to the cast, who saw dark significance in it. The rest of the performance was clearly off-kilter.

S. Miles Baron watched his investment with worry. "Something had changed from the backers' audition," he said. "This piece has to be done as simply as it possibly can, and I felt that the simplicity was gone."

His fears seemed to be realized by the tepid curtain calls. "Friends and backers all sat on their hands," Curley said.

* * *

Despite the dismal opening night performance, nearly everyone associated with the show continued to hope for the best, even to expect it. After a subdued gathering backstage, they retired to cars and taxis and reassembled at about 10:00 P.M. in the East 82nd Street apartment of designer Ed Wittstein and Robert Miller. They had volunteered to host the cast party because they had a living room big enough to manage a crowd, while most of the other folks lived in tiny places.

In honor of the Texas contingent, Charles Blackburn made chili con queso. Miller and Word Baker's wife Joanna did the rest, including pimiento and cheese sandwiches (Baker's favorite) plus the more traditional hot dogs and potato salad. There was plenty of beer and hard liquor, which would become a solace as the evening progressed. The party was burgeoning merrily, Schmidt remembers, until about eleven, when Harvey Sabinson called from his office next to the *Times* building to read Atkinson's review hot off the presses. Suddenly things got very quiet, and Word Baker began to repeat the review word-for-word as he was hearing it.

Considering how long the show has run, one might think the reviews were rapturous. They weren't. According to folklore that has grown up around the show, the reviews were disastrous. But that isn't accurate either.

An impartial observer might say the overnight reviews ranged from mildly disapproving to pleasant. None were outright pans, though none were what Broadway calls "money reviews"—reviews so deliriously enthusiastic that they send ticket buyers scampering to the box office.

Atkinson wrote, "Although the story is slight, the style is entrancing in Word Baker's staging. It seems like a harlequinade in the setting of a masque. The characters are figures in a legend acted with an artlessness that is winning. Jerry Orbach, Rita Gardner and Kenneth Nelson. . .sing beautifully and act with spontaneity, not forgetting that they are participating in a work of make-believe."

He also wrote, ". . . the form of a masque seems original in modern theater. Harvey Schmidt's simple melodies with uncomplicated orchestrations are captivating, and the acting is charming. Throughout the first act, *The Fantasticks* is sweet and fresh in a civilized manner."

Other parts of Atkinson's review were not so pleasant. "Although it seems ungrateful to say so, two acts are one too many to sustain the delightful tone of the first. After the intermission, the mood is never quite so luminous and gay. . . . Perhaps *The Fantasticks* is by nature the sort of thing that loses magic the longer it endures. Any sign of effort diminishes it. But for the space of one act, it is delightful."

His wife's chewing gum notwithstanding, Kerr's review went more or less the same way, praising mildly and disparaging mildly. "It is one of the conceits of *The Fantasticks* that the actors who are not occupied in any given scene do not leave the stage but lounge about lazily watching their fellows perform," Kerr began. "I can't say I blame them. A good bit of the performing is well worth watching."

He saluted the performers and said, "The jazz figures that composer Schmidt has insinuated beneath tunes that have the essential flavor of tea roses climbing a trellis help mightily to give the proceedings a contemporary wink."

Kerr ended with the verdict, "It attracts you, settles back a bit limply, wakes you up again and averages out a little less than satisfactory. But some of these people should be seen and listened to."

In the afternoon papers, Frank Aston in the *World-Telegram & Sun* would call it "a musical pip" but proceeded with some left-handed compliments: "It makes sense out of nonsense, sanity out of foolishness. It develops a point of view to the effect that storybook romance is ridiculous but endearing, parents absurd but lovable. . . ."

Under the headline " 'Fantasticks' a Delight," John McClain

of the *Journal American* wrote, "*The Fantasticks* is a bewitching off-Broadway evening, bright and tasteful. It is wonderfully-well suited to the small environs of the Sullivan Street Playhouse and should enjoy a long and lively occupancy."

In each case, the cast was praised in lavish terms, particularly Orbach and Gardner, though Stauffer and Curley were singled out for laurels in some of the notices. The critics were either charmed or annoyed by Jones's libretto, though "Thomas Bruce" made out somewhat better. Schmidt's score seemed to be a favorite, particularly "Try to Remember" and "Plant a Radish." Unaccountably, Larsen and Thomas were scarcely mentioned.

The general feeling seemed to be that the style of the show was fetching but perhaps too precious. That style made the show distinct, but critics weren't sure whether or not they were happy with it.

Despite the many pluses, the minuses fell most heavily on the ears of those at the cast party. Curley believes part of that can be blamed on the person who read them.

"Word read them like death warmed over," Curley said. "I tell you, never in my life would I have Word Baker read any reviews of any play I'm in."

Things scarcely improved when Nelson took over reading. "Poor Kenny," Schmidt said. "They seemed at the time like not-great reviews though they're not bad really."

Gardner concedes the point but observed, " 'Cute' and 'adorable' and 'whimsical' don't [sell tickets]. Three people would be in the audience. We were so upset and flabbergasted. We thought they'd be great reviews. We had so many previews where people were raving and applauding and crying and carrying on that when we read these reviews we went into shock. I've heard the original reviews of *Pal Joey* weren't great either. I guess we were an unusual little show for that time."

Jones still speaks with bitterness about the opening night reviews. Schmidt reports that his partner was "absolutely crushed." Schmidt said, "Tom always thought it was going to be a huge critical success but people wouldn't go to it. Instead, it turned out to be the opposite."

Anyway, Schmidt said, the reviews were bad enough "that

everyone seemed depressed by them. I remember Kenny crying as he read towards the end. It really cast a pall over the party, and it disintegrated shortly thereafter."

With three decades of hindsight, Nelson said, "The reviews were very patronizing, and we read them as if they were death sentences and insults to our mothers. I was enraged. I couldn't believe it. I proceeded to get very drunk, which I don't do and didn't generally do even then. Rita took it very philosophically. She didn't seem to be as disturbed by those reviews as I was."

Stauffer was happier than most, having been highlighted in nearly every review. Brooks Atkinson called him "a mountebank in a top hat," which he later adopted as a catchphrase.

But a few good personal notices were not what would keep a show running. Curley remembers Powers pulling Lore Noto aside and giving him a pep talk about how important it was to help the show find its audience.

Despite some excellent personal notices, Nelson was unswayed. "I stormed out of the party very shortly after that," he said. "I was absolutely blind drunk and walked home crying and yelling the whole time. It's a wonder I wasn't arrested, because I walked down Park Avenue yelling at all those philistine slobs who didn't know what a wonderful show was going on downtown."

For the producers and the authors, there was one more painful duty to perform that night. As Fred Golden describes it, theatrical managements customarily gather at the ad exec's office on opening night to go over the reviews and put together an advertising campaign. Usually, this takes the form of a "quote ad," filled with accolades from the critics, which appears in daily newspapers a day or two after the opening.

Noto took the elevator up to the Blaine Thompson's office above Sardi's restaurant with a contingent including the creators, Jones, Schmidt and Baker; the associate producers Olim and Baron; the publicists Powers and Sabinson; and the Farbers.

"There was a magnum of champagne waiting for us," Baron remembers. "Blaine Thompson only gave you a magnum of champagne if they thought you were going to go belly-up. And it wasn't Piper-Heidsieck either."

Noto came up to Golden and his partner, Ingram Ash, and asked what the next step should be.

Ash told Noto he'd be wise to close the show that night. Sabinson agreed. Twenty-twenty hindsight shows their counsel to have been flawed. But they weren't being foolish. They were making a business decision, and they based it on years of experience. Because the show had no bankable stars and had maintained such a low profile, the lukewarm reviews were unlikely to generate enough business to pay the weekly operating bills, let alone return the show's investment. Closing that night would mean that the actors would not have to be paid for the rest of the week, which would save a few hundred dollars. Also, what was left of the production could be liquidated so the investors could get back at least a few cents on the dollar and would know that Noto had done the best he could.

Schmidt said, "I heard that, and my heart just sank. I still wanted my friends to see it, and I thought, my God, can't we run one more night?"

Jones was stunned, and Baker began weeping. Olim, too, remembers curling up in a corner of the office and crying, "because I thought the show was so wonderful, it didn't deserve to close. But then I remember hearing something from the corner—I can still see Lore getting up and everyone getting very quiet. He said to us, 'Don't be upset, we're not going to close. I believe in this show, and I'm going to put my money where my mouth is. This show is going to run and be very successful.' "

Farber said that after Noto had sold off the extra 10 percent of the show, he had put his $3,300 life savings back in the bank to be used in case of an emergency. Though it was all the money he had in the world, he decided to gamble it on keeping *The Fantasticks* alive.

"When Lore said, 'I believe in this show, I'm going to make a run for it,' I was so impressed," Schmidt said.

Olim got up and dried her eyes. "This production owes its life and longevity to Lore Noto," she said. "He followed his belief attentively with love, devotion, care, determination and hard work. When Lore stated at the opening-night party that he believed in it, he'd put his money into it and he'd make it work—he did it. Without Lore Noto there would be no *Fantasticks* today."

Baron and Ann Farber departed Blaine Thompson with a mutual feeling of defiance. "We walked out, and we said 'Fuck you!' [to no one in particular]. We were holding hands, saying 'Fuuuuuck you! This is going to run!' "

Afterward, the Farbers and some of the others went back to Rita Gardner's apartment for a late-night post-party party, but Jones had no stomach for it—literally, as it turned out.

As Jones was walking home through Central Park, all the years of frustration, capped by nearly a year of hard work and hope, boiled up inside of him at the thought of the uncharitable reviews. The Mexican food might not have helped, either. In any case, on the opening night of the longest-running hit in American history, the author was throwing up in the bushes.

Schmidt, however, salvaged a reason for elation. "At least it was established that we were going to run the next night so my friends could see it," he said. "I was greatly relieved."

13

May–July 1960

"Who understands why Spring is born / Out of Winter's laboring pain? / Or why we all must die a bit / Before we can grow again."

IN a perfect world, brave speeches like Noto's would sell tickets like mad. Alas, there was no line at the box office on Wednesday morning.

Noto and Farber went back to Blaine Thompson that day, hoping to put a quote ad together. "It wasn't easy," Farber said. "We didn't have a lot of money." They were helped by the reviews in some of the afternoon papers and wire services.

One of the best came from the critic who had seen only half the show, Charles McHarry of the *Daily News*. He proclaimed the show "recommended without reservation" and "an entirely captivating evening." He added, "Jerry Orbach turns in one of the finest performances of the season," and concluded, "Everything about the production . . . smacks of taste and imagination."

In the *Post*, Richard Watts, Jr., pronounced it "A rueful and disarming little romantic fantasy" which he said "has freshness, youthful charm and a touch of imagination." The latter half of that quote landed in the ad, as did the Associated Press's accolade, "A sheer delight."

Like the overnight reviews, none were true critical analyses, but they contained specimens of commercial cheerleading that convinced the show's press agents and ad execs that Noto might have a chance after all.

The three-column-by-nine-inch ad that ran in the papers on Friday also included praiseful quotes surgically removed from reviews in the *Times*, the *Herald Tribune* and the other papers. In larger type were Aston's "A musical pip!" and McClain's "A delight!"

The audience was small but appreciative at the second performance, and afterward there was a subdued reception in the second floor lounge for friends who had not been able to squeeze into opening night.

Making his silent way through that second performance, Blair Stauffer had a chance to reflect on the previous month of his life working intensely on this project. "It had been a bright point in our lives," he said. "I'd been living alone for a couple of years, struggling, and I realized that it had been like a wonderful party."

Thanks to Noto's resoluteness, the party wasn't over yet.

Some salt was rubbed in their wounds the night of the second performance when another Off-Broadway musical, *Ernest in Love*, opened at the Gramercy Arts Theatre and got the kind of lyrical reviews *The Fantasticks* had prayed for. The musical version of Oscar Wilde's *The Importance of Being Ernest* was hailed as the best thing since the previous season's big hit, *Little Mary Sunshine*, though it didn't run nearly as long and has had no major revival.

But as time went on, the *Fantasticks* folks had less to gripe about, critic-wise. Reviews continued to roll in from weekly and then monthly magazines, and they kept getting better and better.

While gently encouraging, Donald Malcolm in *The New York Times* broke ground in equivocation by writing "If you like this sort of thing, this is the sort of thing you'll like."

Cue magazine was better, saying, "The mood is martini-dry, uncommitted, upper-Bohemian, with the main enemy the cliché. I suggest you head to Sullivan Street to catch the brightest young talents on display."

Henry Hewes in the *Saturday Review* finally gave *The Fantas-*

ticks its hoped-for rave, saying, "One of the happiest Off-Broadway evenings in a season that has been happier off of Broadway than on is the new lighter-than-air musical *The Fantasticks.*" Jones and Schmidt "have worked with a professional expertness equaling the best Broadway has to offer. . . ." Hewes concluded by calling the show "the freshest and best new Off-Broadway musical."

Designer Ed Wittstein recalls his elation at seeing Hewes's review. He realized it wasn't just because he had invested in the show, but because he felt it finally had gotten some of its due.

But Jones's personal favorite was Michael Smith's follow-up review in *The Village Voice*: "I am sadly out of practice at writing raves. As any critic knows, it is far easier to pick out a production's faults than its virtues, and I am hard-pressed to explain *The Fantasticks*. With this in mind, I did something for the first time last week. Having seen the show free on Tuesday, its opening night, I bought tickets and went back on Thursday."

Smith continued, ". . . the most elaborate and sophisticated art is employed to catch the audience in its simplicity. There is a breathtaking balance between worldly wit and commitment to naïveté."

That "balance" was exactly what Jones had been striving for.

Schmidt designed little one-column-by-two-inch ads for the show, each including one of the good quotes. That was just one of many tasks the composer took upon himself. "For me," he said, "there was nothing in the air but the show. I came every night to the show. It was fun to relax and just watch it, which is very different than when you're preparing the show for the critics. Also, I felt it was important for morale to be up here. There always seemed to be something to do."

The theater was still being cleaned and repaired, bit by bit, and Schmidt liked to play pastor of the church, personally greeting audience members and guests, sometimes going out with friends afterward.

Part of the purpose was socialization, but another part was helping to stimulate word-of-mouth. The magazine reviews were fine and welcome, but they lacked the impact of the daily newspapers. The show had not gotten the imprimatur of a "must-see," and, as Orbach recalls, "It was very borderline. We were just struggling."

At capacity, the show could gross some $4,400, which would yield $1,000 profit. But the show never got near that in its first three months. According to a report by certified public accountant Harold J. Busch, the show sold only $1,867.79 worth of tickets during the first week of its run, which works out to a little over five hundred tickets—about 40 percent of capacity. As a result, it lost $906.26 the week ending May 8.

Things improved slightly the week ending May 15, when the show earned an aggregate net profit of $31.02, and you better believe that two cents was carefully accounted for. That $31.02 was a triumph for the show: it comprised the show's first profitable week, though it represents less than the price of a single Broadway ticket in 1990.

But the triumph didn't last. The show slipped into the red again the following week, losing $70.15. That loss was covered in the final week in May by a $72.17 profit.

The show continued teetering on the edge of profitability like that for the next two months, though things actually started to slide to the point where it was losing an average of $100 a week. There were some dismal nights when there were as few as four people in the house. Schmidt recalls one night when trouble with the air conditioner drove off all but one patron.

"It was so nip and tuck," Schmidt said. "There were some nights where I'd go there and wonder whether there were going to be any people. I'd arrive around 7:00—nobody. Then it would be 7:30, then 7:45, and there would be maybe four people. They'd continue to trickle in, and finally there would be a sprinkling in the center section."

Orbach recalls, "Some nights we outnumbered the audience. There was a general feeling among the cast that if the audience fell below a certain number of people, we should cancel. But it never happened."

The morning after the opening, Noto's associate producers Olim and Baron had headed off to Saranac Lake to open their summer theater there. Noto was left to manage the show by himself, which usually was how he liked it.

Noto acquired a reputation among the cast members as a penny pincher. Meal allotments were watched carefully. He combined as many jobs into one as he could. Schmidt designed the ads to save the cost of a commercial artist, even at a time when he and Jones were taking half-royalties. The house manager also sold refreshments in the lobby and helped usher patrons to their seats. When Jones fell ill, Word Baker was called upon to play the old Actor. When one of the fathers missed a performance, Noto sometimes stepped in himself.

A lot of empty seats in a theater can be a morale-killer for actors and creates an atmosphere of doom for whatever audience members are there. Press agent David Powers counseled a quick cure — "papering" the house. Translation: giving away tickets for free to groups (like charities) that probably wouldn't have bought them anyway.

Noto refused to follow this time-honored theater tradition. "Lore never ever felt that giving seats away would help the show," Powers said. "Sometimes they played to ten people, but Lore didn't care as long as all ten had paid. Jack Schlissel, who was David Merrick's legendary general manager for years and years [and later was associate producer of *Sugar Babies, The Grand Tour, Bent,* etc.], always said, 'They have empty seats on the subway, but they don't give those away.' Lore felt the same way."

So the seats stayed empty. As Jones observed in a 1967 *World Journal Tribune* interview, "the future looked as bright as the inside of that prop box."

Because the production was unable to afford to buy its own harp or stage lights, Noto rented both for many years. Mann brought her own harp, so the rental augmented her salary and turned into an annuity for later *Fantasticks* harpists. The rentals eventually totaled thousands of dollars, which should have bought both lights and harp many times over, but in the days when the show was crawling from day to day, they were two fewer investments Noto had to make.

Fred Golden said, "If the *Times* made a mistake in the ad, and they do sometimes, and you couldn't read the phone number or something, hm, we'd take the make-good [free ad]. If not a make-good, we'd take a credit. He watched every penny all the time. But you see, it took that kind of penny-pinching to keep that show alive. He did everything possible."

The show's tribulations would have seemed funny if they

hadn't been so desperate. For instance, Noto and the rest of the staff fretted constantly about the theater's rusted and cranky air conditioner. As summer approached, the rattletrap became increasingly crucial to keeping audience members in their seats. The production couldn't afford a new one, but the compressor on the old one was unreliable and could transform the Sullivan Street Playhouse into a steambath within minutes. Even when working, it leaked inside the theater. One patron claimed her jacket was damaged by the rusty dripping and demanded recompense. Still, it was cheaper than paying for a new compressor.

Noto coddled and fussed over the machine, trying to wring yet one more day out of it. But, finally, Jones and Schmidt stuck their hands in their pockets and sprung for a new one, themselves, and made a gift of it to the show.

"We never thought the show would close," Kenneth Nelson said, "though I don't know why we didn't. We sometimes were depressed by the small houses. I guess we were led by Lore Noto's faith, which was extraordinary, and his determination. And there was the word-of-mouth through the business. It was our peers who came to see the show first and spread the word that we were good, and that it was a lovely, special show. We all knew that we had something of value and importance, and it just *couldn't* close."

Noto hung on by his fingernails because to let go would have meant losing everything. The one-performance collapse of *The Failures* had wounded not only his finances but his pride. A second such collapse was just unthinkable. And it wasn't in his nature to abandon something the way he felt he had been abandoned at the boys' home when he was a child. Besides, as everyone connected with the show attests, he believed in *The Fantasticks* with an almost religious fervor. His patience and perseverance reflects that.

Gardner said the cast members were inspired by Noto's faith. "People in the business were looking at us, and we were all getting offers," she said, "but nobody left."

But in the end, sheer force of will and faith isn't what kept *The Fantasticks* from closing; Noto's $3,300 life savings was. He made what was called a "priority loan" to the limited partnership, meaning that it would be paid back first when the profits, if any, came rolling in. Some of the money went to advertising and other audience-building support.

But most of it went to meeting the weekly payroll. Counting the time the money was used to complete the show's financing, it was the second time Noto's life savings had saved the life of *The Fantasticks*.

His philosophy was that if you can make tonight work, you can make tomorrow work. If you do that eight times, you've put another week of performances behind you. If you come out short at the end of that week, dip into the reserve and try harder next week. At times, it seemed that he was still bailing after his boat had gone under.

But he didn't stop, and he even started to get some help. Volunteer boosters began to pitch in. Most Broadway shows have a separate box office staff to arrange group sales and theater parties. That was far too complicated and expensive for *The Fantasticks* to manage during its dicey first twelve weeks. "Soon it became obvious that it would be a tough haul," Farber said. But it was Farber's wife, Ann, who had loved the show since she first saw it with her husband and Noto on that fateful night at Barnard, who took it on herself to scare up such groups.

Ann Farber was well-suited for the work. Sociable and a joiner, she belonged to the PTA, her local temple and other charitable associations on Long Island. She approached these groups with the traditional deal: buy twenty or more tickets at full price, then get a group discount and keep the difference as a donation. "I told them, 'You'll make some money for your organization—and I guarantee you'll like it.' " Her theater parties included dinner beforehand at Punjab's, the Indian restaurant at Bleecker and Sullivan Streets, and a post-performance coffee-and-cake with the actors in the theater's second floor lounge, which was still decorated with theater co-owner Robert Alan Gold's atmospheric paintings of Mexico.

Every filled seat was a blessing. There were nights when Ann Farber's groups from Merrick or East Rockaway were the entire audience.

The show's first and most faithful partisans were the little girls from next door. Later, Jones would write, "We were grateful for them even though they didn't pay. They were so 'willing,' sitting out there in their little starched dresses and grownup white gloves. And they always yelled 'Bravo' during the curtain calls."

The show acquired more influential champions as well. One of the earliest and most faithful proselytizers was actress Anne Bancroft, known then as the co-star of the *The Miracle Worker*, who was impressed not only with the show but with Tom Jones as well. She later told the *Daily News* that she attended eight times during the first ten weeks. Schmidt recalls that she tried to work a little personal miracle for *The Fantasticks* by bringing a fresh group of friends each time.

"I'd see Anne Bancroft," Orbach said, "Lee Strasberg, Kaye Ballard and other friends, and they would tell their friends to go. We started getting curiosity seekers and [inveterate] theatergoers. It really came down to just word-of-mouth among friends. Walter Kerr had been wonderful to me—just a personal rave that got people down to see me. That's why [producer] David Merrick came down. It also brought [choreographer/director] Gower Champion, who later cast me in my first Broadway show, *Carnival*. But the show itself was really on shaky ground because they were saying it was a children's play—cutesy."

When Matt and Luisa have their falling out early in Act II, Matt accuses her of being "childish," and Luisa retorts that she's actually "child*like*." In a way, that distinction applies to the show as well. In one of the show's more perceptive reviews, Donald Malcolm in the *The New Yorker* said, ". . . the author's view of real life is quite as romantic and theatrical as the illusions once shared by the youngsters," but he was willing to overlook this quibble.

Many of the show's earliest partisans felt no need to overlook it. It was precisely the quality they most enjoyed.

Being practically in the audience's lap, Rita Gardner couldn't help but notice that "each night when Kenny and I would sing 'They Were You' and Jerry would sing 'Try to Remember,' everybody would be weeping. It was so touching. But it was a good feeling, like a catharsis. We'd taken them to a peak, and then they could relax and let go and really feel good. They would come up afterward and ask for autographs and say they felt like they'd eaten a wonderful meal. They experienced something. That's what kept this show going."

As Schmidt remembers, the neighborhood ambience helped, too. It was a beautiful time of year; the Village had never been cleaner, safer or more in fashion; and the show sometimes even benefitted from walk-up business on nice days or when the nearby Catholic church was having a fair.

Playwright Marc Connelly and composer Frank Loesser jumped on the bandwagon and began talking-up the show at cocktail parties. Producers Cheryl Crawford and Robert Fryer were impressed enough to enter into negotiations with Jones and Schmidt immediately to do their next musical.

For the cast members not immediately concerned with making the show's ends meet, life began to settle down just a little bit. Rita Gardner sometimes would meet her old *Nightcaps* pal Charles Nelson Reilly after the show for coffee or a ramble around the streets of Greenwich Village. Sometimes he would come to see the show to be supportive of her, and when she got tired of the food at Punjab's, he would cook spaghetti for her between matinee and evening performances.

Press agent David Powers was constantly trying to weave the flax of their personal lives into gold. George Curley recalls Powers coming around once a week and asking, " 'Anything happen to ya this week? Did ya do anything that would make good copy . . . ?' " As a result, there were stories about a party Julius Monk threw for the cast, an interview with Schmidt about his Texas background, a trial balloon about University of Texas classmate Pat Hingle wanting to do Jones and Schmidt's next show—even a society page shot of Nelson hobnobbing at Trader Vic's with a pair of Off-Broadway ingenues, Collin Wilcox of *Camino Real* and Arnette Jens of *The Balcony*.

Richard Stauffer was the subject of an offbeat story in the *World-Telegram & Sun* by a reporter who was unable to speak and who wrote a story on what it was like to play the Mute. The five-foot-two-inch George Curley was the subject of another odd bit of press in *Newsday*. Under the headline "Actor Says Being Short Hurts Careers [sic] on Stage," it was a chronicle of life as a short actor.

Observing Powers's indefatigable tub-thumping, Schmidt

said, "I can't stress enough how important he was to the running of this show during those early months."

Inside the theater, Orbach and Nelson called their ushers "method ushers" because of the dramatic way they would send latecomers scurrying across the stage just after "Try to Remember." George Curley remembers, "They'd point and say 'Go!' "

Whether there were a lot of audience members or just a few, on time or late, Stauffer learned to focus elsewhere. "I never played to the faces," he said. "It was a matter of concentrating on the task I had to do. After we finalized the cues for who needed what and when, it was death to try and anticipate two moves beyond where you were. I just had to focus on the fact that now Rita needed her beads, or now the confetti had to come down and it had to finish on cue. You simply had to think of this one, and then the next one, and then the next one. . . . If you could keep that, you could get through a performance in pretty fine shape. It allowed you to forget mostly about the people, though sometimes there'd be toes: I could feel myself sitting on some lady's sharp pump toe. I remember somebody in the front row throwing up in their lap one night. There was a lot of red wine with it, and it splashed But what could you do? Just keep going."

"Just Keep Going" was the de facto motto of *The Fantasticks* during those harrowing first twelve weeks.

But there were compensations. One of the high points was the recording of the original cast album. It was a particularly exciting moment for Jones and Schmidt, who had discovered musical theater through some of Broadway's first original cast albums in the late 1940s. But Noto also saw the album as a potent marketing tool. After the rest of the show's charm had begun to fade in the mind of a theatergoer, the memory of the show's melodies tended to remain. The cast album, plus sheet music ("Try to Remember," "Soon It's Gonna Rain" and "They Were You") which was published by Chappell Music about the same time, would be ambassadors to an otherwise indifferent public.

Schmidt and Stein worked almost as hard on the cast album as they had on the show itself.

"We wanted a bigger sound for the cast album," Stein said.

"We wanted more instruments. The harp and piano were already written [which he and Mann played on the record]. It was a simple matter of augmenting and dividing. And, of course, I put in percussion [drum] because you can always use the rhythm."

Schmidt said he ad-libbed a second piano part—a throw-back to his original two-piano arrangement—and a second pianist was hired.

Stein said a bass violin was a natural addition because of the bass line in the music. "But I thought there were some lovely opportunities for melody, so I added a cello."

The cello can be detected, with some careful listening, during the third verse of "Try to Remember," but Stein said he was unhappy with the cellist's performance at the recording session and eliminated most of his work during the engineering.

"Piano, percussion, cello, bass and harp," said Stein, "that's a huge orchestra for that show."

The album was recorded in high fidelity stereo for MGM Records at the Olmstead Studios, 80 West 40th Street, just below the Times Square theater district, from 10:00 A.M. to 6:00 P.M. on June 13. It was a Monday, ordinarily the cast's day off. A second, shorter recording session was held that Friday to do some retakes.

Things did not go smoothly. The night before the recording session, Nelson was headed up the aisle after the "Round and Round" sequence when he slipped and fell heavily on his arm. He heard the snap but decided to continue, since he had only the final scene to play, and it called upon him to look wounded and disheveled anyway.

He headed right to the emergency room afterward, where the worst was discovered. The bone was broken. The next morning, he appeared at the Olmstead Studios with his arm in a cast and his head full of woozy painkillers.

"When they showed up, it looked like a war zone," Mann said. "Kenneth had his broken elbow, and Julian had a bad case of bursitis [allegedly from pressing his back and shoulder against the cold side wall of the theater], and it was very painful for him to move his arms laterally. I remember not feeling that comfortable with the part yet, myself. It was still a little bit new to me. So we all sort of agonized through this whole long session. It was sad, but they did valiantly, and it certainly doesn't show up on the record."

The MGM engineer gave Stein some trouble as well. He was uncomfortable with the many pauses in the score and asked Stein for "fills"—runs of two and three notes between phrases on songs like "They Were You." Stein said, "It kind of bothered me to destroy the simplicity of a moment like that. The original is very simple, almost like a guitar part, which I thought was more effective. But the recording people did not. They thought it sounded too bare."

The lovely piano and harp fills that can be heard throughout the album were ad-libbed by Mann and Stein on the spot.

All the anxieties of the recording session were left in the studio. The original cast recording is one of the most lovely ever made, displaying the elusive paradoxical quality of sounding like it was made up on the spot (which it partially was), yet being carefully crafted and inevitable. It plays like a music box.

Noto was delighted. Once he got his hands on the LP, the only significant format in pre-cassette, pre-CD 1960, he wouldn't let go of it. The front artwork was similar to the poster, except that Schmidt's purple logo was on a white background surrounded by the credits. On the back was a synopsis of the plot surrounding an intriguing group shot of the cast.

"For as long as I was in the show," Orbach said, "Lore would ride the subway with me going uptown and always carried the album of *The Fantasticks* like an ad. He was a walking advertisement at all times."

Ad manager Fred Golden said it wasn't just the subway. "The show was Lore Noto's whole world. He used to walk up and down Broadway with the album, making sure the front of the album was facing outside. He used to call that our 'outdoor campaign.' I'd tell Harvey that Lore was up to see me and he'd say, 'Is he working on our outdoor campaign?' "

Noto suddenly became a social butterfly, showing up at society parties armed with the cast album. Anyone naïve enough to ask about it would get an immediate sales pitch.

But Noto wasn't the only one pushing the album. Charles McHarry reported in his *Daily News* column, "On the Town," that Anne Bancroft had bought fifty of the albums for her friends on the West Coast. Sales of the album were surprisingly brisk, and by mid July, it was on turntables all over Manhattan.

But despite all Noto's efforts, the labors of *Fantasticks* irregulars like Bancroft, the nightly efforts on stage and the "outdoor campaign," the little show was not quite making it into the black on a regular basis. "We were close to closing," Orbach said.

But then, Noto got another of his periodic brainstorms.

Conrad Thibault, chairman of the John Drew Theater at Guild Hall in East Hampton, New York, contacted Lore Noto about producing something at his summer stock playhouse near the beach on the eastern tip of Long Island. Thinking that this was a chance to let his cast have a vacation but continue to earn money at the same time, Noto suggested that the entire original production of *The Fantasticks*, lock, stock and moon, pull up stakes and play a week at the John Drew.

The contract with the East Hampton theater was perhaps the biggest inducement. For a show that had been making $100 profit one week and losing it the next, the eight performances August 2 to 7 would net some $600.

The New York production wasn't closing; it was going on abeyance, a contractual theater term meaning that a play may suspend performances for an agreed period of time without technically ending its run. Usually it's used for changing theaters or changing stars or if there is some unforeseen problem with a production. Using it to pop out of town was unusual, to say the least.

"Nobody does that," Schmidt said. "You don't close a show in New York and go out to the beach for a couple of weeks when you're barely hanging on here. Well, Lore thought it would be good. He said a lot of the right people would see it."

So at the end of July 1960, just after celebrating its one-hundredth performance with a party at Punjab's Restaurant, *The Fantasticks* hung out a sign inviting audiences to come back in a week and headed for the Hamptons.

14

August–December 1960

"Item—one moon"

BAKER called the East Hampton move "a bold stroke" but did not accompany the cast. He had been awarded a Fulbright Scholarship to study in Europe and decided to leave the show in Tom Jones's hands.

In retrospect, East Hampton was a move to precisely the right place at the right time.

In Julius Monk's *Demi-Dozen*, Jones had poked fun at New York City's slogan "New York is a summer festival." In fact, there is very little festive about non-air-conditioned New York in the summer. It's hot and humid and, on weekends, deserted because anyone with the wherewithal heads for the eastern beaches. Summer colonies for the theater community are Fire Island, Quogue, Martha's Vineyard, Bridgehampton, Sag Harbor—and East Hampton.

When *The Fantasticks* hung Schmidt's oddly lettered poster outside Guild Hall, it didn't attract curious potato farmers; it drew the cream of Broadway. Many of the people who bought tickets wouldn't have dreamed of slumming down to Sullivan Street. But served on a platter in the country like a glass of iced tea, *The Fantasticks* seemed worth a look.

The John Drew Theater is an auditorium within Guild Hall, a

low-slung structure that includes an art gallery and other civic facilities in the center of the village of East Hampton.

"The theater was very beautiful," Stauffer said. "It was made for the famous classical actor, John Drew, and he delivered all the famous Shakespearean monologues there. It's a beautiful thing, but playing on it is hell. There's a distance between the stage and the audience that's just like a black pit. We had gone from a very intimate situation to facing this darkness. It was difficult to penetrate."

It was the first time the musical had been done on a standard proscenium stage with a curtain and an orchestra pit. Jones adapted the show's style to the conventional space as well as he could. Working in that pit, in front of the actors for the first time, Julian Stein said that the show "lost its intimacy. Getting up close to the audience is important to this show. "When we did it in the Hamptons it didn't feel right, didn't have the same touch. But I realize now that the show was better than the performers thought it was. It went over well there. The audience liked it."

The audience that filed into the seats at Guild Hall August 2 to 7 had a lot on its mind. Two weeks earlier, on July 16, John F. Kennedy had been nominated in Los Angeles by the Democrats to take the White House back from the Republicans. Just the previous Wednesday, July 27, Vice President Richard Nixon had been nominated in Chicago to defend that beachhead. To the largely liberal audience, the campaign getting underway was an apocalyptic showdown between good and evil, and as the incumbent evil, Nixon looked like he would be hard to beat.

The Fantasticks helped take the weight of the world off their shoulders. It showed idealistic young people coming through a serious trial and surviving with their love intact. In an age of waste and ostentation, an age when Broadway musicals seemed to be getting bigger but somehow hollower, *The Fantasticks* offered a compact and streamlined alternative, full of heart yet bursting with theatrical inventiveness.

When the show played a return engagement at the John Drew (directed by Jones's future second wife, Janet Watson) in 1981, Jones was asked by *The New York Times*'s Long Island section to analyze the unorthodox 1960 engagement. He said,

first audiences were almost exclusively theater people
saw something avant-garde in the way we used the obvi-
theatrical devices. 'Is this a strange, aberrant new form?'
all wondered. Anne Bancroft and Elia Kazan and Jerome
bins and Bob Fosse and Agnes de Mille came to see it and
ame active supporters. They mounted campaigns. When
returned to New York, everything was different."

Miriam Javits, wife of New York Senator Jacob Javits, also
w it and began spreading the word in political precincts as
ell.

Orbach remembers becoming a celebrity in East Hampton.
His idols suddenly wanted his autograph. "Word-of-mouth
started to spread very quickly because a lot of people from the
theatrical community saw it there," he said.

By the time that word-of-mouth began shifting into high
gear, the East Hampton engagement was over. But the show's
newly recruited platoon of influential fans returned to Manhattan and began spreading the word.

Those returning from East Hampton had a chance to listen to
the original cast album and to take a second look at the July 17
Times photo feature, which had somehow included *The Fantasticks* with *The Threepenny Opera*, *Leave It to Jane* and *Little Mary
Sunshine* as one of "Off-Broadway's Durable Musicals."

In the same 1981 story, Lore Noto, the Mysterious Man in
White, said, "By the time we returned to Sullivan Street we
were transformed from an endangered artistic success with an
uncertain future to a commercial enterprise which has since
endured."

Though the box office phones were ringing at last, Noto
didn't stop his "outdoor campaign" or relent in his personal
promotion of the show. *The Fantasticks* might prove to be just
another summer romance for the East Hamptonites, and Noto
was in for the long run. So he kept pushing. One day, he told
the *Christian Science Monitor* in 1966, his efforts paid off in an
incident that may be apocryphal but reveals something of
Noto's innocent aspirations. "I was taking an outside turn—to
show the [record] cover better—at Fifth Avenue and Forty-fifth
Street," Noto is quoted saying, "when I noticed a happy young
couple just behind me. They stopped, they kissed, and then

the man said, 'Honey, let's see *The Fantasticks* again.' At that moment, I knew we'd made it."

The show acquired a staunch, if offbeat, champion in Janice Mars, a classmate of Farber's (from Lincoln High School in Lincoln, Nebraska, of all places) who had become involved with Lee Strasberg's Actors Studio, eventually appearing in its production of *The Three Sisters* and *Blues for Mister Charlie*. To provide her friends with a safe, homey haven where no one would stare at them, she opened a nightclub in Julius Monk's neighborhood on West 55th Street near Sixth Avenue in the late 1950s. Called The Baq Room, the intimate space attracted a minuscule but enviable clientele including Marlon Brando, Lauren Bacall, Jason Robards, Jr., Maureen Stapleton, Judy Holliday, Kim Stanley, Betty Comden and Adolph Green.

"I was surprised that *The Fantasticks* wasn't doing better," Mars said. "It seemed so direct, so sincere, so un-New Yorkish—so innocent and wise at the same time."

In addition to being the manager, Mars also served as the entertainment, singing her heart out for hours to the accompaniment of pianist Beau (Baldwin) Bergersen.

Mars got her hands on the sheet music and began singing the numbers, particularly "Soon It's Gonna Rain," each night at the club, talking up the show as the East Hampton crowd had done. "I wasn't trying to promote it," she said. "I just liked it and told everyone so."

In that tight circle, *The Fantasticks* cast, but particularly the youngsters, Gardner, Nelson and the Studio-trained Orbach, became "in," as Schmidt and Benton might have put it, and suddenly were besieged by invitations to dinners and parties.

"Everybody was coming down to see it," Gardner said. They'd go out to Figaro, Portofino or the Cafe Borgia. She remembers going out with William Daniels, later star of TV's *St. Elsewhere* but then an icon of Off Broadway for his performance in Edward Albee's *Zoo Story*.

She also began pulling around with Eileen Brennan, then star of the operetta spoof *Little Mary Sunshine*. "We would meet and be hysterical," she said, "because we'd say, 'Did you ever think the two of us would be the ingenues of the year?' "

Ken Nelson remembers the then-blind James Thurber coming to the show. "His wife very quietly and very softly told him all through the show what was happening visually," Nelson said, "but it wasn't the least distracting, not to us at any rate."

On another night, Nelson looked up "straight into the eyes of Ingrid Bergman. I nearly fell down. She came backstage that night. She was incredibly beautiful. She was wearing a fur coat and had very long hair. She was like a Valkyrie. When she threw her head back, which I've seen her do a hundred times in the movies, and her hair fell back over her coat, I thought, 'Where's the camera?' "

Nelson had another brush with stardust when actress Tallulah Bankhead showed up. As Schmidt tells it, "She just plowed into the actors' dressing room, went straight to Kenny and said, 'Oh, you're that divine boy who never says a word all evening.' She thought he was the mute. Kenny pointed to Blair Stauffer and said, 'No, that's him over there.' And she turned back to Kenny and said, 'Oh, you're that divine boy who never shuts up.' "

Adlai Stevenson came in a limousine that barely fit down Sullivan Street. Esther Williams was named an honorary usher so she could see a sold-out performance. Vivien Leigh checked her Siamese cat at the box office. John Gielgud left after Act I, which, Schmidt said, "was unusual. I think he hated it. But most theater people loved it. They always made very good audiences."

Along those same lines, "Kids picked up the music and began auditioning with the songs when they went for Broadway musicals,' Curley said, quoting intelligence gleaned from his buddies at the Theater Bar. "And the Broadway people were saying, 'Where's that from?' "

A lot more of the Broadway people got to see the show when Actors Equity Association went on a brief strike against the Broadway theaters but not the Off-Broadway ones. Not only were audiences diverted downtown, so were the uptown actors.

Curley began inviting agents to see the show, and he started getting TV commercials for shaving razors and other products. He even was sent on an audition for the title role in the national touring company of *Fiorello!* Though he wasn't hired, it was a tribute to the show's incremental success that someone in the smallest role of *The Fantasticks* was even considered for the lead in a Broadway show.

Soon, however, the show's reputation began to spread beyond New York. Negotiations commenced for the rights to produce the show in stock companies around the United States and to tour it to the larger cities. There even was talk of a London production.

These were due partly to South African singer Miriam Makeba, who heard "Try to Remember" and brought the sheet music to Harry Belafonte. He was the first to "cover" the song in a new arrangement, which Schmidt described as "kind of an African folk song" with a second singer in the background creating an echoing countermelody. Of the many versions of the song done over the years, Schmidt said Belafonte's remains one of his favorites.

Barbra Streisand put two of the songs in her nightclub act and made "Much More" her signature song until "People" came along with *Funny Girl* in 1964.

* * *

After clinging to the limelight for seven months, the show finally became, if not a hot ticket, at least a warm ticket. It began to sell out, first on the weekends, then during the week. In the four months between East Hampton and New Year's Day, it managed to earn back Noto's life savings, and then the backers' entire investment.

"We got our money back at Christmas-time as our Christmas present from Lore Noto," Curley said. "By the first anniversary, we had made $220 [on a one percent investment] and from there on it was 'Katy bar the door.' "

15

1961–90

"You must always leave the wall."

Aº²ND so *The Fantasticks* ran happily ever after. The show celebrated its thirtieth anniversary at the Sullivan Street Playhouse on May 3, 1990, and has played in excess of 12,500 performances, making it the longest running musical in history.

It didn't go from trumpeted milestone to trumpeted milestone, though David Powers and, later, Dorothy Olim (and, still later, Lore's son Tony Noto) sent out press releases at each anniversary.

No, the show just kept not closing—much to everyone's surprise. In the early 1970s, Schmidt took out an ad saying, "Is that show *still* running?"—which captured the attitude of a lot of New Yorkers. Nearly two decades later, the attitude is the same.

Jones, Schmidt and company were as amazed by the show's success as anyone else. Everyone figured it would ride out the spurt of hipness that followed the East Hampton sojourn. But long after that had dissipated, the show was still puttering along.

Hoping to capitalize on the many celebrity partisans, Noto ran an advertisement in March 1961. It listed eighty celebrities, from Alfred G. Vanderbilt to Henny Youngman, who invited readers to ask them why they liked *The Fantasticks*. The ad cost

Farber months of detective work but paid off in eager praise from some of the brightest lights in show business. Among those Farber convinced to make an unprecedented endorsement of a show not their own were George Abbott, Tallulah Bankhead, Bennett Cerf, Barbara Cook, Hermione Gingold, Ruth Gordon, Garson Kanin, Myrna Loy, Tony Perkins, Anthony Quinn, Richard Rodgers and Leonard Sillman.

In May, Jones and Schmidt were named winners of the Vernon Rice Award for "outstanding achievement" in the Off-Broadway theater; specifically "For music and lyrics with gayety, freshness, imagination and wit."

The original cast played another out-of-town engagement at the Poinciana Playhouse in Palm Beach, Florida, but soon began to answer calls for their services in new projects.

Rita Gardner was the first to leave, to take a role in what turned out to be a minor film, *One Plus One*, about the Kinsey Report. She then was cast by Word Baker for *A Family Affair*. Gardner was replaced in *The Fantasticks* by Miss America finalist Carla Huston, a former Miss Montana.

Jerry Orbach was next, winding up as the male lead in David Merrick's musical *Carnival*, which opened April 13, 1961. He was succeeded by Gene Rupert.

After music director Julian Stein left, Beverly Mann put down her harp and became the show's keyboardist. She, in turn, taught the piano part to a young composer named David Shire, who, with his lyricist, Richard Maltby, Jr., wrote a musical titled *The Sap of Life*, inspired partly by *The Fantasticks*. Kenneth Nelson left *The Fantasticks* after seventeen months as Matt to play a featured role in *Sap*, which opened Off-Broadway at the Sheridan Square Playhouse at the end of 1961, but which closed soon after. Maltby and Shire went on to write *Closer Than Ever* and *Starting Here, Starting Now*.

Schmidt said finding replacements for the original cast of *The Fantasticks* was a surprisingly difficult chore. "Nobody seemed as good," he said, "because the first cast was so extraordinary. I don't think we've ever had anybody who 'had it all' the way Jerry did. And Kenny and Rita were strangely right too, even though they were older. There was a classiness about everybody. And with Tom playing the Old Actor—it's never been played that well since. It never will be."

Harder still, though far more pleasurable, was accepting May

3, 1961—the show's first anniversary. Schmidt paid for an ad to mark the date and designed a new poster for the show. The logo was rendered in white on a solid purple background with Schmidt's own sketch of the Act I tableau and the simple slogan, "Second Year at 181 Sullivan Street." That started a tradition which endured into the show's fourth decade. Each year, a new ad and a new poster appear, courtesy of the composer. It's the only commercial artwork he did after 1980.

Noto and Farber broke tradition by striking a deal with Music Theater International to make rights for *The Fantasticks* available for stock and amateur productions. "Usually you waited until a show closed in New York before you let those rights out," Schmidt said. "If we had done that, we still wouldn't have any secondary rights."

MTI was owned by *Guys and Dolls* composer Frank Loesser, one of the original *Fantasticks* irregulars, who had formed MTI as a licensing agent to challenge the power of the two giants in the field, Tams-Witmark and Samuel French. Rodgers and Hammerstein had formed a licensing company of their own for a similar purpose.

Trying to build up his catalogue with commercial hits, Loesser approached Noto soon after *The Fantasticks'* opening. But negotiations stretched until March 1961, as Farber sought to make a deal for the authors that would enable them to profit from productions at summer theaters, regional companies, colleges—even high schools and summer camps. Once available to those groups, *The Fantasticks* quickly became a staple because it was so accessible, so much fun to perform and comparatively inexpensive to mount.

Not only did this arrangement enrich the producers and the authors—Noto finally was able to move out of the 211th Street tenement and into a spacious house in Queens—it also helped cultivate audiences for the show in New York. Thousands of nascent thespians who made their debuts in one or another of the roles then made pilgrimages to Mecca on Sullivan Street.

Of fifty-two people responding to a 1977 audience survey at the Playhouse, twenty-two said they had seen the show before and twenty others had been in school productions of the show. These included playgoers from as far away as Los Angeles, Tokyo and Capetown.

Schmidt reported in 1990 that the number of stock productions "has been almost religiously as strong year in year out" as it was in the early 1960s.

Professionals were just as eager to try their hands at the mighty mite. Unfortunately, the first one fell flat on its face— and it was a big one. *The Fantasticks* opened in London, September 7, 1961, under what seemed like ideal circumstances. It was a first-class production at the Apollo Theatre, with Word Baker directing a cast led by John Wood as the Old Actor.

Unfortunately, the production was greeted with luxuriant antipathy. J.W. Lambert's pan begins, murderously, "The centre of the stage is occupied all too invitingly by what appears to be a scaffold. . . ."

The critics complained that the show was toothachingly darling, though the consensus among its creators is that the show was removed from its open-stage concept and placed in a traditional proscenium environment, breaking the important connection between actor and audience. The play had survived such a transition in East Hampton but was not as lucky in the West End. It ran less than a week.

That didn't stop New York's Shubert Organization from offering *The Fantasticks* a chance to transfer uptown to a full-size Broadway theater. Noto and the authors declined. "We were scared to disturb it," Schmidt said. "We'd discovered the charm of our little theater. We'd realized by then that it was all a part of the whole experience."

In October 1964, for the nth time, Lore Noto flouted conventional wisdom to the benefit of *The Fantasticks*. He agreed to allow the *Hallmark Hall of Fame* to adapt *The Fantasticks* as an all-star TV special. Such adaptations were thought to be death for stage plays. After all, why would audiences then pay to see something they had gotten on TV for free?

"It was an unorthodox thing to do," Schmidt said, "but we had already broken the rules by having it done all over the country." Besides, he'd worked with some of the same production people when he was employed at NBC.

The cast may have tempted them as well: Ricardo Montalban as El Gallo, Bert Lahr and Stanley Holloway as the Fathers and, for sentimental value, Susan Watson, the original Luisa at Barnard, as The Girl. The then-unknown John Davidson played Matt.

Jones trustingly put his script into the hands of director

George Schaefer, who proceeded to cut it down from ninety minutes to fifty, eliminating the Mute and merging the Old Actors with the Fathers.

"Anyone who knew *The Fantasticks* was horrified and aghast at the way they cut it down," Schmidt said.

Ed Wittstein's minimalist set was jettisoned as too bare and replaced with sets that resembled storybook illustrations. Watching it at home, Curley hooted at "Ricardo Montalban singing 'Try to Remember' up in a tree. He looked scared to death."

But the reaction to the TV version was exactly the reverse of the London production's. Though the creators and the original cast hated it, critics applauded.

Jack Gould in *The New York Times* called it "sixty minutes of enchantment." And though it was beaten in the ratings by *Candid Camera*, it had the perverse effect of giving Sullivan Street a shot of adrenaline.

Variety reported that the network presentation "seems to have helped rather than hurt the box office."

Television helped the show in another way as well. When Ed Ames sang "Try to Remember" on *The Tonight Show*, "the song just took off," Schmidt said. "After that, everybody recorded it."

The show began to sell out solidly during the week as well as the weekends, a situation that persisted well into the late 1960s.

* * *

As early as August 1960, producers had come sniffing around the theater with grand schemes to make *The Fantasticks* into a movie. Louis de Rochemont was first, somehow envisioning it as a vehicle for Shirley Knight. He was followed by Murray A. Gordon and others. Disagreements about money and artistic control generally sank the various deals.

Jones and Schmidt had hoped that at some point a film director might come forward with a special vision of how to transfer to film what was very much a stage piece. Finally deciding it would never happen, they tried writing a screenplay of their own.

The script was never completed, but one summer when

Schmidt was departing for a European vacation, Jones suggested that he keep his eyes open for possible locations.

Visiting Sicily for the first time, Schmidt took hundreds of photos of that bleak but somehow theatrical and seductive landscape. A movie shot there would be played out in locations where genuine sixteenth-century *commedia* troupes might have capered. Upon his return home, Schmidt mounted the best of his photos in a book, with accompanying text outlining the plot of *The Fantasticks* in cinematic terms.

Jones became intrigued by this new possibility, and, together, they mounted a second volume of photos, incorporating the actual text of the play. This became their film "treatment," which they showed to anyone who expressed interest.

Among them was emerging film director William Friedkin (*The French Connection*), who confessed to being a fan of the show. He said he loved the new approach but soon became deeply immersed in shooting *The Exorcist*, so their collaboration eventually was shelved.

About the same time, Charles Bludhorn, president of Gulf + Western, which recently had acquired Paramount Pictures, approached Noto about filming *The Fantasticks*. He put Jones and Schmidt in touch with line producer Howard W. Koch, who allowed them to hunt more intensively for appropriate directors and cinematographers by watching films in the Gulf + Western screening room in Manhattan.

Since no director's work was deemed right, Schmidt said they went back to Paramount with the name of stage director Gower Champion, who had done *I Do! I Do!* In addition to having danced in Hollywood films early in his career, Champion also had directed a few, including *My Six Loves* and *Bank Shot*.

Getting a green light from Paramount, Schmidt returned to Sicily with Champion and Jones to pin down specific locations and assemble a shooting script.

After it was completed and submitted, Schmidt and Jones were informed that Paramount was still willing to consider Italy but not Champion. Paramount wanted Franco Zeffirelli, who recently had given the studio one of its biggest money-makers, *Romeo and Juliet*. Whether the studio was aware of *The Fantasticks'* pedigree as Rostand's parody of the Shakespeare piece is not clear.

ramount president Frank Yablans flew to Rome to court
talian maestro. But in a preproduction meeting, Yablans
Jones and Schmidt Zeffirelli literally went down on his
es and begged the studio executive not to pressure him to
e the movie.

. can't understand what this movie's about," Yablans quot-
im as saying. "It's too American."

the early 1980s, Jones and Schmidt tried courting opera
ctor Jean-Pierre Ponnelle, whose La Scala *Cenerentola* Jones
seen on PBS and deeply admired. Ponnelle never had
rd of *The Fantasticks* but saw it for the first time at Jones's
itation. He was enchanted and immediately visualized it as
a film. Action would open at the Sullivan Street Playhouse,
showing the facade as the audience is coming in, and then
backstage as the actors get into makeup. As the story got
underway, however, it would be filmed in the larger venue of a
sound stage that would suggest Italy.

Jones and Schmidt worked closely with Ponnelle on developing the screenplay, but Hollywood studios that were shown
this version were leery of a director who may have staged
operas all over the world and on television but who had never
done a movie. There was talk of doing it in Europe with
European financing, but that, too, fell through. A heart attack
took Ponnelle shortly afterward.

The gods that blessed *The Fantasticks* probably are the same
ones that have cursed a movie version. And perhaps wisely so.
As the *Hallmark Hall of Fame* version suggested, a translation to
film would be problematic. So much of the show's White Magic
and effectiveness depends on live actors interacting with a live
audience. Pushing it behind a fourth wall would be like putting
it under glass. It might be pretty, but it would be dead. Born
out of theories of Elizabethan open-stage technique, it is inex-
tricably a creature of the legitimate stage.

* * *

Like the fabled tortoise, *The Fantasticks* won its race slowly
but steadily. The first anniversary was a revelation and a relief,
but there were many more to come.

On August 29, 1962, *Little Mary Sunshine* closed, and on the
following night, *The Fantasticks* became Off-Broadway's

longest-running attraction. Less than a month later, it played its 1,000th performance, though it was noted that this was not half of what *The Threepenny Opera* had attained.

On August 5, 1966, it surpassed *Threepenny* to become the longest-running show in the history of Off-Broadway. A *Wall Street Journal* story quoted Jay Hampton, who by then had played five of the show's roles, boasting that it would run "another seven years."

That was fine for Off-Broadway, but what about Broadway? Later that year, it surpassed *My Fair Lady* to become the longest-running musical in New York. But what about straight plays? In 1967, it outstripped *Life With Father*, up to then the longest-running professional production in U.S. history.

As *The New York Times* pointed out, rightly, at the time, the all-time American record holder was not *Life With Father* at all, but the temperance melodrama *The Drunkard*, which had run from 1933 to 1953 at a non-Actors Equity theater in Los Angeles. That was a tough one, but *The Fantasticks* bided its time. In 1980, it puttered quietly past *The Drunkard*.

But as the *Guinness Book of World Records* points out, *The Fantasticks* does not hold the world's record, and the show may never attain it. Agatha Christie's murder mystery, *The Mousetrap*, which opened in London November 25, 1952, and was still going as of 1991. To best it, *The Fantasticks* would have to continue running nearly eight years after *The Mousetrap* closed.

For those who love statistics, there is one thing that *The Fantasticks* can hold over its British rival. *The Mousetrap* switched theaters in 1974 after 8,862 performances, meaning that since 1981, as Sullivan Street Playhouse owner Jules Field loves to boast, "I have the record for the longest-running play at any one theater in the history of the world."

Field paid for the right to make the boast. Having bought out Robert Alan Gold's half-interest, he maintained the theater until 1979, when the owner, Phillip Edwards, opted not to renew Field's twenty-year lease, and to sell out and tear down the building to make way for a larger residential complex.

Field said that in order to insure that *The Fantasticks* reached its milestone under his stewardship, he met the owner's price and bought the Playhouse himself. It turned out to be a tidy investment as well, but Field said he regularly turns down offers for the building, which he continues to own and operate as a personal hobby.

In its one-hundred-forty-nine-seat theater (later upped to one hundred and fifty-three), the show sold its millionth ticket on October 3, 1980.

Field and Noto oversaw a silver anniversary renovation of the theater and its facade in 1984. On May 3 of that year, Mayor Edward I. Koch renamed that stretch of Sullivan Street "Fantasticks Lane." Both street signs are displayed at the corner of Bleecker Street above where the long-vanished Punjab restaurant dispensed alleged curry. Ten days later, the musical gave its 10,000th performance. On February 26, 1989, it gave its 12,000th performance.

* * *

Speaking of world's records, the show survived its 1961 London thrashing (and an equally unhappy return in 1979) but has done well elsewhere. There have been more than two hundred and seventy-seven productions in sixty nations, including Canada, Australia and New Zealand.

Elsewhere in Europe, it's been done in The Netherlands, France, Belgium, Germany, Sweden, Norway, Denmark, Austria, a very successful production in Yugoslavia, Czechoslovakia and Poland.

Middle Eastern productions have been mounted in Israel and Saudi Arabia. It was seen in Africa in Kenya, Zimbabwe and South Africa. Translated into Spanish by Luis del Llano and Martha Fisher, *Los Fantastikos* was seen in Argentina, Chile and Mexico (at the Teatro del Bosque, the theater where Schmidt was inspired to write "Soon It's Gonna Rain"). A Spanish-language production was done in New York City in May 1977.

Perhaps owing to its Oriental stage techniques, the show has been a favorite in Asia, particularly in Japan, which has done a production annually, as *Peter Pan* is done in London. Two English-language tours of Japan were mounted in 1988 and 1990, featuring Jones as the Old Actor and Schmidt at the piano. In 1987, it was presented, with *The Music Man*, by the Beijing Opera Company. Played in Mandarin and in Caucasian makeup at a thirty-five-hundred-seat theater, they were the first American musicals to be performed in the People's Republic of China since the 1949 Revolution.

Other Asian productions include ones in The Philippines, Singapore and Hong Kong. During the Vietnam War, an American actor named Bob Sevra played El Gallo in places where performances were interrupted by incoming Vietcong rockets. He'd been inspired by the original cast album and had fallen in love with Rita Gardner based on the sultry-eyed photo of her on its jacket. Sevra survived that experience to meet and marry Gardner after her divorce from her first husband.

The most recent (1989) figures for American productions show that more than two hundred actors have appeared in the roles on Sullivan Street. There have been 4,753 professional performances in two hundred professional productions in the U.S. and Canada. The figures for amateur productions are much higher: 39,079 performances in 6,717 productions.

The San Francisco production ran 1964 to 1970; the Los Angeles company, from 1964 to 1968; Denver, from 1968 to 1973. Los Angeles hosted an all-black company (featuring Ken Prymus) in 1968 in the wake of David Merrick's successful Pearl Bailey-led *Hello, Dolly!*

The Fantasticks has gotten every sort of review over the years, some gently approving, some even worshipful. The most glowing remains Henry Hewes's valentine in *Cue* that reads like a press agent's handbook: "sophisticated," "happy" (twice), "distinguished," "delightful," "clever," "lovely," "delicate and breathless," "compelling," "whimsically charming," "attractive," "appealing," "riotous," "subtle," "precise," "memorable," "effective," "wonderful," "imaginative," "freshest" and, naturally, "best."

The worst review the show ever got had to have been a poisonous 1967 notice by Roger Dettmer in the *Chicago American*. It slammed the text as "self-preeningly effete, self-consciously campy, as epidemically cute as a Walt Disney cartoon feature crossed with another Walt Disney cartoon feature. But with this difference: *The Fantasticks* is larded, like a lean roast of beef, with dirty jokes and maggoty ideas. The big production number in Act One is 'Rape Ballet' and the big production number in Act Two a sadomasochistic shivaree called 'Round and Round.' "

The show survived Dettmer's pan, and others like it, to be done in the cities of Athens in Greece, Alabama, Georgia, Ohio, Tennessee and West Virginia. Among its more unusual venues have been the White House, the White Sands Missile Base in New Mexico and Yellowstone National Park. In 1962, B. Iden Payne's original students at the University of Texas did a production at Hogg Auditorium, a little more than ten years after their *Time Staggers On* bowed there.

* * *

For the fifty-six intrepid investors, each one percent invested of $330 earned back $44,056 as of December 1989—a 13,350 percent return. But the dividends did not flow smoothly.

If you owned one percent of *The Fantasticks*, you would have gotten back your investment in 1960, earned (in current dollars for each year) $220 in 1961, $605 in 1962, $625 in 1963 and $915 in 1964, when the *Journal American* reported the show had grossed its first million dollars. Investor income rose to $1,180 in 1965, $1,490 in '66, and $1,660 in '67.

Income fell to $1,620 in 1968, $1,130 in 1969, $1,075 in 1970 and then tumbled to $530 in 1971, when the show underwent its second real financial crunch and was in danger of closing. Noto dismissed the understudies, personally took over the role of Hucklebee and tried special incentives, like a rebate plan for customers coming to the theater on public transportation, that soon vanished. Ticket prices rose, too, and in the early 1970s, Actors Equity demanded that Noto raise the actors' salaries to keep pace. Instead, he cut ticket prices from $8.75 top to a $7 top. Salaries, have, however, risen comparably to those of other Off-Broadway theaters.

Eventually, Noto told the *Newark Evening News* that busloads of students and other tourists from New Jersey and other suburbs brought income back into the black. "Thank God for New Jersey," he was quoted. "It saved my show."

Income hovered around $1,000 per percent each year during the 1970s then dipped dangerously in 1979, when the show had its third crunch. Salaries, ticket prices and investor income began ballooning to catch up with inflation, and in 1986, the figure was $3,700. It still was in that neighborhood at the dawn of the 1990s.

Don Farber estimated that the $16,500 show would cost $500,000 to $600,000 to produce at 1990 prices.

* * *

An adding machine can't do full justice to all the riches produced by *The Fantasticks*. It's been a prolific breeding ground for acting talent as well.

Among the thirty-four (as of 1990) actors who played El Gallo in New York are Gene Rupert, Bert Convy and John Cunningham (the first three replacements); also Keith Charles (who would star in Jones and Schmidt's *Celebration*), David Cryer, and Richard Muenz.

The thirty-two Luisas have included Leta Anderson, Carole Demas (original lead in *Grease*) and Betsy Joslyn (ditto, *A Doll's Life*).

The twenty-seven Matts included perennial Michael Glenn-Smith (another Jones-Schmidt collaborator) and composer Craig Carnelia.

The Old Actor attracted the talents of Edward Everett Horton and Oscar-winner F. Murray Abraham. Dick Latessa (later star of the Jones-Schmidt *Philemon*) played Hucklebee in 1967. Richard Thayer, the carpenter who had built the platforms for the theater's seats and who had executed Ed Wittstein's set design, later performed on that set as the Mute.

Others who did the show in its many productions around the world: Liza Minnelli, Elliott Gould, Ed Ames, Glenn Close, Bill Bixby, John Carradine, Kevin Kline, George Chakiris, Richard Chamberlain, Jones's old pal Tom Poston, John Raitt, even Florida Governor Bob Graham, who played Hucklebee.

Rita Gardner's standby, Sybil Lamb, held that position for more than seven years. By January 7, 1967, she had gone on 295 times.

Noto told an interviewer that he found no difficulty in recruiting replacements. "They want to do the show," Noto said. "They bring with them that mystique we talk about. They also expect to be discovered overnight like Jerry Orbach and Rita Gardner. . . . When they find that not happening in three or four months, they start to lose some drive. So then we put them in touch again with the material, which is what originally interested them."

Chappel/Intersong compiled a list of forty artists who have recorded songs from the score, including Roger Williams, Roy Orbison, George Shearing, Blossom Dearie, Duke Ellington, the Kingston Trio, Gladys Knight and the Pips, Patti LaBelle, Liberace, Jim Nabors, The Temptations and Rick Nelson.

* * *

As soon as *The Fantasticks* returned from its lifesaving spree in East Hampton, it started accruing memorabilia. People wanted to save Wittstein and Schmidt's costume and staging sketches, so Schmidt had them framed and hung in the second floor lounge. When magazines did layouts on the show, those went up, too, along with some of the original sheet music.

As the show began to be produced around the world, Schmidt began to collect the posters. Soon, people started sending things on their own: photos, letters, caricatures, even needlepoint. "Where do you put it all?" Gardner asked, having watched the answer. "The walls started to fill up."

One of Schmidt's friends commissioned cloth artist Norman La Liberte in 1966 to render the Act I tableau on a tapestry—one of the show's favorite pieces of memorabilia. Robert Alan Gold's paintings gave way before this rising tide of *Fantasti*ana, and eventually, by consensus, the lounge was rechristened the *Fantasticks* museum.

* * *

The Fantasticks hasn't changed much over the years, but there have been fine-tunings and even one controversy.

Some of the fine-tunings have been obvious. A curtain on a runner was rigged in the dressing room to give The Girl, whoever she might be, some privacy. The tiny concession stand next to the phone-booth-like men's room got even more crowded as the show began offering records, sheet music, T-shirts, sweatshirts and even a *Fantasticks* mug. The concession space is so cramped that only one each of these revenue-enhancers can be displayed at a time.

Though tiny, the theater is honeycombed with crawlspaces equipped with peep holes so the stage manager can monitor the evening's performance. These have been enhanced and made more comfortable over the years, though the theater has never added a prompt box. Often as not, when actors go up on their lines, someone in the audience will do the prompting for them.

The oranges El Gallo juggles early in the show and the plum that is "Too Ripe" in Act II originally were fresh produce that had to be hunted down and purchased daily. In the mid-1960s, one of the oranges rolled under the harp during a song. When the song was done, the harp came down hard and squirted an arc of fresh-squeezed right into the face of a first-row patron in a way that would have warmed the hearts of the Three Stooges. To top it, the actors went "Round and Round" in the sticky juice. Starting the next night, the produce was artificial.

Costumes have changed slightly. The Old Actor's devil costume was eliminated in favor of something less distracting (and easier to change out of). Jones tried to introduce a greater use of masks throughout the play, but these, too, were cumbersome and pulled audience attention.

The *Sunday News* of November 9, 1969, noted how short The Girl's dress had become. What had been mid-calf for Gardner, had crept six inches above-knee for the miniskirt era's Girl, Carolyn Mignini. It also was the *Oh! Calcutta!* era, and the writer speculated that the Luisa of 1979 would be performing nude.

Musically, the show has not changed, though tempos tend to drift, much to Julian Stein's dismay. He said "This Plum Is Too Ripe" is a constant problem. "I would go back to find it was going like lightning with too much of a jazzy beat. The way it is on the cast album is the way I liked it."

Schmidt said the whole show tends to have that problem. "People think they're doing it the same, but it picks up a millimeter every night. If I'm not down there for a while, I'll come in and it will be just moving at a hysterical pace and everybody thinks they're still doing it the same."

The show's tender spot, furiously poked by Dettmer in his famous 1967 pan, has always been "It Depends on What You Pay," better known as "The Rape Song."

Schmidt said some of his relatives complained about the use of the word "rape" in a comic context early in the show's run, and he knows of a Catholic school where the nuns changed the word to "snatch," which fits into the music but doesn't necessarily improve the situation. "I've never told this to Tom," Schmidt said, "but when we wrote it, I thought it was a little like college humor. Tom loved it. But we've totally reversed roles since then. In recent years, he's been wanting to change it, and I'm always saying it's fabulous as a product of our youthful work and we should leave it."

Jones said that while one dictionary definition of "rape"

continues to be "to seize and carry off by force," that's not the meaning perceived by audiences, especially not after a widely publicized 1989 rape and near-fatal beating of a female jogger in New York's Central Park. Jones said his own consciousness about the word was raised long before that. Jones changed the introduction to the song and several of the opening lines to emphasize what sort of "rape" is being discussed.

When Bellomy expresses horror at the word, Hucklebee now explains, "He doesn't mean a real rape, he means a literary rape: *The Rape of Lucrece, The Rape of the Lock.* . . ."

And Bellomy answers, "I've heard her [Luisa] mention Sabine women. . . ."

Nevertheless, Jones said he feels that's not good enough and has gone ahead and written an entirely new song. To maintain the integrity of the show, Jones used music already in the score. He put lyrics to the main theme featured in "The Rape Ballet," now retitled "The Abduction Ballet." It begins, "Abduction, abduction/ Theatrical abduction . . ." and goes on to list the various types, as per Rostand, Fleming, et al.

The new song, however, has not been put into the Off-Broadway show. Jones said Noto, for obvious reasons, is unwilling to tamper with any iota of the show and has been steadfast in his refusal to replace the song.

In mid-1991, the title of the rape song was changed to "The Abduction Song."

16

The Long Run

"There is a curious paradox /
That no one can explain."

From 1963 on, every time anyone has sat down to write about *The Fantasticks*, they invariably have attempted to account for its longevity.

Variety's late theater critic Richard Hummler told *Newsday*, "It's famous for being famous, for having a long-running mystique about it."

Doubtless that's true. *The Fantasticks* has become almost as much of a sightseeing destination for New York tourists as the Statue of Liberty and the Empire State Building. It even is touted as such by the New York Visitors and Conventions Bureau.

But surely, if people weren't enjoying the show, the hollowness would have sunk it years ago.

Fred Golden, who makes his living advertising theater, acknowledges that what keeps *The Fantasticks* open are not the one-column-by-two-inch ads run periodically in *The New York Times*, the ABC listings, or the TV commercials twice a week on *CBS This Morning* (to save money, they don't specify time).

No, it's "word-of-mouth, purely word-of-mouth," Golden said.

But word-of-mouth doesn't generate itself. Could it be the

reviews? All the energies (and prayers) of a show are directed toward getting good reviews. *The Fantasticks* got a few, but the memory of them faded long ago. As Schmidt points out, it's almost impossible to get publicity for the show anymore. Lisa Anderson in the *Chicago Tribune* wrote that the little musical "fades in and out of public consciousness like a theatrical *Brigadoon*. It surfaces most visibly on its anniversaries. . . ."

Which is true. But which means that good press isn't what is keeping *The Fantasticks* running.

Maybe it was just dumb luck. The chemistry was right and never will be duplicated. Without Tom Jones, the show wouldn't have its verbal delight, its mystical connection with a literary tradition stretching back through the Renaissance to the Romans and the Greeks and even to ancestral nights around the campfire.

Of course, without Schmidt, there wouldn't be those melodies that everyone remembers. Almost anyone can whistle "Try to Remember" all the way through, but how many people can remember past the second lyric line?

And lastly, without Word Baker, what would the words in the word-of-mouth be about? People may hum Schmidt's tunes, but they describe Baker's staging: the stoic Mute whisking props on and off the tiny wooden platform, the dashing El Gallo stamping his heels, the whirling rainbow mist of confetti.

Well, heck, maybe it's just magic. After all, the show has an undeniable and consistent ability to delight. As associate producer S. Miles Baron said, "There is something very beautiful and very pure about it. It was so simple and so simply done that it goes right to something very central and very innocent in all of us. And that's where I think it stays. That's why people come back over and over again and bring their kids. There's something very universal about it. It's a classic story: two fathers putting something over on their kids, and then it goes all wrong. There's a certain kind of innocence it requires."

That sounds very lovely, and probably is true. But there have been other simple, pure, colorful love stories, and none have come close to running thirty years. We're not there yet.

Let's be cynical. Perhaps the show perpetrates that most dreaded of artistic cop-outs: it panders to its audience and reaffirms what it already believes. That may be true about the idealistic first act, but the whole point of the show and its source material is to puncture that sort of nonsense. Many of the show's critics confuse it with the thing it is satirizing. Reduced to a sentence, the "message" of the show—as far as a *commedia* allows itself to have a message—is not "Don't worry, be happy," but "This is going to hurt, but you may learn something."

But do audiences buy tickets to learn lessons? Maybe the show is seducing them on a different level. Maybe it has to do with the spirit of the times. Though the song, "It Depends on What You Pay," has dated poorly, the rest of the show has exhibited a chameleon-like timeliness as it has moved through some sharply different epochs.

In the late 1950s, its Beat-ish poetry was, like, infra-dig, man. Its fervent idealism thrilled the New Frontier generation in the early 1960s. Its kaleidoscopic staging and floral imagery spoke to the flower children of the late 1960s, when Lore Noto asserted to the Associated Press, "It created today's youth life-style."

But it didn't stop there. The nostalgia boom of the 1970s could find no better anthem than "Try to Remember." Luisa captured the watchcry of the "Me" generation when she chanted, "I am special/ I am special," and when she and Matt broke up and went separate directions to discover themselves.

By the early 1980s, the show had run long enough to be part of the cherished cultural matrix of the newly adult baby boomers. In the profit-worshipping mid-1980s, what could be more fascinating than an investment that had returned more than 10,000 percent? Never mind the content—think of the box office!

Some say the 1990s will be a hangover decade in which newly sober society faces up to its responsibilities and gains a little wisdom from hard experience. If so, the whole and true point of *The Fantasticks*—"without a hurt the heart is hollow"—will be waiting.

But do ticket-buying audiences really think about those things when poring over the ABC listings? Is that really what enables Lore Noto to meet the payroll every week?

Think of it in the purest commercial terms. For a product to last this long, it must have been consistent. That makes sense—Jones and Schmidt personally did all casting and rehearsals for the first ten years, treating the show as their cottage industry. Some of those tasks have been handed over to production stage manager James Cook, but the two writers still often take part.

They know precisely what they want from the show, and even after an actor has been in a part for a year or more, the two authors will hold rehearsals to calibrate the show and keep it toned and focused.

You couldn't pay for that kind of tender loving care.

And when you peel away all the sentiment and cynicism from speculation about *The Fantasticks*, that's what you find: TLC you couldn't pay for.

When *The Fantasticks* opened, theater-owner Jules Field signed a run-of-the-play contract for peanuts. The contract may have been updated in the late 1970s, but the rent was $600 at a time when most Off-Broadway theaters of one hundred and forty-nine to one hundred and ninety-nine seats were paying $5,000. Field didn't mind. It warmed his heart to foster the show. But that little cardiac incandescence has kept bills low.

Ed Wittstein designed sets that would last forever and several costumes that look better as they wear out. Big savings there.

What if Jones and Schmidt billed the production for all the hours they spent rehearsing and casting it with just the right people? What if they had insisted on all those cowboys from *Joy Comes to Dead Horse*? What if they hadn't agreed to royalty cuts when the box office was low. What if they hadn't bought that air conditioner back in 1960?

It would have been where *Ernest in Love* is today.

"It has run a long time because that's what we designed it to do," Word Baker said.

And yet . . .

It can't all be money. Even one-man shows with no set don't run forever.

"People can take it on many different levels," Schmidt said. "Children love it. To them, it's just like a fairy tale. But there are so many different levels for many different people. For very sophisticated people, there are a lot of witty inside references, both theatrical and literary, that they can appreciate."

Maybe audiences are like Harvey Schmidt. After all these years, Schmidt said he still finds himself drawn to the theater. "I often stand just where I did opening night," he said. "If it's not working, it can be drudgery. But if the show works at all, it's a very pleasant experience. Funny—it doesn't seem old. Sometimes someone will do a fresh line-reading that's never been done before, and it's like you're hearing the show for the first time. I still can be surprised by performance and bits of business. And I sometimes will even laugh out loud."

17

1986

"Deep in December, our hearts should remember, / And follow . . ."

Fans of *The Fantasticks* took one look at the May 2, 1986, *New York Times* and suddenly found themselves on their feet, shaking.

There in the Weekend section was an ad topped by Schmidt's familiar logo and followed by nineteen lines of fateful type:

> Today THE FANTASTICKS completes its twenty-sixth consecutive year at the Sullivan Street Playhouse in Greenwich Village. During these many years, this remarkable Jones/Schmidt musical has burst out of its tiny 150-seat house to be seen on larger stages throughout the world, where it continues to be produced and enjoyed by many thousands of people. At a midnight preview in 1960, THE FANTAS-TICKS began its historic run.
>
> And so, appropriately, the final curtain of the New York City production will be hung at midnight. The date has been set for June 8, 1986. In case you have been putting off seeing the show, or have been meaning to see it again, we suggest you make your reservations now by calling OR4-3838.

It was the first that most people connected with the production had heard of Noto's decision to close the show.

Stauffer said, "When I heard that was happening, I found myself getting a little bit shook up. In a selfish way, I'd just taken the show for granted. It was like losing a great-aunt or something. I never really expected to be shook up by it, but I certainly was."

The first reaction was disbelief. "Everyone was convinced that it was a ploy," Don Farber said, "that Lore was doing it as a gimmick to raise public interest in the show."

He went to the theater with Jones and Schmidt for reassurance, but they were told that, yes, the closing notice was for real. In fact, Noto had called Schmidt and Jones for a meeting in April and explained that for certain reasons (described below) it must mean the end of the "Lore Noto production." The two writers were sorrowful but resigned to it. They helped prepare the wording and layout of the ad. What followed in the ensuing five weeks was a battle to keep the show open. Lawyers were marshaled, strategies plotted, salvos of legal papers fired. When the smoke cleared, the show was still running. But its rescue constituted a saga of youth and age that would have befitted Jones and Schmidt's *Celebration*.

Perhaps the most remarkable aspect of the battle is that so little of it ever made its way into the press. The official story was that the farewell prompted such a cry of protest from the theater community and such a surge in ticket sales that a grateful Lore Noto was compelled to tear up the closing notice.

The cry and the surge certainly occurred, and Noto indeed was compelled to keep the show running, but there was no direct cause and effect there.

The second reaction among the show's fans was *why?*

Commercial stage productions typically close when they stop making money, or when they fall below a certain agreed-upon weekly gross and the theater owner wants the space for a more profitable show. Thanks to Jules Field's benevolence, *The Fantasticks* had no such "stop clause," and a certified public accountant's reports show that *The Fantasticks* still was earning a profit of between $900 and $2,000 a week.

Noto gave several reasons for closing the show, none of which had to do with business. Most were personal, which prompted the legal battle, but at least one was esthetic.

Pieces of the story emerged in two interviews Noto gave *New York Newsday*. He acknowledged that the show was still making money, but he wanted to close it due to the "numerology" of his own age. He was thirty-six when *The Fantasticks* opened, and he wanted to close the show when those numbers reversed—when he was sixty-three.

The date chosen for the final performance (the 10,864th) was the eve of Noto's sixty-third birthday, and he told the paper he hoped the post-performance party would spill over well into the big day.

Noto also told the paper he wanted to be the last man to play Hucklebee at Sullivan Street. An encroaching frailness brought on by age and cancer meant he would not be able to play the part much longer.

Noto's reasons seemed fanciful, but there seemed to be an edge to them as well. The paper reported that Noto was "angered" when costume designer Dee Meyers handed him pages and pages of a petition she'd circulated to keep the show from closing. They bore the signatures of some whole Broadway companies including those of *The Mystery of Edwin Drood* and *A Chorus Line*. But Meyers wasn't alone. The Sullivan Street Playhouse was clogged with letters from the show's fans all over the world, imploring that some way be found to keep the theatrical landmark from vanishing. The remainder of the run promptly sold out, and for the first time in years, *Fantasticks* tickets were being offered by scalpers.

Noto was unmoved but was prompted to give another motivation for the closing. He said he wanted the show to "go out with style, grace and nobility. Why does a show have to close under the worst conditions? Why not close under the best, during a successful run?"

In a similar vein, he told the *Times*, "It will be a joyous occasion, going out a winner."

Joe Papp would employ similar reasoning in his decision to close *A Chorus Line* in 1990, though the financial situation of the long-running Broadway musical was genuinely dire.

Noto deserves credence for his remark. He had believed in *The Fantasticks* when few others did. He had put his family's tiny fortune on the line to bring the show into the world, and he had striven against critics, unions and economic storms to keep it alive. It's fair to say that without Noto, there would have been no *Fantasticks* to close on June 8, 1986.

In a way, perhaps, he looked at it like a pet owner: he had nursed it when it was a puppy, cared and fed it all its life, and now that it was old, he felt it was his responsibility to put it out of its misery.

The only problem was, the show wasn't *in* misery. The show was still in blooming health. It wasn't the show that was getting older, but Noto.

Whatever Noto's reasons, the backers were ready with an answer. The show belonged to them as much as it did to him. It wasn't his to close. They were determined to keep it open. And with that, the battle was joined.

As an investor, Don Farber advised Noto that he was not in a position to liquidate the limited partners' asset. Jones, Schmidt and Farber met May 5, and the partners met May 6.

Several plans were considered, most involving buying Noto out. Some of the partners wanted to let the show close, then reopen it under their control at another theater. Some wanted to transfer the existing production to another theater, as *The Mousetrap* had been moved. Jones came up with the idea of working a deal to revive the show annually.

The notion of closing for several weeks and reopening seemed to have the most support. Farber and associate producer Dorothy Olim entered into negotiations with Eric Krebs to move *The Fantasticks* to the one hundred and ninety-nine-seat Douglas Fairbanks Theatre on 42nd Street near Tenth Avenue. Conservatively estimated, and presuming reduced royalties for the authors, the new production was budgeted at $125,000. A tentative reopening was set for August, after a two-month vacation for the actors and staff.

The limited partners made an offer to buy Lore Noto's share, and that stopped him. Noto had envisioned himself continuing without *The Fantasticks*, moving on to other projects, maybe acting a part other than Hucklebee for the first time in more than a decade.

But what Noto hadn't envisioned was a *Fantasticks* without him. The partners made it clear that if he tried to liquidate their asset, they would sue and win. The decision to close the show was taken out of his hands.

Reluctantly therefore, Noto acquiesced to flouting numerology and continuing things more or less as they had for twenty-six years. But protesting that he no longer wished to either act or manage the production, he negotiated the introduction of a new co-producer, Donald V. Thompson, to rule as his regent.

A tennis buddy of Noto's, Thompson wrote the libretto to *The Revelations of St. Paul* presented at Avery Fisher Hall with music by Alan Hovhannes. Thompson's producing record included concerts at classical halls in Manhattan. Since taking control of *The Fantasticks*, he produced the Peter Link musical *The River*, which had a brief run Off-Broadway in 1988.

Variety published the official story on May 28: "Publicity from the announcement a few weeks ago of the show's imminent closing quickly sold out the balance of the then-scheduled run, which now will continue indefinitely."

The Man in White, as mysterious as ever, opted to continue, though now in the shadows. And, having survived a hurricane and a change of skippers, the little craft sailed into its fourth decade, steady as she goes.

* * *

In a cycle typical of Jones, he and Schmidt returned to their roots in 1990, mounting a thirtieth-anniversary national tour of *The Fantasticks* starring Robert Goulet as El Gallo. "For the first time," Schmidt said, "we did a larger production for larger houses. It's something we talked about for years."

Ed Wittstein designed a stage much like the one used at Portfolio Studio, and Jones, who directed it in Word Baker's place, broke up the part of the Mute into a half-dozen ubiquitous assistants, who also serve as a chorus.

Most interestingly, Jones and Schmidt collaborated on a new song for this tour. Titled "This Is the Perfect Time to Be in Love," it precedes "Soon It's Gonna Rain" in the glen scene, following El Gallo's line "It is September,/ Before a rainfall—A perfect time to be in love."

> . . . This is the perfect day to give your heart away,
> To share your secret dreams with one another.
> This is the perfect time to risk it all
> Forget about the clouds that come tomorrow.

I know what you should do
For I myself have been there, too.
This is the perfect time to be in love,
Don't let it slip away
For it may never come again . . .
Don't miss this perfect time to be in love.*

Not only was the number a gift to Goulet, it also opened the door a crack on El Gallo's life before Luisa and Matt. "This was the key element to me," Jones said. "I always felt that El Gallo had a love story that didn't work out, and that this [the moment of intimacy between the two young lovers] was the place in his own life where his opportunity was lost. So I wrote a short, simple ballad, emanating from an appropriate place in the script, yet stressing his own lost opportunities."

The writers also used the tour as an opportunity to cut the "Rape" song ("It Depends on What You Pay") at last and replace it with "Abduction." Schmidt acknowledged that in tampering with the show's magnitude and text, he and Jones were risking another 1961 London debacle. But "after thirty years," Schmidt said, "we felt we could take the chance."

* * *

To mark *The Fantasticks'* twenty-ninth anniversary, *The New York Times* published a rumination by author Vivian Gornick, bearing the headline "THE FANTASTICKS": AT 29, A PACIFIER MORE THAN A PLAY.

It was one of the chunkier brickbats that had been hurled at the musical, an indignant denunciation of the show for not being more reflective of the counterculture, gay rights, the women's movement and generally "what's happening in the streets." She wrote, "For one minute, *The Fantasticks* may have looked as if it were art, but for 25 [sic] years, it has been a startling demonstration of the power of kitsch. When the lines stop forming at the Sullivan Street theater, we'll know some important social change has been accomplished."

In Texas, Sam Houston, the Rev. Parrish of Word Baker's long-ago Alabama production of *The Crucible*, saw the story and got riled. Though he hadn't seen or spoken to Baker since the 1950s, he was moved to write a reply, which was published in the same paper three weeks later. His defense was floridly heartfelt, but it ended with the central incontrovertible fact of *The Fantasticks'* phenomenal run:

"How is it that one innocent little musical creates fear and loathing throughout its history in writers like Vivian Gornick? . . . Like those before her who've mounted their heavy profundities of destruction, their words become the wrappings of yesterday's garbage while the music box plays on without pause, decade after decade."

The same anniversary that had inspired Gornick also inspired journalist Linda Ellerbee, who wrote, "Will Durant said civilization is a stream with banks. He said the stream is sometimes filled with blood from people's killing, stealing, shouting and doing the things historians usually record, while on the banks, unnoticed, people build homes, make love, rear children, sing songs, write poetry and whittle statues. He said historians (and journalists) are pessimists because they ignore the banks of the river. But the story of civilization, he said, is the story of what happened on the banks.

"Sixteen years ago, I saw *The Fantasticks* for the first time. This week, I will see it for the sixteenth time. Why? Because at least once a year I need to be reminded about the importance of what goes on on the banks, and how to get back to them. Deep in December, it's nice to remember. The rest of the time, it's necessary."

Coda

THE golden age of *The Fantasticks* alumni must have been 1969–70 when Orbach was starring on Broadway in *Promises, Promises*, Gardner was starring Off-Broadway in *Jacques Brel Is Alive and Well and Living in Paris* and Nelson was on the road re-creating his Off-Broadway performance in *The Boys in the Band*.

Orbach has enjoyed the highest-profile career, going on to star in Broadway musicals like *Chicago* and *42nd Street*, and films including *The Gang That Couldn't Shoot Straight*, *Dirty Dancing* and Woody Allen's *Crimes and Misdemeanors*, as well as frequent starring roles on TV.

Nelson's career, which had been in a slide after *Seventeen*, was revived by *The Fantasticks*. His credits include *Hamlet* at the Stratford Festival in Canada. He's since settled in England.

Gardner appeared in *To Be Young, Gifted and Black* at Off-Broadway's Cherry Lane Theatre and toured in her one-woman nightclub show. She appeared regionally at Hartford Stage Company and the Actors Theatre of Louisville and finally got into the coveted Theatre De Lys in 1989 when she replaced the lead in *Steel Magnolias*. She directed a production of *The Fantasticks* at the Burt Reynolds Dinner Theater in Jupiter, Florida, in 1989.

William Larsen established a career as a solidly dependable supporting player in musicals such as *Dear World*, *Prettybelle*, and the Word Baker-directed *Caravaggio* before returning to Texas with his wife, June Larsen, who wrote a college thesis on *The Fantasticks*.

Hugh Thomas wrote and acted for several years before devoting himself to his antique business in New Jersey. He died June 27, 1981.

Blair Stauffer gradually became less and less involved in acting and finally converted his friendship with Jerry Orbach into a job. He worked for several years as Orbach's dresser, then eased himself out of show business. At one of the *Fantasticks* reunions, he read a clipping on the wall of the second floor museum which said he had retired from show business. "Sometimes if you don't see it written on the wall," he said, "you never know, kid." He has since become a physical therapist.

George Curley continued as a sometime-actor, sometime-lighting man and sometime-Santa Claus. Mortimer remains his signature part, and he still keeps a bag with his costume packed and ready by the door as a perpetual stand-in for the role. In all, he has played Mortimer 848 times as of 1990.

After *The Fantasticks*, Julian Stein was in greater demand than ever and worked on a number of 1960s musicals, including *What Makes Sammy Run?*, Lore Noto's *The Yearling*, Word Baker's *Smiling, the Boy Fell Dead*, *Half Past Wednesday* and others, before moving to Florida with his wife Tao and running a cruise business.

Beverly Mann played harp in one major musical after another—*Milk and Honey*, *The Sound of Music*, *Carnival*, *How to Succeed . . .*, *No Strings*, until she was hired for Jones and Schmidt's *110 in the Shade*, where she met her husband, Arthur, a trumpeter. She worked for three and a half years in the original Broadway production of *Mame* and frequently returned to *The Fantasticks* before moving to Seattle in 1976.

Lore Noto never thought that he had the Midas touch and waited patiently before choosing his next project. It wasn't until 1965 that he found a property that struck the right chord in him: a musical based on Marjorie Kinnan Rawling's Pulitzer Prize-winning novel *The Yearling*, about a boy who comes to terms with the fact that he and his pet deer will someday have to go separate ways.

The show had a book by Noto and Herbert Martin, lyrics by Martin, and music by Michael Leonard. Unfortunately, Noto's experience was much closer to that of *The Failures* than that of

The Fantasticks. Unable to overcome several basic problems, like needing to show a live deer on stage, the show closed quickly, losing $360,000. Included was $20,000 of Noto's own money and a friend's $24,000 nest egg. The friend wept.

The experience broke Noto's heart, and he never produced again. He dedicated his life to tennis and *The Fantasticks,* even taking over the role of Hucklebee and playing it close to six thousand times between 1971 and 1986, which he claims is the most times any actor has played any role. Guinness is mute on the point.

According to Schmidt, it wasn't just a vanity performance. "He had that thing we always tried to trap: he seemed *commedia*-like, stylized, almost like a drawing, and yet he had a reality, too. It's a hard thing to achieve."

Word Baker was constantly in demand during the 1960s, flying all over the world and across the United States to do offbeat projects. He never worked with Jones and Schmidt again (Jones wanted to direct his own material, as he had been trained), but he formed a fruitful collaboration with the song-writing team of Nancy Ford and Gretchen Cryer. Failing eyesight and precarious health prompted him to retire to his hometown of Honey Grove, Texas, though he did make a pilgrimage to New York for the show's thirtieth anniversary.

Schmidt went on to write music for two movies, Robert Benton's 1972 film, *Bad Company,* and an art film titled *A Texas Romance, 1909.* In his reference catalogue *TV Movies and Video Guide,* Leonard Maltin wrote that *Bad Company* is "aided immeasurably by . . . Harvey Schmidt's piano score."

Jones and Schmidt wrote four more shows that got major productions in New York by 1990. Their *Ratfink* musical (about a janitor at the American Museum of Natural History), announced right after the opening of *The Fantasticks,* wound up being delayed for nine years and emerging in a different form with a different story and a different title: *Celebration* (1969). First they satisfied their desire to do a big Broadway musical set in Texas: *110 in the Shade* (1963), based on N. Richard Nash's *The Rainmaker*; and then a vehicle for Harvey's NBC buddy Mary Martin and for Robert Preston, the two-character musical *I Do! I Do!* (1966), based on Jan de Hartog's *The Fourposter.*

About the time of *Celebration,* they opened the Portfolio Studio, a theater on West 47th Street (named after their long-imagined nightclub revue), where they could experiment with new forms of musical theater and stage techniques. They poured a large share of their *Fantasticks* earnings into the project, which yielded a new play series, *4 at Portfolio*, in 1974–1975. Its first production was *Philemon*, about an acrobat-turned-martyr in the ancient Middle East. It was successful enough to continue with a limited Off-Broadway run and be televised on PBS, and revived in 1991 at Manhattan's York Theater.

Aside from a revamped *Celebration* and, at last, a *Portfolio* revue of their songs and skits, the Portfolio studio series brought forth one more musical, *The Bone Room*, which went back to their original *Ratfink* idea, but the show was flawed and not done again.

Ed Wittstein designed the basic Portfolio studio unit stage, as he had the Broadway *Celebration*, and has worked steadily in New York and regional theaters and opera companies.

Since Portfolio closed in 1976, Jones and Schmidt have worked on two long-term projects, a musical based on the life of French writer *Colette* and another based on Wilder's *Our Town*, called *Grover's Corners*.

The former began as a play by Jones's first wife, Elinor Jones. It had a successful run Off-Broadway starring Zoë Caldwell, Mildred Dunnock, Keene Curtis, Barry Bostwick and Holland Taylor. Five songs and some incidental music were written by Jones and Schmidt.

These five songs later were developed into a full musical for a large, pre-Broadway tryout tour starring Diana Rigg, Robert Helpmann and John Reardon. It closed out of town.

Several years later, a somewhat smaller version, *Colette Collage*, had a limited run at York Theatre.

Grover's Corners was given a workshop production at Westbeth studios in Manhattan and a full production with a successful run at the Marriott Lincolnshire Theatre in Chicago. A national tour was announced but then cancelled when the star, their old friend Mary Martin, withdrew for health reasons. As of early 1991, Jones and Schmidt still were rewriting *Grover's Corners*.

The Closing Night of
The Fantasticks
January 13, 2002

"Don't let it slip away / For it may never come again."

On the closing night of *The Fantasticks* there were plenty of omens for the superstitious.

A huge shroudlike tarp covering construction work on the adjacent building flapped so hard on the cold, blustery Sunday evening that it pulled loose and nearly fell on several of the early birds who had gathered in front of the playhouse.

Act I of the show is full of moon imagery; Act II, of sun imagery. Perhaps it was another omen that the final performance came after dark on a moonless night. The show is also filled with the imagery of passing seasons and youth growing into age. It talks about May and September and even deep in December. But it doesn't mention January or the dead of winter, and January is when *The Fantasticks* finally passed away. But not without one last fling of the Mute's confetti.

* * *

By 2001, *The Fantasticks* had survived well into the age of the Internet. And in July of that year message boards and chat rooms were suddenly burning up with the news: *The Fantasticks* was in

233

trouble and planning to close. Actually, it was burning up with a question much more to the point: was *The Fantasticks* really closing this time?

After the aborted closing in 1986, the show had won a special Tony Award in 1992, and for a short while business was good. Producer Lore Noto posted another closing notice in August 1994, but quickly rescinded it when the box office once again rebounded. During the hard months of January and February throughout the mid and late 1990s, the show played to as few as twenty people. One press account said there was one forlorn night (for the cast anyway) when the show was performed for a single patron. Even with top-price tickets going for forty dollars, that didn't add up to much on a weekly basis. It became harder and harder to cover the show's $15,000 weekly operating "nut." They tried a few strategies. There was "Monday Night Magic," a series of magic acts on *The Fantasticks'* night off. There were some concert bookings on those nights as well, the most memorable Rita Gardner's solo show. *The Fantasticks* also launched a website, www.thefantasticks.com. When receipts were averaged over a period of months, the show was still turning a small profit.

But the first death blow was struck when Robert Alan Gold, longtime owner of the Sullivan Street Playhouse, sold it to a speculator named Braden Bell, whose company he christened 181 Sullivan LLC. In early 2001, Bell approached Noto to say that he wanted to make some changes at the theater.

Along with the rest of Greenwich Village, the area had become increasingly gentrified. Artists and writers were being replaced by the dreaded bourgeoisie, who liked living in former garrets— as long as they had undergone million-dollar makeovers. The new owner planned such a refurbishment of the four-story building that housed *The Fantasticks*. Bell had an ambitious plan to expand the apartments, add office space, and even refurbish the little theater to bring it up to twenty-first century standards and address concerns by Actors' Equity Association, the actors' union, which had never been happy with the cramped dressing room area. The catch was that *The Fantasticks* had to suspend performances for many months or move elsewhere.

This, ultimately, is where the line was drawn. There was no money for such a move, and Tom Jones was not alone in feeling that although the show had played in theaters all over the world, the original was inseparable from its performing space.

In July 2001, *The Fantasticks'* ABC listing in *The New York Times* began carrying the following headline:

FINAL
WEEKS
?

That question mark made the ad look to cynical *Fantasticks* watchers like another marketing ploy. But by August, Noto was giving interviews insisting that he was not crying wolf. The show was really in jeopardy of closing.

Noto told the Playbill On-Line internet news service on July 27, "Our biggest concern now, because of a lot of things happening internally—new contracts, the financial drain of maintaining our own theatre without landlord support, the economy slump—we might have to close in a day. . . . The landlord wants to raise our rent significantly to ask our support for [his] overpaying for this building. He hounds us with proposals to not just renovate but reconfigure it so he can add apartments. But if he does that, the theatre would be dramatically different: the upstairs gallery would disappear, the physical space would be smaller. It would not be the same. We did make some compromises with the previous landlord, but this is different. Nobody wants to put the actors in the basement. All we want to do is just run our show. Quite frankly, we just wish this guy would go away."

Noto also privately worried about the departure of another crucial "guy"—himself. Now seventy-eight he realized he was finally losing his long battle with cancer. His mortality was upon him, and he wanted to close the books. Still brilliant and eccentric, he identified so closely with the show that he told Jones, Schmidt and others in the surviving inner circle that he wished to fold the show's tent before he made his own exit. Considering the financial realities facing the production, they agreed.

Jones said "It came down to the fact that Lore knew he was dying. I think he wanted it to close with his death."

He said he respected this final wish because "Lore's spirit was very much why it ran so long. He also kept saying to us, 'If you guys want to take it, you can have it.' But after all the huge hoopla, I just didn't feel right. It seemed much classier to let it close than to extend it."

Once the decision was made, Don Farber recalls, there was surprisingly little grief. "I wasn't happy about it closing, but I accepted that was what life was all about. You get to the stage of life when you understand that life goes on. This is the cycle of life, like in the play. And it's winter. It's no longer springtime. It had to close. It was time."

The show, which had survived so many twists and turns in the culture and had ridden through both its time to be "in" and time to be "out," had finally missed a turn. It's tempting to say that the culture had lost its innocence. But why not? *The Fantasticks* was a parable of innocence lost.

On September 4, Noto made the closing official in a press release, which blamed the closing on "dwindling grosses combined with escalating operating costs."

It went on to say, "The new purchasers of the building that houses the Sullivan Street Theater had certain plans in regards to us, and we felt that we couldn't accommodate them. We came to an amicable agreement and let them have the building for their purposes. We felt we had to be honest and fair to our cast and crew who have supported the show for these many years."

And something new: a firm closing date was listed, *sans* question mark. *The Fantasticks*, the release said, would play its final performance on January 6, 2002, allowing it to benefit from one last holiday season's worth of box office bump.

The September 4 announcement noted that as much as they had hoped *The Fantasticks* would "beat out" London's (non-musical, 1952 vintage) *The Mousetrap* as the world's longest runner, that became "too unobtainable a goal."

As it began to dawn on people that this time the closing notice was for real, the phone in the box office began ringing early in the morning and barely stopped. At first, the final performance was announced as an invitation-only event, but there were still more than twelve weeks left. People who had been putting off seeing the show (or seeing it *again*) now realized their last chance had come. The Sullivan Street Playhouse quickly began selling out on weekends, then began selling out every performance. There were a lot of children those final weeks, as people who had seen the show when they were young began ushering in their kids and grandkids.

Boosting the trend was the press attention the show began to attract. Newspapers and TV stations around the world began sending reporters and photographers to interview Noto, his son and anyone else who would sit still for a photo shoot or even a phone call.

Demand for tickets was such that an extra week was added, rescheduling the closing night to Sunday, January 13, and making the final tally of performances 17,162. A ticket for that final performance became a sought-after prize. Tickets were set aside for any of the original company or investors who wished to attend, plus significant others, plus people who had been special friends of the production through the years. A small number of tickets were also released for sale to the fans who simply *had* to be there.

The closing made the front page of *The New York Times* on January 9, accompanied by a photo of the gray-haired Schmidt and Jones of 2001 next to a photo of their more hirsute selves in 1975. Writer Peter Marks said, "The ancient-looking stage lights will be switched off on an essential piece of theatre history." Noto was quoted talking of "the right to retire gracefully." ABC-TV's *Nightline* devoted a special feature segment to the closing, as did news magazine shows across the United States.

On that windy closing night, the faithful began arriving, clutching hats and turned-up collars, in taxis and limousines and on foot. They arrived blinking in the bright lights of TV cameras, with reporters interviewing almost everyone in sight, including those standing on line in the recessed area beside the sidewalk, quixotically hoping for last-minute cancellations.

Composer Harvey Schmidt and lyricist-librettist Tom Jones greeted the closing-night crowd out front, with Jones telling those who offered condolences, "You can't be sad for a show that has run forty two years."

A lot of the arrivals had known each other for decades. Many were friends, enemies, lovers, former actors and grateful investors. Among the attendees: original Luisa, Rita Gardner; original Off-Broadway Mortimer, George Curley; Oscar-winner F. Murray Abraham (one of many El Gallos throughout the run); former theater owner Robert Alan Gold, new owner Braden Bell and original set/costume designer Ed Wittstein.

Among those in the show's final cast was Bill Tost (as Bellomy), who had played Mortimer in the show's first incarnation at Barnard College.

Notably absent was the original El Gallo, Jerry Orbach, who had achieved TV stardom as Detective Leonard "Lennie" Briscoe in the drama *Law & Order*. He also created the voice of Lumiere, the enchanted candlestick, in the Oscar-nominated Disney animated film musical *Beauty and the Beast* and its sequel. Orbach would finally succumb to prostate cancer on December 28, 2004. The following night, all the Broadway theaters dimmed their lights for one minute at curtain time. His obituary appeared on the front page of *The New York Times*.

Original Mute, Blair Stauffer, said he did not attend the final performance of *The Fantasticks* because he had not been notified of the show's closing.

Also there that night was filmmaker Eli Kabillio, who had gotten permission not only to attend the final performance and interview the guests, but also to film the final performance itself. The resulting movie, *Try To Remember: "The Fantasticks,"* had only the briefest of releases, playing on May 17 and 19 of 2004 at the Walter Reade Theater in Times Square, and was scheduled for DVD release in 2005. The film is invaluable for *Fantasticks* fans because it offers a rare glimpse of Word Baker's staging and demonstrates how well the little show worked in its native space at the Playhouse. The film featured interviews with celebrities who had been associated with the show, including local TV weatherman Ira Joe Fisher, who had gone into the show for a time as one of the fathers. He let down his jocular mask for a moment to tell Kabillio, "I was never happier than when I was doing that show." Fighting back tears, he said, "Maybe if I cry on camera, they'll bring it back."

The film also captured some of the craziness outside the Playhouse as people tried their best, legitimately or not, to get inside. The mob was a bittersweet sight for Jones and Schmidt. They had had two minor hits on Broadway, *110 in the Shade* and *I Do! I Do!*, plus a notable flop, *Celebration*, but never again had a Broadway show, and certainly never enjoyed anything approaching the success of *The Fantasticks*. They had a critical success Off-Broadway in the 1970s with *Philemon*. But their larger-scale musicals, *Colette*, also known as *Colette Collage*, and *Grover's Corners* (based on Thornton Wilder's *Our Town*), were long in development but never got the major New York productions their creators sought. Another musical, *Mirette*, debuted at Goodspeed Opera House in the 1990s; *Roadside* was performed at York Theatre Company in 2001. The pair was inducted into the Theatre Hall of Fame in 1999. They reunited very briefly with Rita Gardner, who sings one number (with the cumbersome title "Part I: 'Willy': The Claudine Craze: Love Is Not a Sentiment Worthy of Respect") on their studio album of *Colette Collage*.

* * *

In the crush of people at the Playhouse door, several held up forlorn penciled signs saying things like NEED 1 TICKET PLEASE!!! Their hope was not completely in vain. One man who was openly begging all arrivals for a spare ticket actually got one from the Noto family, which found it had one extra.

Firmly pressing forward, the lucky ticket-bearers entered the narrow passageway and shuffled past the tiny merchandise and refreshment stand, past the stairs on the left and the cast head shots on the right, then through the droopy black curtain and into the Playhouse. In the end, every seat was occupied, of course. Several dozen more people packed into the upstairs museum, where a closed-circuit television had been set up amid the posters for productions around the world and photos of actors who played the roles through forty years of trendy haircuts. The final performance started nearly a half hour late, as the show's alumni, who hadn't seen one another in years, made tearful reunions and ignored ushers' attempts settle them down.

Final performances can be odd things, especially on long-running shows. The final performance of *Cats* was a celebration, with composer Andrew Lloyd Webber using it to debut a song that had been cut from the show, making the closing also a premiere of sorts. It came complete with fireworks and a speech on Broadway from Mayor Rudolph Giuliani.

The final performance of *A Chorus Line* was a celebration of the show's performing family. As producer Joseph Papp said farewell, it was remarkable to notice how, without prompting, all the original cast members were either holding hands, squeezing one another's shoulders, rubbing knees, and so on, creating a kind of physical circuit.

The final performance of *The Fantasticks* had a different kind of electricity. For one thing, there was a large age range. Many in the closing-night audience were middle-aged or elderly—creators, investors, fans—a forest of gray heads full of memories. But there was also a sprinkling of beautiful children, some of whom perhaps might have been considered too young to have seen the show under ordinary circumstances, but who were brought by their elders because the chance to see the original production would never come again. When they grew older and came to understand such things, they would brag that they were present at the final performance.

Several were director Word Baker's grandchildren, which provided a momentary disconnect to surviving original participants who remembered their parents, who looked very much the same, playing around the theater in the weeks leading up to opening night. These children looked like sweet-faced living memories of the previews long ago.

And they served as a reminder of the people who were not there. Original fathers Hugh Thomas and William Larsen had died long before. Kenneth Nelson, the original Boy, had moved to London, where he died on October 7, 1993, of complications related to AIDS.

And Word Baker himself was not there. He had died in 1995 after a long illness. In a memorial service at the Sullivan Street Playhouse on November 19 of that year, one of the eulogies described what he had meant to the show:

> In a time when falling chandeliers and rising helicopters are believed necessary to make a theatrical point, Word Baker's faith in the simple magic of floating confetti—and the even deeper wonder of a wall indicated by nothing but a man holding a stick—continues to be vindicated. That's why *The Fantasticks* is Word Baker's greatest monument. It somehow manages to coax the audience's imagination out of its box every night, and

uses this wondrous instrument as the show's most spectacular special effect. Word Baker was an arch-sorcerer in the amazingly durable magic of the human imagination. Word Baker was the ultimate Fantastick.

Finally, the lights went down on the final performance, and bearded lighting technician John LaRocca took the stage. Gazing out at the faces, some lined, some smooth, all glowing, he said simply, "Welcome to the seventeen thousand one hundred and sixty-second performance of *The Fantasticks*." And the staccato harp notes of the overture struck up for the last time. Upstairs in the gallery one man called a less lucky fan on his cell phone and held it up toward the video monitor so the person at the other end could bear electronic witness, too.

Paul Blankenship, the final El Gallo, began to sing the show's signature tune "Try To Remember." There was a gasp after he sang the first line, as if someone was startled by a realization of where we were and what we were doing. People seemed to cling to each word, and then gave the song a frenzied hand. But a real show couldn't be watched like that. When Jeremy Ellison Gladstone, as The Boy, said, "There is this girl," and El Gallo dryly riposted, "That is the essence," the show got its first laugh. Everyone relaxed a little bit.

"Try To Remember" is such a natural opening for the show, setting the mood the way it does. But not everyone saw it that way. One who did not was film director Francis Ford Coppola, director of *The Godfather* and *Apocalypse Now*. He arrived in the world of *The Fantasticks* down something of a bureaucratic rabbit hole. After many false starts and failed concepts from other directors and writers, Michael Ritchie came forward in the early 1990s with an idea that appealed to Jones and Schmidt. The film would be set in a small western town—so small that the only two houses for miles around would be Luisa's and Matt's. A magical carnival would come to town, much like the ones that so stimulated Schmidt's imagination when he was a child in West Texas. El Gallo would serve as the carnival's enigmatic manager and ringmaster.

On the basis of his success with the films *Smile* and *Fletch*, Ritchie secured financing from United Artists-MGM and populated the new project with a variety of interesting actors. Bellomy would be played by Joel Grey, star of Broadway's *Cabaret* and *George M!* The role of Hucklebee went to crusty character actor Brad Sullivan. Barnard Hughes—a real-life old Shakespearean actor—would play The Old Actor. The role of Mortimer, The Man Who Dies, went to Teller, the usually silent half of the "new vaudeville" team of Penn and Teller.

In the main roles, former New Kids on the Block singer Joey McIntyre would play Matt; *Mr. Holland's Opus* and *Into the Woods* actress Jean Louisa Kelly won Luisa; and incarnating El Gallo would be Jonathon Morris, who had done the part successfully in London. The movie was filmed in wide-screen Panavision in the same Arizona valley where the movie *Oklahoma!* was shot, and the orchestrations were lushly expanded by veteran Jonathan Tunick, whose resume included many of Stephen Sondheim's best-known shows. The film combined a starkly beautiful backdrop with numerous surreal touches, like the fact that the two houses were jammed cheek by jowl though surrounded by miles of waving grass stretching away toward purple mountains. The carnival was populated by dwarves and oddities who served as a chorus and sang, apparently unnoticed for the most part, just beyond the action. El Gallo conducted "Soon It's Gonna Rain" from a sturdy-limbed tree.

There were also many lovely moments, including a brief pas de deux for the dainty Jean Louisa Kelly and veteran hoofer Joel Grey. In addition to the rain of "Soon It's Gonna Rain," Ritchie filmed scenes in bright sun, gathering clouds, crimson dawn and even a whirling snowstorm. Bellomy's neat side of the "wall" bristled with sunflowers; Hucklebee's run-down yard contained ranks of ragged cornstalks. It might have been nice to have seen some drowned magnolias, if not a kumquat. But Ritchie found many original visual ways to make the show's points.

Things looked very promising for the project, and trailers teasing a 1995 holiday season opening began appearing at New York area cinemas. But a July sneak preview of the film in Los Angeles elicited mixed reactions. Some in the audience who wrote evaluations reportedly complained about the previously uncontroversial scene where El Gallo takes Luisa's necklace. Soon the debut was pushed back to January 1996 and then indefinitely.

Post-production problems continued. This was still the pre-*Chicago* "dark age" of film musicals, and the UA-MGM marketing department told the creators that they were having trouble figuring out how to sell the film.

"There were two schools of thought in management at that time," Jones was quoted as saying. "One school thought it was an interesting film with a family market. Part of it seems like a very na ve, simple fairy tale for a family [but] part of it seems very sophisticated, knowing and theatrical. . . ." It was not clear to executives who the audience was, he said.

Schmidt marveled that the corporate descendant of his beloved MGM would be stumped at how to market a musical. The film sat on the UA shelf for five years. Jones and Schmidt took the time to screen it and suggest changes, but it wasn't until film legend Coppola took a look that the wheels began to turn again.

In his production notes, Ritchie wrote, "When *The Fantasticks* was not released five years ago, it was a painful experience. But as the years passed I began to have a very profound regret. I had been too faithful to the original theater piece. While there were many changes to the seven original characters, there were too many 'set pieces' still included. At this point, my old friend from San Francisco, Francis Ford Coppola, offered to look at the film in his capacity as MGM board member, and then, in his role as guru and fellow filmmaker, he put his suggestions on film."

Coppola, who had directed two big-screen musicals, *Finian's Rainbow* and *The Cotton Club*, re-edited the film, shortening it by cutting "Plant a Radish" and other bits (resuscitated in an addendum to the DVD) and making one major and controversial change. He moved "Try To Remember" from the opening to the end, on the theory that the song serves as the story's summary, not its prologue.

UA-MGM still wanted to release the movie direct to video, but Ritchie's contract barred just such a move. So in its revised form the film opened on September 22, 2000, in a tightly limited release in single theaters in New York, San Francisco, Los Angeles and other select cities. Where it was marketed at all, it was positioned as an art-house film that would get a wider release if the public responded in droves. The public didn't. Reviews were mixed to negative, most charging the film with having an uneven tone and a clotted whimsy. It was widely felt that the magic of the stage version did not translate to film.

In *The New York Times*, A. O. Scott wrote, "As a film *The Fantasticks* . . . wobbles between the timeless and the anachronistic. For all its robust good cheer it's a timid and uncertain creature, a mewing kitten wandering out into the world in search of a big-hearted 11-year-old girl to tie ribbons around its ears and give it a bowl of warm milk. . . . *The Fantasticks* is, at bottom, a tribute to the transformative power of theater, and the theater is where it should have been allowed to remain. The movie version overflows with affection and good intention, but unwittingly turns a bauble of cheerful fakery into something that mostly feels phony."

In *Rolling Stone* magazine, Peter Marks observed, "Disaster? Pretty much. . . . [But] Even as the movie threatens to derail, the charm of the score, by Tom Jones and Harvey Schmidt—'Try to Remember,' 'Soon It's Gonna Rain,' 'I Can See It'—keeps breaking through."

The movie was released on DVD and VHS in early 2001. The stage version survived it for more than a year.

Fans of the show should note two other important recordings. In 1993, DRG Records released an album of the Japanese touring version of the show, which was performed in English with an American cast led by Alfred Lakeman as El Gallo. The recording preserves a great deal more of the show than the original cast album, including several stretches of dialog. Tom Jones recreates his role as The Old Actor (under his own name, at last), and the piano part is played in its entirety by Harvey Schmidt. Rather than the sweetened-up mini-band on the original cast album, this recording uses a single piano accompanied throughout by only a harp, so it sounds much more like *The Fantasticks* actually did on Sullivan Street. A bonus track captures "A Perfect Time to Be in Love," the new song written for Robert Goulet to sing in the aborted 1980s U.S. tour. On the CD, it's Schmidt who croons the song, to his own piano accompaniment. The epigraph of this chapter is taken from that lyric.

Also, in honor of the fortieth anniversary of the show, on April

25, 2000, Decca Broadway re-released the remastered original cast album of *The Fantasticks* on CD with new liner notes and illustrations. For those who wore out their old LP versions, the sound is beautifully crisp, and you can hear much more of the ad-libbing cello, especially on "Soon It's Gonna Rain."

* * *

The intermission of the final performance came quickly, and it was hard to believe the show was going by so fast. Sitting in the worn, red-upholstered seats, it was also hard to imagine this space being used for a restaurant or a store or someone's apartment. Can fictional characters leave ghosts? If so, then Matt, Luisa, Hucklebee and Bellomy would be singing here for many years to come, no matter what happened.

The intermission gave people another chance to chat, to catch up with old friends, and to walk around touching the space one last time. On the China-silk curtain that hung over the stage, you could feel the thickness of the purple paint where composer Schmidt had hand-lettered the title. You could see the worn spots on the poles where many hands had swung on them. The prop box looked as if it had been on tour with Mortimer and Henry's old troupe—as indeed it had.

* * *

El Gallo turned the crescent-moon disc around to reveal the yellow sun, and act 2 began. The audience tried to hang on to every word, as the show slipped quickly through their fingers. Memories of the many times most of them had seen the show lay like multiple exposures over the show they were seeing now. It was as if the show were already being seen in memory. In the scene where Matt is carried out by the two old actors, they exit up the aisle to the main access door. Audiences could hear the old floorboards creak, hear the rustle of the costumes, smell the sweat, as they sang, "Beyond the road lies an episode, an episode, an episode . . ." as they disappeared en route to Venice, "Indja" and the lobby.

At the end, El Gallo hung up the curtain for the final time, and the cast took their bows. The applause went on and on and on, as if they knew that their clapping was truly the end of the show, and that as long as they were still applauding, the show was still technically running. But the actors didn't linger too long. They linked hands and ran off.

Afterward there were a few brief speeches. Standing on the tiny stage of the Sullivan Street Playhouse with multicolored confetti from the show still unswept around his feet, Jones told of a Good Friday ceremony in Athens, Greece, in which coffins are opened in churches at midnight, and people celebrate the fact that they are empty. He said he wanted to celebrate not the fact that the show was closing, but the fact that it had had such a bountiful life, when so many other projects close quickly. "It's been given a real life. It will live on in the minds of hundreds of thousands of people. All of you," he said, gesturing to the crowd, "breathed life into it."

Schmidt recalled that he was twenty-nine when the show debuted at Barnard, and he was now seventy-two. "It's always been a part of my life," he said. "I love every one of you and will remember until I die all the contributions all of you made."

Noto told the audience, "We set the bar at 17,162 [performances]. God bless and good luck to anyone who wants to try to jump over that."

Outgoing New York City Council President Peter Vallone told the crowd, "It will never end. It will be in our hearts, be in our minds, be in our souls, as long as love exists. It's the greatest play ever."

Afterward Schmidt said, "There was such a jam. We were onstage with Lore, and people kept coming up and talking to us. People wanted me to sign programs on the stage. I sat on the bench signing for what seemed like several hours." It would prove to be the last time the two men saw each other.

As the audience filed out, many bent down, holding one of the stage poles for support, to pick up bits of the final crop of confetti. Some touched the piano or the prop box, or patted the poles one more time for good luck, and filed up the aisle to the exit.

Afterward while the guests were partying and hugging and having reunions and farewells in the upstairs gallery, Kabillio and his film crew sat the creators down in the now empty theater space for some final interviews. The results were poignant and well considered, though many of the questions had been asked and answered many times over the years.

One of the most interesting comments came from Tony Noto, Lore's adult son, who reflected that as long as it looked as if the show might live forever, those involved in it might fool themselves into thinking they might live forever, too. But now that it was closed, well . . .

The little musical about a boy and a girl and the wall their fathers built to keep them apart remains secure in its status as the world's longest-running musical, as perennial in *Guinness World Records* as it seemed on Sullivan Street. It's a distinction the show is likely to hold for a long time. To put the 17,162-performance run in perspective, compare it to the run of *Cats*. *The Fantasticks* ran nearly 10,000 more performances than *Cats*.

* * *

Lore Noto died on July 8, 2002, at age seventy-nine. The Associated Press gave credit where it was due: "It was Noto, a former actor and artists' agent, who saw the possibilities in a small one-act show written by Tom Jones and Harvey Schmidt when it was first produced in 1959 at Barnard College in New York."

Noto was joined soon thereafter by longtime stage manager James Cook, who had worked on the show, in one capacity or another, for nearly as many years as Noto.

A few weeks after the show closed, composer Harvey Schmidt walked past the Playhouse and made a heartbreaking, but lucky, discovery. A Dumpster stood outside the building filled with costumes, photos and pieces of what once had been the dressing room. He salvaged what he could and added it to his own collection, parts of which were sought by the Smithsonian Institution, including the hand-lettered curtain and the prop box. Schmidt said he also sent along one of the painted plywood discs that had served as moon and sun.

Meanwhile, though its seats and most decorations were removed, the Sullivan Street Playhouse did not undergo the threatened renovation. As of this writing in late 2004, it was still standing as it had during the show. Even the purple awning over the box office window was still there, but graffiti had appeared on the locked stage door. Upper-story windows and the box office were covered with plywood, and the metal frame of the show's marquee hung from the front of the building, though the sign itself was long gone.

And the building itself was again for sale. Brock A. Emmetsberger of real estate broker Massey Knakal said there had been six offers for the building, including three who said they wanted to refurbish the theater space, but none had yet been accepted.

The listing for the space on the Massey Knakal Web site read, in part:

> Built shortly after the Civil War, this five story brick townhouse housed the Sullivan Street Playhouse on the ground and second floors, where the show, *The Fantasticks*, ran for over 40 years. Today, the ground floor space might be suitable for a variety of commercial uses. The property will be delivered vacant. . . . With restoration, this property would serve as an ideal candidate for a live plus investment or single family conversion opportunity. Alternatively, the property could be converted into a boutique condominium development. Asking Price: $4,250,000."

Though composer Harvey Schmidt had virtually retired to Texas as of this writing, Jones was still living in New York City and continuing work on various projects, including a revised version of his and Schmidt's *Colette Collage*. He also held out hope for a revival of *The Fantasticks*. He mentioned in particular his admiration for Amon Miyamoto's staging, which toured fourteen Japanese cities in 2003. Miyamoto became the first Japanese to direct a musical on Broadway with a revival of *Pacific Overtures* in 2004. Jones said he was fascinated by Miyamoto's environmental approach to *The Fantasticks*, completely different from Word Baker's, in which actors would sit with the audience when they weren't onstage. In a November 28, 2004, interview with *The New York Times*, Miyamoto promised that his next project would be a major revival of *The Fantasticks* in Tokyo.

Jones said he doesn't believe that New York has really seen the last of *The Fantasticks*, whether in that form or another. "I do think the time will come when *The Fantasticks* will be done again."

* * *

On January 14, 2002, for the first time in more than forty years, *The Fantasticks* wasn't playing at the Sullivan Street Playhouse. It was, however, opening that week at Weathervane Community Playhouse in Akron, Ohio. And Broadway West Theatre Company in Fremont, California. And Carousel Dinner Theatre in Fort Collins, Colorado. And Hedgerow Theatre in Rose Valley, Pennsylvania. And Greenville High School in Greenville, California. And Wichita Children's Theatre in Wichita, Kansas. And Riverfront Theatre in Reno, Nevada.

And those are just the ones tracked by Music Theatre International's Michael McDonough in North America. *The Fantasticks* was opening that same week in theaters all around the world. And, probably, it always will.

PLAYBILL®

SULLIVAN STREET PLAYHOUSE

The Fantasticks

FIFTH DECADE

Final performance...
January 13th, 2002
17,162 performances

The cover of the special *Playbill* created for the final performance. Property of Playbill Inc. New York City. Used by permission.

Index

About the Authors

Donald C. Farber is one of the foremost theater, film and entertainment industry attorneys in New York. He has written seven books on the business of show business. *Producing on Broadway, Actor's Guide: What You Should Know About the Contracts You Sign, Producing Theatre: A Comprehensive Legal and Business Guide, From Option to Opening: A Guide to Producing Plays Off Broadway,* and *Producing, Financing and Distributing Film* (the last with coauthors Paul A. Baumgarten and Mark Fleischer). He served as attorney, business consultant, and adviser for the original production of *The Fantasticks.* He is the general editor of ten volumes of *Entertainment Industry Contracts* (author of the theater volumes), published by LexisNexis Matthew Bender, which are updated three times per year. He taught a course on Producing Theatre at the New School for Social Research in New York City and has lectured on theater all over the world. Donald enjoys being the grandfather of Justin and Miranda.

Robert Viagas, in addition to serving as historian of *The Fantasticks,* is founder and former managing editor of news services for Playbill On-Line and Theatre.com. As program director of Playbill Broadcast, he hosts the *Radio Playbill* show on Sirius Satellite Radio, and has hosted the webcast of the annual Tony Awards since 2002. His books include *The Back Stage Guide to Broadway* and *On the Line: The Creation of A Chorus Line,* and he was editor of Louis Botto's acclaimed history of the Broadway theaters, *At This Theatre.* His articles have appeared in *Playbill, USA Today, American Theatre, InTheatre, The Times of London,* and *Show Music* magazine, and he was a theater critic for various Connecticut newspapers for fourteen years. He has served as editor of programs for New York City Opera and New York City Ballet, and edits the special *Playbill* for the annual Tony Awards ceremony. An alumnus of the BMI Musical Theatre Workshop, he has written the librettos for two musicals, *City of Light* and *In a Perfect World.* His parents took him to see *The Fantasticks,* his first experience with professional theater, when he was twelve years old.